Post-AIA Patent Professional's Handbook

A TRAINING TOOL FOR ADMINISTRATIVE STAFF

• • •

Susan Stiles

ISBN: 1535517565
ISBN 13: 9781535517560

Post-AIA Patent Professional's Handbook

Table of Contents

*(A Step-by-Step Guide for Support Professionals in
Patent Law Firms and IP Departments)*

Preface

• • •

THE PURPOSE OF THIS PATENT Professional's Handbook is to be a reference source for Patent Professionals or Administrative Staff in the patent field, who provide administrative assistance for a Registered Patent Practitioner. The Patent Professional can turn to it for assistance and guidance in his/her many duties as an employee in a law office or IP Department. As a reference book, it will reduce the amount of instruction time a Registered Patent Practitioner must spend with his/her staff.

The Supreme Court calls a patent application one of the most difficult legal instruments to prepare. Registered Patent Practitioners have shelves of treatises and practice guides to help them. What do Patent Professionals have? Until now, nothing. The Patent Professional's Handbook is intended as a compilation of information a Patent Professional needs in one convenient source.

The Patent Professional's Handbook lists the administrative requirements for Patent Office filings, and goes on to show what the filing documents should contain and how they should be formatted. The Patent Professional's Handbook is intended as an easy-to-use guide for the Paralegal staff with step-by-step instructions for submitting documents to the U.S. Patent and Trademark Office associated with the filing and prosecuting of U.S. patent applications. By describing each facet of the U.S. Patent and Trademark Office procedures from the Patent Professional's viewpoint, the Patent Professional's Handbook can be a valuable tool for training new staff. With its checklists, tips and sections on advanced topics, the Patent Professional's Handbook can improve the efficiency of experienced staff while reinforcing best practices.

This Patent Professional's Handbook is further intended to take much of the confusion out of the patent process by providing checklists, step-by-step instructions, timelines, by answering common questions, providing examples, and giving detailed instructions.

All material provided herein is to be used only as a general guide and not as a substitute for legal advice for any specific application. It should be used strictly under the supervision of the Registered Patent Practitioner and never without his/her permission. If legal advice for a specific matter is required, the services of a competent professional person should be sought. The author accepts no responsibility for errors, omissions, or the misuse of this Patent Professional's Handbook.

Acknowledgements

• • •

I WISH TO ACKNOWLEDGE THAT most of the material in this Patent Professional's Handbook comes from the U.S. Patent and Trademark Office at *www.uspto.gov.*

While responsibility for the contents of this Patent Professional's Handbook is entirely mine, I also wish to acknowledge the help and advice initially with Stephen W. Aycock II, Esquire, Registered Patent Practitioner, of Cygnet IP Law, P.A of Lakeland, FL. Also, I wish to acknowledge Cameron K. Weiffenbach, Esquire, Registered Patent Practitioner, for his advice on ethical and technical issues. Mr. Weiffenbach is with the law firm of Miles & Stockbridge P.C., Tysons Corner, VA. With gratitude for their assistance I also acknowledge that neither they nor Miles & Stockbridge P.C. have exercised any supervision, authorship or endorsement of the contents of this Patent Professional's Handbook.

About the Author

● ● ●

SUSAN STILES HAS BEEN A Legal Assistant for more than 30 years, with 24 years' experience in Intellectual Property. Working at several major law firms in the Washington, DC metro area, Mrs. Stiles helped prepare, file, and prosecute thousands of U.S. and international patent applications. Mrs. Stiles earned the Professional Legal Secretary (PLS) certification (2003-2013) and Professional Paralegal (Paralegal) certification (2009-2014) through NALS...*an association of legal professionals*. Mrs. Stiles is currently an IP Assistant Administrator/IP Paralegal with Miles & Stockbridge P.C., Tysons Corner, VA.

Disclaimer

● ● ●

THIS PATENT PROFESSIONAL'S HANDBOOK is not intended for use as a legal guide book or to provide legal advice to law issues. This Patent Professional's Handbook is simply a resource manual to give guidance to the Patent Professionals in how to prepare documents and guide them through the many steps in order for an invention to become patentable under a Registered Patent Practitioner's supervision. Ultimately, the Registered Patent Practitioner is responsible for the final product outcome.

List of Abbreviations

• • •

AAU	Application Assistance Unit
AIR	Automated Interview Request
ADS	Application Data Sheet
AE	Accelerated Examination
AFCP 2.0	After-Final Consideration Pilot Program 2.0
AFR	After-Final Rejection
AIA	America Invents Act
APJ	Administrative Patent Judge
AU	Art Unit
ASD	Assignment Services Division
CFR	Code of Federal Register
CIP	Continuation-in-Part
CN	Customer Number
CON	Continuation Application
CPA	Continued Prosecution Application
CRU	Central Reexamination Unit
DIV	Divisional Application
EBC	Electronic Business Center
EFS	Electronic Filing System
EFT	Electronic Funds Transfer
EMP	Extended Missing Parts Pilot Program
ePAS	Electronic Patent Assignment System
ET	Eastern Time
FAI	First Action Interview
FIG	Figure
IB	International Bureau
IDS	Information Disclosure Statement
IFW	Image File Wrapper

IP	Intellectual Property
IPEA	International Preliminary Examining Authority
ISA	International Searching Authority
ISR	International Search Report
LIE	Legal Instruments Examiner
L&R	Licensing and Review
MPEP	Manual for Patent Examining Procedures
NOA	Notice of Allowance
ODM	Office of Data Management
OED	Office of Enrollment and Discipline
OPAP	Office of Patent Application Processing
PAIR	Patent Application Information Retrieval
PALM	Patent Application Location Monitoring
PCT	Patent Cooperation Treaty
PDF	Portable Document Format
PE	Prioritized Examination
PG-PUB	Pre-Grant Publication Division
PLT	Patent Law Treaty
PLTIA	Patent Law Treaties Implementation Act of 2012
Paralegal	Patent Professionals or Administrative Staff
PPH	Patent Prosecution Highway
PTA	Patent Term Adjustment
PTAB	Patent Trial and Appeal Board
PTE	Patent Term Extension
QPIDS	Quick Path Information Disclosure Statement
RAM	Revenue and Accounting Management
RCE	Request for Continued Examination
RCFR	Request for Corrected Filing Receipt
SE	Supplemental Examination
SPE	Supervisory Patent Examiners
TC	Technology Center
TD	Terminal Disclaimer
USC	United States Code
USPTO	United States Patent and Trademark Office
USRO	United States Receiving Office
WO	Written Opinion
WIPO	World Intellectual Property Organization

CHAPTER 1

Introduction

● ● ●

THE PATENT PROFESSIONAL'S HANDBOOK IS geared toward Patent Professionals or Administrative Staff ("Paralegal"), who are not licensed, but provide service for the administrative side of the Registered Patent Practitioner ("Practitioner").

1.1 WHAT IS A PATENT?

So the inventor has come up with a conception for a new invention. How will the Practitioner keep competitors from unfairly capitalizing on the inventor's invention? The answer is to get a patent for the invention.

Patent law is a sub-set of the broad category of intellectual property (IP) law. IP law serves to protect creations of the mind, whether they are intangible or ethereal products. In addition to patents, there are several other types of IP, such as trademarks, copyrights, and trade secrets. This Handbook will focus on patents.

A patent document delineates an inventor's conception of an invention in sufficient detail such that the public can make and use the invention. This is part of the *quid pro quo* of the patent system. In return for the full disclosure of the invention, the inventor has the right to exclude others from making, using and selling, importing, offer to sell his/her invention. The continual disclosure of new ideas through the patent system is designed to promote a constant evolution of technology, both in serving as a foundation for new ideas and in motivating innovation in concurrent technology to avoid infringement.

Once issued, a patent gives the patent owner the right to exclude other people from making, using, and selling, importing, offering to sell the invention claimed in the patent. Contrary to popular belief, however, obtaining a patent may not enable the inventor to make, use, or sell his/her invention, if his/her patented invention incorporates patented inventions of others.

1

There are essentially three categories for patent protection: utility, design, and plant. The most common type of patents are utility patents, which are granted for any new and useful process, machine, manufacture, composition of matter, or improvements. Design patents protect the non-functional appearance or design of a manufactured article. Plant patents are granted for a new and distinct variety of plant.

This Handbook will focus on utility and design patents, as these are the most common in traditional patent practice and the ones most likely to be encountered by the inventor. However, the Paralegal should be aware of other types of patents and IP protection, especially since the guidance provided in this Handbook may not be applicable to the other types of patents and IP protection. Accordingly, the Paralegal should consult with a Practitioner in these instances to determine the appropriate prosecution methodology for the inventive subject matter.

The USPTO is an agency of the U.S. Government that examines patent and trademark applications with authority to grant patents and trademark registrations. The term "USPTO" will be used throughout this Handbook refer to the U.S. Patent and Trademark Office, the Patent and Trademark Office, the Patent Office, or just the Office.

1.2 A Patent Story

As you become experienced in the field of patent prosecution, the terminology commonly employed will become second nature to you. However, the variety of specialized terms may seem daunting. To assist in your understanding, this Handbook will endeavor to explain the parlance associated with the patent practice, as well as variations, in an appropriate place in this Handbook. In *Sections 1.2.1 to 1.2.3*, certain fundamental terminology, which will be used throughout the remainder of this Handbook, is introduced.

We present in *Sections 1.2.1 to 1.2.3* a patent prosecution story for a typical invention. The following is by no means intended to be exhaustive, as various deviations, additions, and omissions from the following story are possible and often occur. Rather, it is meant to be informative for the Paralegal on what to expect in typical patent prosecution, from beginning to end.

1.2.1 Preparing and Filing the Patent Application

Steve is working on his car during a hot day in August. He is trying to change the oil in his car, but, between the heat and the cramped engine interior, he is having trouble removing the oil filter using the oil filter wrench he bought at the local auto supply store. In a moment of desperation, he yanks too hard on the wrench and bangs his head on the engine hood. While recovering from his injury, Steve has a moment of inspiration and conceives an idea for a new oil filter wrench which will, among other things, prevent him from banging his head in the future. He immediately begins to think about obtaining a patent for his new oil filter wrench.

In order to obtain a patent, a patent application must be filed with the USPTO. An inventor may draft the patent application himself/herself or consult with a Practitioner. When working with a Practitioner, an inventor may draft an invention disclosure, which documents the relevant details of the invention. Such relevant details usually include a background of the invention, how it was developed, the components and description of the invention, and whether or not the invention was discussed with others. The Practitioner will interview the inventor to obtain the relevant details of the invention before drafting the patent application.

A Practitioner is a person who has been licensed and given a registration number by the USPTO to represent clients in matters related to patent prosecution before the USPTO. To be licensed, a Practitioner must (i) possess the requisite scientific and technical training, (ii) take and pass a registration examination to demonstrate knowledge of USPTO practice and procedure, and (iii) possess good moral character and repute. A Practitioner may be a Patent Agent (a Practitioner who does not have a law degree or who is not a member of a State bar) or a patent attorney (a member of a State bar). The Practitioner may employ the assistance of Paralegals in the drafting and subsequent prosecution of the patent application for the Practitioner's supervision and review.

> NOTE: The Paralegal cannot give legal advice and the Practitioner has the ultimate responsibility to supervise and be responsible for the work that is being done on the client's behalf.

Steve meets with a Practitioner who is a patent attorney in California. Steve has not had a chance to write down any details of his invention, but is very excited about getting a patent. "There's nothing like this out there on the market," Steve tells the Practitioner. The Practitioner proceeds to interview him about the details of the invention and confirms that he has not told anyone else about the invention. The details of the interview are documented by the Practitioner and appended to a file for Steve's matter. The Practitioner and Steve agree on a budget for the patent application, after which the Practitioner begins work on drafting a suitable patent application.

In general, the patent application includes several parts related to the invention and several formal aspects. The formal aspects will be addressed in greater detail later in this Handbook. The specification, together with the drawings, describes the invention in sufficient detail that the public can recreate the invention from the application. The abstract provides a brief summary of the invention and is often used to determine the relevance of the patent in a specific information (or patent) search. The claims are the most important part of the patent application, as they set forth the legal definition (and uniqueness) of the invention the inventor wants to protect.

> *The Practitioner finishes the draft patent application, including the claims. Because Steve asserts that no one else has ever done this, the Practitioner drafts fairly broad claim language. The Practitioner then submits the draft application to Steve for review. Steve notices a few errors in the application and also wants to include some additional ideas that were not discussed in the interview. He makes a note of the changes on the draft application and sends it back to the Practitioner. The Practitioner has her assistant, Joyce, make the appropriate changes and also instructs Joyce to prepare Declaration and Power of Attorney forms for the patent application for Steve's signature.*

> *After Joyce completes the changes, she forwards the patent application to Steve for final review and execution of the Declaration and Power of Attorney forms. Steve reads the final draft application and is pleased with the results. Having read the application, he signs the Declaration attesting that the invention is indeed his. He also signs the Power of Attorney giving the Practitioner the power to represent him before the USPTO.*

Effective September 16, 2012, the USPTO revised the rules of practice to permit a person to whom the inventor has assigned or is under an obligation to assign an invention to file and prosecute an application for patent as the Applicant, and to permit a person who otherwise shows proprietary interest in the matter to file and prosecute an application for patent as the Applicant on behalf of the inventor(s).

The patent owner (or the Applicant, if the application is not assigned) may designate a Practitioner to receive USPTO correspondence and prosecute the application on behalf of the inventor by filing a Power of Attorney with the USPTO. After filing a Power of Attorney, the USPTO will only communicate with the designated representative or someone who has authority, unless the Power of Attorney is subsequently revoked.

> *Joyce receives the executed Declaration and Power of Attorney from Steve and notes his approval of the final draft. She then prepares the application for filing with the USPTO by uploading the patent application to the USPTO electronic filing system ("EFS-Web"). The Practitioner reviews the patent application for formal requirements one last time, signs the appropriate transmittal, and files the application via EFS-Web. The USPTO immediately indicates receipt of Steve's patent application and assigns its Application Number 99/999,999.*

The patent application can be filed in person, by mail, or electronically via the EFS-Web. The EFS-Web employed by the USPTO will be explained in details later.

The other options will also be explained to a lesser extent in appropriate sections. Once the application is received, the USPTO assigns an application number, which consists of a two-digit series code followed by a six-digit number. All subsequent correspondence directed to the USPTO must include the patent application number, as well as the first named inventor, filing date, and a confirmation number assigned by the USPTO.

1.2.2 EXAMINING THE PATENT APPLICATION

The USPTO sends Steve's application to the Office of Patent Application Processing ("OPAP") to make sure it complies with certain formal requirements. OPAP confirms that the basic formal requirements are present and sends an Official Filing Receipt to the Practitioner, who instructs Joyce to confirm that the information on the Official Filing Receipt matches the information in the file for Steve's matter.

When the USPTO receives a patent application, it examines the application for compliance with the relevant patent laws and rules. The Manual of Patent Examining Procedure ("MPEP") is a guide for patent applicants, Practitioners, the public and USPTO personnel on the patent statutes, rules of practice, policy, and procedure for patent prosecution. When in doubt on how to proceed with a pending patent matter, the Paralegal should always consult with the Practitioner for guidance.

The USPTO consists of several divisions, each of which plays an important part in making the prosecution of patent applications more efficient. Once OPAP reviews the patent application and determines that it complies with certain formal requirements, it is then forwarded for examination on the merits. The Office of Licensing and Review ("L&R") also reviews for foreign licensing and national security purposes before going to Examiner.

The USPTO sends a copy of Steve's application to the publication division. The publication division prepares the application for publication by the USPTO eighteen (18) months after the filing date.

Unless the Patent Applicant (Inventor or Assignee) requests nonpublication of his or her patent application, the USPTO will publish patent applications eighteen (18) months from the earliest filing date. Each published application has a publication number. The published application includes the abstract, specification and claims of the patent application and drawings. Nonpublication should not be requested if the Patent Applicant desires to submit for patents in a foreign country. A request can be made for nonpublication at the time of filing, but if a counterpart foreign application or international application under the Patent Cooperation Treaty ("PCT") is to be filed, it would be improper to file such a request if inventor knows at the time of filing request, a foreign or PCT application will be filed. See **Chapter 11 - Publication of Patent Applications**.

Simultaneously, the application is routed to Examiner Monroe, who specializes in the art of oil filter wrenches. Examiner Monroe will pick up Steve's application for examination in the order it was received.

The examination divisions of the USPTO are organized into Technology Centers ("TC") based on basic technology areas, such as biotechnology, chemistry, electrical, computers, communications, and mechanical. There is also a TC which examines design applications and another TC which handles plant applications. One or more Group or Center Directors are in charge of each TC. Each TC is further subdivided into Art Units ("AU") based on more specific technologies. Each AU is supervised by a Supervisory Patent Examiner ("SPE").

Each AU is composed of 10 or more Patent Examiners, who have scientific and technical training. The Patent Examiners within an AU are the ones who actually examine a particular patent application. An examiner may be a Primary Examiner or an Assistant Examiner. Primary Examiners are experienced examiners who have been certified by the USPTO to make independent decisions on patentability of patent claims, and thus have the authority to sign official USPTO communications without supervisory review. Assistant Examiners are less experienced and do not have the authority to sign official USPTO communications. Accordingly, Assistant Examiners work under the supervision of an SPE or Primary Examiner.

A Legal Instruments Examiner ("LIE") serves as an assistant to an Examiner (Assistant and Primary Examiners as well as SPE's). In particular, the LIE forwards communication from the patent application (or representative) to the Examiner and vice versa. The LIE also reviews communication for compliance with certain formal requirements, such as compliance with amendment guidelines.

After two years, Steve is getting anxious that he has not received an update on the status of his patent application. The Practitioner reassures Steve that this time frame is normal. Serendipitously, Examiner Monroe picks up Steve's case for examination. Examiner Monroe reads Steve's specification and claims, after which he performs a prior art search for the claimed subject matter. Examiner Monroe finds a single patent reference, issued to Noah, which discloses an oil wrench having all of the elements of the broad claims in Steve's patent application. He prepares a first Non-Final Office Action rejecting Steve's claims as being anticipated by Noah's patent. The Practitioner receives the Non-Final Office Action and forwards it to Steve for his review.

After the initial examination, the Examiner assigned to examine a patent application will perform a prior art search for the claimed invention. The purpose of the search is to find any references that predate the Applicant's filing date, anticipate the claimed subject matter, or render the claims obvious. These references need not be patents, but can be any type of publication or disclosure dated prior to the filing date of the patent application. If the Examiner finds a reference that discloses all of the elements of the Applicant's claim, the Examiner can reject the claims as being anticipated. If the Examiner finds references disclosing some of the elements of the claimed subject matter, the references can be combined with other prior art references to reject the claims for obviousness.

Steve receives a copy of the Non-Final Office Action forwarded by the Practitioner. After his initial shock over the rejection wears off, he realizes that there is a key distinction between his oil filter wrench and Noah's oil filter wrench. This distinction was not in the claims, but it was disclosed in the written description of the invention (the specification of the patent application). After consulting with Steve, the Practitioner rewrites the claims to emphasize this distinction and prepares an Amendment to the claims with remarks to distinguish the amended claims from Noah's invention. After approval of the Amendment by Steve, the Practitioner signs the Amendment and has Joyce efile the signed Amendment with the USPTO via EFS-Web.

After receiving a Non-Final Office Action from the USPTO, the Practitioner has a chance to respond to the rejections or objections noted therein. Rejections are based on statute or judge-made law (e.g., obviousness-type double patenting) and are typically directed to the claims, while objections are based on rules and typically relate to formal matters. The Practitioner may request reconsideration of the patent application and file a response to the Office Action with or without changes to the specification, claims, or drawings. Changes that are made are termed Amendments. The response includes remarks supporting the changes and arguments as to why the Examiner's rejections or objections are in error. This response is labeled an "Amendment". A response without any amendments is labeled a "Response".

After the Amendment is filed, it is routed to Examiner Monroe by the LIE for his AU. Within two (2) months, Examiner Monroe reviews the Amendment and agrees that Noah's patent is deficient with regard to the new feature in Steve's claims. Examiner Monroe performs an additional prior art search for this new feature. Examiner Monroe finds a Japanese patent to Oshi which discloses the new feature. The translated abstract of Oshi's patent clearly suggests the new feature and the attending advantages. Examiner Monroe prepares a Final Rejection, rejecting Steve's claims as being obvious over

Noah's patent in view of Oshi's patent (a rejection for obviousness). The LIE then forwards the Final Rejection by mail or electronically together with Oshi's Japanese patent to the Practitioner, who receives the Final Rejection and Japanese patent, and notes the new ground of rejection. The Practitioner reports the Office Action to Steve with a copy of the Office Action for his review. She advises Steve that the Examiner has made a new ground of rejection and that the action is Final. She also advises Steve of his options after a Final Rejection.

After an Amendment or Response is submitted to the USPTO, the Examiner will evaluate the changes and/or arguments in view of the prior Office Action. The Examiner may perform an additional search based on the changes and/or arguments. The Examiner may continue to reject the claims on the same grounds, or may make a new ground of rejection and issue a Final Rejection. A Final Rejection significantly limits further prosecution, and the application will go abandoned unless a Request for Continued Examination ("RCE") or an appeal of the final rejection is filed or an Amendment is filed placing the claims in condition for allowance as a patent.

Steve receives the reporting letter and copies of the Final Rejection and the Oshi patent from the Practitioner. He is shocked and dismayed by this latest rejection. The Practitioner consults with Steve about the options set forth in her reporting letter. Unfortunately, it does not appear that an appeal is a plausible route, as Oshi's patent does suggest this new feature and in combination with the disclosure of Noah's oil filter wrench, the Examiner has presented a prima facie case of obviousness taken alone. However, the Practitioner notices another feature in the specification that does not appear to be suggested by Noah or Oshi, or in combination. The Practitioner suggests filing an Amendment After Final to amend the claims by adding the new feature. Steve agrees. The Practitioner revises the claims as discussed and drafts Remarks corresponding thereto. After Steve has reviewed and approved the Amendment After Final, the Practitioner signs the After Final Amendment and has Joyce efile the signed Amendment in the USPTO via EFS-Web.

After a Final Rejection is received, the prosecution options for the Practitioner are limited. The Practitioner can file an Amendment After Final, but such Amendments are not entered as a matter of right. Rather, the Examiner has discretion to permit the Amendment to be entered. The Examiner will only enter the Amendment if it places the application in condition for allowance without further examination. Such Amendments are typically very time sensitive, since the application will go abandoned if certain actions are not taken within six (6) months from the issuance of the Final Rejection.

The Amendment After Final is routed to Examiner Monroe by the LIE for his AU. Within 10 days, Examiner Monroe reviews the Amendment and agrees that the combination of Noah's patent and Oshi's patent is deficient with regard to the new feature of Steve's claims. However, the Examiner notes that he would have to do an additional search to evaluate the patentability of this new feature. Accordingly, he prepares an Advisory Action stating that the claim amendments have not been entered because they require further search and consideration. The LIE then forwards the Advisory Action to the Practitioner within 30 days after the Practitioner submitted the Amendment After Final.

The Practitioner receives the Advisory Action and reports the Advisory Action to Steve for his review and also advises Steve of his options.

The Practitioner advises Steve that the Advisory Action and is not a determination of the patentability of the revised claims. She suggests filing a Request for Continued Examination, commonly referred to as an RCE, to have Examiner Monroe consider these new amendments to the claims. Steve agrees. The Practitioner instructs Joyce to prepare the RCE. After it is prepared, the Practitioner reviews and signs the RCE. At the Practitioner's direction, Joyce efiles the signed RCE and pays the appropriate fees via EFS-Web.

To have amended claims denied entry after a final rejection and in order to prevent an application from going abandoned, the Practitioner must file an RCE and pay the appropriate fees. Another option, if the Practitioner considers the Examiner's final rejection to be in error, is to file a Notice of Appeal with payment of the appropriate fees. In practice, an RCE continues prosecution of the application and removes the finality of the Final Rejection. Any Amendments submitted with the RCE are thus entered as a matter of right. If any Amendments submitted after the Final Rejection was not entered, these Amendments are entered with the filing of the RCE. The Examiner would either allow the claims or continue to reject the claims in a Non-Final Office Action.

The USPTO also has a separate adjudicating body for resolving legal disputes between the Examiner and the Practitioner on a particular patent application. This body is called the Patent Trial and Appeal Board ("PTAB") and is composed of a number of Administrative Patent Judges ("APJ"). When a patent application continues to be rejected by an Examiner, for example, after a Final Rejection, the Practitioner may appeal the Examiner's decision of unpatentability to the PTAB, if the Practitioner believes the Examiner's decision is in error.

The LIE receives the RCE, changes the status of the application, and enters the previously filed Amendment After Final. The LIE then forwards the Amendment to Examiner Monroe. Within two (2) months, Examiner Monroe reviews the Amendment and, after conducting a prior art search, determines that the claims as amended are patentable. Examiner Monroe therefore issues a Notice of Allowance indicating that the claims proposed in the RCE are allowable over the prior art of record. The LIE takes the

Notice of Allowance and appends a "Notice of Allowance and Fees Due" form before sending it to the Practitioner. After she receives the Notice of Allowance, she forwards a copy of the Notice of Allowance and Fees Due form to Steve.

Steve is ecstatic and instructs the Practitioner to pay the Issue Fee. She instructs Joyce to review the application file history to make sure all formal matters are in compliance (or have been met). After confirming that the application is in good order, the Practitioner signs the Issue Fee Transmittal. At the Practitioner's direction, Joyce efiles the signed Issue Fee Transmittal and pays the appropriate Issue Fee via EFS-Web.

If the Examiner finds that the claims pending in an application are patentable over the prior art, the Examiner issues a Notice of Allowance. After the Notice of Allowance is issued, prosecution is effectively closed. However, for a patent to issue from the patent application, the Issue Fee must be paid within three (3) months from the date of the Notice of Allowance. The time is not extendable. If the Issue Fee is not timely paid, the patent application becomes abandoned.

1.2.3 ISSUING THE PATENT

After payment of the Issue Fee, the Practitioner receives an Issue Notification from the USPTO indicating the date the patent will issue and the patent number. When the patent issues, the Practitioner receives a formal copy of the Patent Grant and forwards it to Steve and advises him that he can begin enforcing his patent and that he will need to pay maintenance fees at 3 ½ years, 7 ½ years, and 11 ½ years to keep his patent in force.

A Patent Grant is a formal document issued by the USPTO which grants patent rights to the Patent Owner. The USPTO grants patents every Tuesday, regardless of whether the Tuesday is a national holiday. Each patent granted is assigned a patent number.

In order for the patent to remain in force, the USPTO requires the payment of a maintenance fee at 3 ½, 7 ½, and 11 ½ years. There is a 6-month grace period for each maintenance fee. Thus, if the maintenance fee is not paid by the 4, 8, or 12 year marks, the patent will lapse and be unenforceable.

NOTE: The maintenance fees increase significantly the longer the patent is in force.

1.3 AMERICA INVENTS ACT

The Leahy-Smith **America Invents Act** ("AIA"), H.R. 1249, was passed by Congress and signed into law by President Barack Obama on **September 16, 2011**. The law represents the most significant patent reform legislation since 1952.

Named for its lead sponsors, Sen. Patrick Leahy (D-VT) and Rep. Lamar Smith (R-TX), the AIA switches the U.S. patent system from a "first to invent" to a "first to file" system, eliminates interference proceedings, and develops post-grant opposition.

1.3.1 SUMMARY OF SIGNIFICANT CHANGES IN THE PATENT STATUTES

First to File

The AIA switches from the "first-to-invent" system to a "first-to-file" system for determining who is entitled to a patent for patent applications filed on or after **March 16, 2013**. The "first-inventor-to-file" system creates simple procedure for determining who is entitled to a patent in case of two or more patent applications claiming the same invention. Under the first-to-invent system, the determination of who is entitled to a patent was determined by a costly interference proceeding. The AIA also expanded what constitutes prior art.

Track One Prioritized Examination

Track One prioritized examination was implemented for utility and plant patent applications and must be requested at the time of initial filing of the application. When an Applicant opts into prioritized examination, the application will be accorded special status during prosecution before the Patent Examiner. The goal is to provide a final disposition of the application within twelve (12) months from the date prioritized status is granted. The fee to request a Track One prioritized examination is $4,000 for regular undiscounted (large) entity, $2,000 for small entity (50% discount), and $1,000 for micro entity. The fee is in addition to the filing, search, examination, and Track One processing fees under 37 CFR 1.17(i)(1). Requests for Track One prioritized examination was effective on **September 26, 2011**, and is only available for patent applications filed on or after the effective date.

A Track One utility and plant patent application cannot have more than four (4) independent claims and the total claims cannot exceed thirty (30). No multiple claims are permitted. Utility patent applications must be filed via EFS-Web, and plant patent applications must be filed by paper.

Continuation, Divisional, and Continuation-in-Part applications are eligible for Track One prioritized examination, but Reissue applications are not.

The resource page for Track One prioritized examinations can be located at *www.uspto.gov/aia_implementation/track-1-quickstart-guide.pdf*. Also, refer to **Chapter 26 - Track One Prioritized Examinations** for more details.

Micro Entity Fee Reduction
Micro entity means an Applicant qualifies as a small entity*, and has not been named as an inventor on more than four (4) previously filed patent applications, other than applications filed in another country. Institutions of higher education may qualify under the micro entity status. There is a 75% reduction of fees for filing, searching, examining, issuing, appealing, and maintaining patent applications if the Applicant qualifies as a micro entity.

Inventor's Oath or Declaration
An application for a patent that is filed must include in an executed oath or declaration the name(s) of the inventor(s) for any invention claimed in the application. In lieu of executing an oath or declaration, the Applicant for patent may provide a substitute statement under certain circumstances. A substitute statement is permitted if the inventor or Applicant is (i) deceased, (ii) under legal incapacity, (iii) cannot be found or reached after diligent efforts, or (iv) refuses to sign the oath or declaration. Identification of each inventor or Applicant's citizenship is no longer required, and there is no requirement for foreign priority applications to be in the oath or declaration. The rules for the inventor's oath or declaration were effective on **September 16, 2012**, and apply to all patent applications filed on or after the effective date.

Electronic Filing Incentive
An additional fee of $400 (regular-undiscounted*) or $200 (small entity*) is required for each application for an original patent (except for a design, plant, or provisional application) that is not filed electronically using EFS-Web. This fee went into effect on **November 15, 2011**.

Third Party Submissions of Prior Art for Patent Applications
Third parties may submit patents, published patent applications, or other printed publications of potential relevance to the examination of a pending patent application. The submission must include a concise

explanation of the asserted relevance of each document submitted. These submissions may be made by (1) the later of (i) six (6) months after the date of publication or (ii) the date of a first Office Action on the merits rejecting any claims, or (2) before the date of a Notice of Allowance. This provision went into effect on **September 16, 2012**.

For any questions, the AIA Helpdesk phone number is 1-855-435-7242 or email *helpAIA@uspto.gov*.

1.4 AIA TECHNICAL CORRECTIONS ACT

Many of the changes described in *Section 1.3* are the result of provisions in the Leahy-Smith America Invents Act (the "AIA") which became law on September 16, 2011. The AIA Technical Corrections Act was enacted into law on **January 14, 2013**, to correct and improve certain provisions of the AIA.

Inventor's Oath or Declaration

Under the AIA, the Applicant was required to file an executed oath or declaration by the time the application was in condition for allowance. Under the AIA Technical Corrections Act, Section 1(f), an oath or declaration may be properly filed any time before the date on which the issue fee is paid.

Patent Term Adjustment

Section 1(h) of the AIA Technical Corrections Act revises the patent term adjustment ("PTA") and is applicable to any patent issued on or after **January 14, 2013**. The USPTO will transmit a notice of the PTA no later than the date of issuance of the patent, but not at the time when the application became allowed. Accordingly, the patentee should wait until the grant of the patent to determine whether or not a request for reconsideration of the PTA indicated on the patent is warranted.

If the Practitioner receives a PTA indicating on the front of the patent that is longer than expected, the Practitioner must disclose the error to the USPTO within two (2) months from the date the patent was granted. This time period is extendible for an additional five (5) months.

1.5 PATENT LAW TREATY

In December 2012, Congress passed the Patent Law Treaties Implementation Act of 2012 ("PLTIA") to implement the provisions of the Patent Law Treaty ("PLT"). The provisions focused on harmonizing and streamlining many of the formal procedures for filing and processing patent applications.

Some of the most notable changes are directed to: (1) the filing date requirements for a patent application (non-design); (2) the restoration of the right of priority to a foreign or provisional application in a patent application filed after the expiration of the priority period; (3) the restoration of patent rights via the revival of abandoned applications, acceptance of delayed maintenance fee payments, and acceptance of delayed patent owner response in reexamination; and (4) the time period for responding to certain office communications and amounts due for issue and publication fees. The PLTIA and ensuing changes became effective on **December 18, 2013**. The changes affected the patent application filing date, restoration of priority and patent rights, and setting a minimum two (2)-month reply period to respond to Office actions unless otherwise specified in the USPTO rules. The changes are summarized below.

1. **Patent Application Filing Date:**
   * Filing date is accorded the patent application on the date the USPTO receives a specification with or without claims.
   * No claims or drawings are required to establish filing date.
   * Claims or drawings filed after the filing date must be supported under 35 USC 112(a) in application as filed.
   * Any drawings necessary to understand invention will be required during examination.

2. **Restoration of Priority Rights:**

   Patent Applications filed after expiration of the twelve (12)-month period (six (6) month period for designs) for filing an application claiming the benefit of a prior foreign application can have the right of priority restored if the delay in filing the subsequent application was unintentional.

   Applications filed after expiration of the twelve (12)-month period for filing an application claiming the benefit of a prior provisional application can have the right of priority restored if the delay in filing the subsequent application was unintentional.

   An application filed after the twelve (12)-month period (six (6) month period for designs) must be filed within two (2) months of the expiration of the twelve (12)-month period (six (6) month period for designs).

   A petition under 37 CFR 1.78(b), including the foreign priority claim or specific reference to the provisional application, petition fee and a statement that the delay was unintentional is required.

3. **Restoration of Patent Rights:**

The USPTO rules were amended to eliminate "unavoidable" delay as a basis for reviving an abandoned application, accepting a delayed patent owner response in reexamination, or accepting an unintentionally delayed maintenance fee payment.

A petition for unintentional delay is the only basis for reviving an abandoned application, accepting a delayed patent owner response in reexamination, and accepting a delayed maintenance fee payment. A petition fee is required.

The amended rules eliminated the twenty-four (24)-month time period requirement for petitions to accept an unintentionally delayed maintenance fee payment.

4. **Minimum two (2)-month Reply Periods:**

Unless otherwise specified by USPTO rules, the PLT provides for a reply time period of at least two (2) months in many situations. The USPTO will provide a period for reply of at least two (2) months for replies to Office Actions for applications not involved in voluntary pilot programs or in proceedings before the PTAB.

1.6 HAGUE AGREEMENT

As previously stated, the Patent Law Treaties Implementation Act of 2012 ("PLTIA") was signed into law on December 18, 2012, and included provisions implementing the 1999 Geneva Act of the Hague Agreement Concerning the International Registration of Industrial Designs ("Hague Agreement"). These provisions (Title I of the PLTIA) took effect on **May 13, 2015**.

The Hague Agreement is an international registration system, which offers the possibility of obtaining protection for up to 100 industrial designs in designated member countries and intergovernmental organizations (referred to as "Contracting Parties") by filing a single international application in a single language either directly with the International Bureau of the World Intellectual Property Organization ("WIPO") or indirectly through the office of Applicant's Contracting Party.

Effective May 13, 2015, U.S. Applicants can file international design applications through the USPTO as an office of indirect filing, and Applicants filing international design applications can designate the United States for design protection. In addition, U.S. design patents resulting from such applications will have a fifteen (15)-year term from issuance.

WIPO provides an electronic filing system for filing international design applications or they can be filed electronically through USPTO via EFS-Web. International design applications can also be filed in paper with either WIPO or the USPTO, though additional WIPO publication fees may apply for paper submissions.

An international design application must include:

1. The "official form" and any required annexes.
2. Reproductions (form of drawings and/or photographs of the industrial design).
3. Payment of applicable fees.

Information concerning the Hague system, including geographic coverage and a guide for users, is available at WIPO's website *www.wipo.int/hague/en*.

The Role of the Patent Professional

• • •

2.1 INTRODUCTION

IN TODAY'S HIGHLY COMPETITIVE MARKETPLACE, the Paralegal is instrumental in developing a cost-effective patent prosecution team that produces a high quality work product under the Practitioner's supervision. The legal and time-sensitive nature of patent prosecution requires that the Paralegal be highly skilled and function well in a team environment, with one or more Practitioners at its head. In view of the breadth of work and the demands of patent prosecution, the Paralegal may assume a multi-faceted role to help with (or perform) his/her Practitioner's administrative and/or clerical functions.

In general, the role of the Paralegal is to assist the Practitioner in administrative and/or clerical functions relating to patent prosecution and maintaining existing patents. The purpose of this section and the following subsections is to make the novice Paralegal aware of the responsibilities typically associated with the Paralegal. Various responsibilities may be assigned based on the preferences of the Practitioner as well as the experience and level of competence of the Paralegal. Accordingly, it should be noted that the following discussion is meant to be representative, not exclusive, of the duties that may be assigned to the Paralegal.

In addition to those duties specifically assigned to the Paralegal, it is always important that the Paralegal communicate effectively with the Practitioner. The Paralegal should reach out to the Practitioner to establish a system of communication as well as responsibilities so that they can both be comfortable with each other. Moreover, it is imperative that the Paralegal communicate with the Practitioner so that there is a mutual understanding of any docket deadlines and work product style and content, as each Practitioner has his/her own style.

The ultimate responsibility for handling a particular patent matter is always with the Practitioner. However, the actions of the Paralegal can have a direct and significant impact on the Practitioner's practice. Adverse impacts can include allegations of malpractice, lawsuits, and revocation of a Practitioner's license to practice before the USPTO. Actions of the Paralegal may also have a direct impact on the ability of a client to obtain or enforce a patent. It is thus necessary for the Paralegal to exercise due care and diligence to ensure that the work performed is proper. It is also the responsibility of the Paralegal to bring any issues that may arise to the attention of the Practitioner as soon as possible. In some cases, delay in attending to an issue may be detrimental in terms of correcting the issue.

2.2 Administrative Support

Many Practitioners rely on the Paralegal for administrative support. Most Practitioners are familiar with computerized word processing, thus lessening the reliance on the Paralegal for many word processing projects. Nevertheless, the Paralegal should be competent with computerized word processing skills in order to assist the Practitioner when required. The Paralegal may be called upon to perform dictation and/or transcription in addition to standard word processing. The Paralegal may also be required (or asked) to perform other administrative functions, as needed, such as conversing with the USPTO help desk on formal matters.

The Paralegal should be familiar with the Practitioner's preferences for formal communications with the USPTO. He/she should be able to draft standard documents or shells for the Practitioner's use. For example, the Paralegal is often called upon to generate an Amendment shell for response to an Office Action.

The Paralegal should be familiar with USPTO forms and formats, as well as any Patent Cooperation Treaty ("PCT") International Bureau forms and formats used by the Practitioner. For example, the Paralegal may need to prepare and complete a Utility Application Transmittal (optional) in preparation for filing a new patent application by the Practitioner. With regards to the International Bureau, the Practitioner may file a PCT International Application with the USPTO as the Receiving Office. Thus, the Paralegal should be familiar with the Request Form required for filing an International Application.

The Practitioner may have developed several forms or documents for USPTO submission which need to be completed by the client and/or inventors. For example, a Declaration for a new application would need to be executed by the inventors and filed with the USPTO. The Paralegal should be familiar with these forms as well and be able to complete these forms with little or no guidance from the Practitioner.

2.3 USPTO Filing

Filings with the USPTO can be submitted in person, by mail, or by EFS-Web. Some filings may also be eligible for submission via facsimile. Always consult with the Practitioner to determine whether or not a submission is eligible for a particular mode of transmission before filing. All papers must be signed by a Practitioner before being submitted to the USPTO.

When filing in person or by mail, all documents should be neatly and professionally presented to the Practitioner for final review and signature. They should be sorted in the order noted on any transmittal and with sufficient bindings to prevent mix-up of the documents. Stapling, binder clips, or paper clips are appropriate according to the preferences of the Practitioner. Once the Practitioner has signed the documents, they should be copied or scanned, as appropriate, for the Practitioner file copy and the client file copy. The documents should then be placed into an envelope in the appropriate order and sealed for transmission to the USPTO. If filing by mail, a certificate of mailing or mailing by priority mail express should be used, as appropriate.

When filing by EFS-Web, consult with the Practitioner regarding the preferred method of review. The Practitioner may elect for an online review as opposed to a hard copy review, especially if he/she prefers the electronic signature option. Since filing by EFS-Web yields an immediate Acknowledgment Receipt, a copy of the Acknowledgment Receipt should be made of record in the Practitioner and client files as well.

Regardless of the manner in filing, the documents must be checked by the Paralegal to ensure that the documents conform to the USPTO formal format requirements for the specification and claims as well as the drawings. The documents should also be checked to make sure all pages are present and accounted for and to make sure there is no spelling or typographical errors. Preferably, this review will include an automated spell check as well as a visual review by the Paralegal. Remember that it is ultimately the Practitioner's responsibility for any filings to be made at the USPTO, not the Paralegal.

2.4 DOCKET MANAGEMENT

Practitioners will have a docketing system to track proposed patent applications, pending patent applications, and issued patents, as well as their respective due dates. Accordingly, it is important for the Paralegal to become familiar with the docketing system. In many cases, the Practitioner may request that the Paralegal add items to the docket, rearrange items on the docket, or add comments to items on the docket. The Paralegal should solicit feedback on docket items with due dates when it is unclear what the disposition of the docket item may be. This inquiry should occur early enough to attend to the due date if work on the docket item has not yet begun.

When an Action is received from the USPTO, it may have a due date or deadline for response associated with it. It is the responsibility of the Paralegal to ensure that the Action is docketed to the appropriate matter and with the appropriate due date. When docketing is performed by someone besides the Paralegal (e.g., a docketing clerk), the Paralegal should confirm that the correct action and date have been docketed.

It is also the responsibility of the Paralegal to manage the workflow associated with the docket to make sure matters on the docket are brought to the attention of and handled by the Practitioner in a timely manner. This may include notifying the Practitioner, in person or by email, on a weekly or monthly basis of Actions with impending deadlines. For example, the Paralegal may prepare a task list for matters with upcoming deadlines. He/she may also prepare Response/Amendment shells, as necessary, for the Practitioner to use in handling matters with upcoming deadlines.

On a daily basis, the Paralegal should review any deadlines requiring immediate attention to make sure a deadline is not missed. This includes ensuring that any filings that may be required are prepared and ready for the Practitioner's signature on or before the due date and that any fees that may be required are prepared and ready for submission to the USPTO.

2.5 BILLING

Paralegals may be asked by their Practitioners to assist with the billing of clients for services rendered and fees paid. Billing statements or invoices may be prepared monthly or at the completion of a particular project. The Paralegal should consult in detail with the responsible Practitioner on the various preferences and requirements for the billing process. In general, the Paralegal will generate billing statements or invoices from Practitioner marked-up time records. The billing statements or invoices should be prepared on appropriate letterhead. A cover letter to accompany the billing statement or invoice may also be included depending on the preferences of the Practitioner and the client.

2.6 REPORTING OFFICE COMMUNICATIONS TO CLIENTS

Any and all written communications between the Practitioner and the USPTO relating to a particular client matter should be promptly reported to the client. It is the responsibility of the Paralegal to prepare the reporting letter and supporting documents for the Practitioner's signature, and after the Practitioner has signed the letter to forward the letter and documents to the client in a timely fashion. Different Practitioners may require different procedures when reporting official USPTO communications to clients. For example, some Practitioners may require a narrative on letterhead directed to the nature of the forwarded communications. In such cases, a draft letter should be prepared for revision and signature for the Practitioner. At a minimum, reporting communications to the client should include a clean copy of the communication. Reporting may be accomplished by mail or by email, based on the preferences of the Practitioner and the client.

2.7 FILE MANAGEMENT

When a new patent application file is to be opened, a request may be sent from the Practitioner. Alternatively, the client may separately request that a new matter be opened for a new invention that he/she would like the Practitioner to work on. Such requests may be in the form of an instruction letter from the client and may include an invention disclosure, foreign priority document, and/or provisional application.

Prior to acknowledging receipt of the new matter, the Paralegal should follow any new intake policies established by the Practitioner. For example, a conflict check based on the client and/or matter should be performed when appropriate. An appropriate tracking number should also be assigned to the new matter, in accordance with the Practitioner's docketing system. In accordance with the docketing system practice, due dates, specified by the Practitioner or the client, should be noted for different tasks associated with the new matter.

The Paralegal should ensure that the docketing of these due dates occurs in a timely fashion, preferably on the day the instruction letter is received. Due dates noted in the instruction letter (or by the Practitioner) may signify bar dates. Once the invention has been disclosed either in public use or on sale in this country, the bar date is the one (1)-year deadline to file a patent application in the United States and any foreign countries. Bar dates are important and may preclude the client from obtaining a patent for the invention. If any due date is impending, the Paralegal should notify the Practitioner immediately.

After docketing, the Paralegal should then prepare an acknowledgement letter to the client for the Practitioner's signature. The acknowledgement letter indicates receipt of the instruction letter and includes any attachments as well as the assigned tracking number. After the acknowledgement letter is reviewed and signed by the Practitioner, it must be promptly sent to the client.

A hard copy file for papers relating to the new matter should be created. The instruction letter, along with any relevant attachments, should be included in this hard copy file, along with the acknowledgement letter and copies of any future correspondence relating to the prosecution of the matter. This includes copies of any communications from or to the USPTO by the Practitioner.

In addition to hard copy files, many Practitioners currently use electronic databases to create electronic file wrappers. The Paralegal should consult with the Practitioner regarding the policies and procedures associated with electronic file wrappers. For example, the Practitioner may direct the Paralegal to store all shells created for the matter on the electronic database. In recent years, Practitioners have increasingly used electronic databases as a replacement for the hard copy files for client matters. Accordingly, the Paralegal may use the electronic database as the repository for all communications from or to the

USPTO by the Practitioner and any client communications as a supplement to or in place of the hard copy files.

Once a patent application has expired (as in the case of provisional applications), becomes abandoned, or is issued, the hard copy of the file may no longer be necessary since the application is no longer pending. The file may thus be placed in storage after a certain period, in accordance with the retention practice of the Practitioner. Some Practitioners may have retention schedules and policies regarding files in storage. For example, the Practitioner may wish for extraneous documents in the file to be removed. The Paralegal should consult with the Practitioner on storage procedures and timely send any expired, abandoned, or issued patent application files to storage, as appropriate. However, patent applications which are in the same patent family as other applications that remain pending should be retained on site so that any information in the parent or child applications is immediately available when prosecuting the currently pending application.

Conducting Business with the Uspto

● ● ●

3.1 CONTACT PATENTS

USPTO Customer Support Centers (*www.uspto.gov/learning-and-resources/support-centers/uspto-customer-support-centers*)

Customer Support is available Monday-Friday, 8:30 a.m. through 8:00 p.m. ET (except Federal holidays)

Phone: (800) 786-9199 (toll-free) or (571) 272-1000 (local) or
        (800) 877-8339 (TTY)

Email: *usptoinfo@uspto.gov*

Patent Central Facsimile Number: (571) 273-8300

Mail: Mail Stop _____
                Commissioner for Patents
                P.O. Box 1450
                Alexandria, VA 22313-1450

Hand-delivery: U.S. Patent and Trademark Office
                Customer Service Window, Mail Stop _____
                Randolph Building
                401 Dulany Street
                Alexandria, VA 22314

Website: *www.uspto.gov*

CUSTOMER SUPPORT OFFICES:

Patent EBC Customer Service Center *(www.uspto.gov/learning-and-resources/support-centers/patent-electronic-business-center)*:

* (866) 217-9197 (toll-free) or (571) 272-4100 (local) or send email to *ebc@uspto.gov*

Customer support for electronic filing and PAIR access. Customer Numbers and Digital PKI Certificate issuance and maintenance.

Inventors Assistance Center *(www.uspto.gov/learning-and-resources/support-centers/inventors-assistance-center-iac)*:

* (800) 786-9199 (toll-free) or (571) 272-1000 (local) or (800) 877-8339 (TTY)

Provides patent information and services to the public. The IAC is staffed by former Supervisory Patent Examiners and experienced Primary Examiners who answer general questions concerning patent examining policy and procedures.

AIA Helpdesk *(www.uspto.gov/patent/laws-and-regulations/leahy-smith-america-invents-act-implementation)*:

* (855) 435-7242 (toll-free) or (571) 272-0300 (local) or send email to *helpAIA@uspto.gov*

Provides information regarding the America Invents Act, including the new legal provisions and rules.

Application Assistance Unit *(www.uspto.gov/learning-and-resources/support-centers/application-assistance-unit-aau)*:

* (888) 786-0101 (toll-free) or (571) 272-4000 or (571) 272-4200 (local)

Provides information regarding filing receipts, missing parts letters, abandonment notices, express abandonments, change/withdrawal of attorney, change of address, Power of Attorney, status inquiries regarding newly filed and allowed patent applications; pre-grant publication or eighteen (18)-month publication, and processing of Certificates of Correction.

Assignment Recordation Branch (www.uspto.gov/learning-and-resources/support-centers/assignments-recordation-branch-arb)**:**

* (571) 272-3350; Facsimile (571) 273-0140 or send email to *epas@uspto.gov*

Provides assistance in recording a new assignment or obtaining information on a pending assignment, questions on assignments, liens on patents, recordation forms, and trademark assignments.

Petitions Help Desk (*www.uspto.gov/patents-application-process/petitions*):

* (571) 272-3282

Provides information regarding petitions, the filing of patent applications, and related matters.

International Legal Administration Help Desk (*www.uspto.gov/patents-getting-started/international-protection/international-patent-legal-administration-formerly*):

* (571) 272-4300

Provides assistance with applications filed under the Patent Cooperation Treaty.

Patent and Trademark Copy Fulfillment Branch (*ebiz1.uspto.gov/oems25p/index.html*):

* (800) 972-6382 (toll-free) or (571) 272-3150 (local) or Facsimile (571) 273-3250 or send email to dsd@uspto.gov

Copies of official USPTO documents are available for sale from the Patent and Trademark Copy Fulfillment Branch. Request for copies must include payment and identification of the patent number(s) being requested. Telephone, fax, email, mail and walk-in services are provided Monday through Friday 8:30 a.m. to 5:00 p.m. ET.

Ombudsman Program (*www.uspto.gov/patent/ombudsman-program*):

* (855) 559-8589 (toll-free) or (571) 272-5555 (local)

When there is a breakdown in the normal application process, including before and after prosecution, the Patents Ombudsman Program can assist in getting the application back on track.

Receipts Accounting Division (RAD) (*www.uspto.gov/about-us/organizational-offices/office-chief-financial-officer/office-finance/receipts-accounting-2*):

* (571) 272-6500

Provides information on fee payments, including maintenance fees, Deposit Accounts, and refunds. Assistance is available Monday through Friday (except Federal holidays) from 8:30 a.m. to 5:00 p.m. ET.

Patent Legal Administration Help Desk (*www.uspto.gov/about-us/organizational-offices/office-commissioner-patents/office-deputy-commissioner-patent-18*):

* (571) 272-7701

Provides information regarding rule changes, PG Pubs, Patent Term Adjustment and Extension.

Scientific and Technical Information Center Library Public Access Information (STIC) (*www.uspto.gov/learning-and-resources/support-centers/stic-library-openings*):

* (571) 272-2520 or (571) 272-3547

Provides extensive collections of foreign patents, non-patent literature, and intellectual property law, as well as assistance for Sequence Listing questions/filing. Open to the public.

Public Search Facility (PSF) (*www.uspto.gov/learning-and-resources/support-centers/public-search-facility*):

* (571) 272-3275

Provides public access to patent and trademark information in a variety of formats including on-line, microfilm, and print.

3.2 FILING PAPERS IN THE USPTO

3.2.1 FILING REQUIREMENTS
If filing a U.S. patent application by paper, make sure that the utility transmittal is signed and dated by a Practitioner, along with his/her registration number. The signature can either be hand written

or by S-signature, e.g., /John Doe/. Otherwise, a Notice to File Missing Parts will be issued by the UPSTO for a missing signature. If it is a National Phase filing in the U.S., a Notice to File Missing Requirements will be issued if the signature is not present (see ***Chapter 28 – Entry into the U.S. National Phase***).

If filing a U.S. patent application via EFS-Web, the utility transmittal is optional if the application is filed with a signed Application Data Sheet ("ADS").

3.2.2 SUGGESTIONS

When preparing documents for the USPTO, place the Practitioner docket number, e.g., 999999, on the upper right-hand corner on every page for identification purposes. This will be of great value if pages get separated and need to be rematched with the application file.

Another suggestion is to have an indication of who prepared the documents, along with the Practitioner's initials on the last page, underneath the Practitioner's signature.

3.2.3 NEXT DAY BUSINESS RULE

The USPTO is not open for filing of correspondence on Saturday, Sunday, or a Federal holiday within the District of Columbia on or days the Office is officially closed due to bad weather or for some other reason. Except for correspondence by facsimile or filed electronically, no correspondence is received on these days.

3.3 IN PERSON - CENTRALIZED HAND-DELIVERY

Except correspondence for Maintenance Fee payments, Deposit Account Replenishments, and Licensing and Review, address correspondence to be delivered by other delivery services (Federal Express, UPS, DHL, etc.), documents to be filed can be hand-delivered to the Customer Service Window located at:

U.S. States Patent and Trademark Office
Randolph Building
401 Dulany Street
Alexandria, VA 22314

Documents can be delivered to the Customer Service Window at the USPTO until midnight weekdays, Monday through Friday (except when a Federal holiday falls on a weekday), and such documents will be stamped as being received on that day. Best practice is to have a pre-prepared filing receipt that can be date-stamped by the clerk at the Customer Service Window. The filing receipt should identify the document(s) being filed.

3.4 Mailing of Papers - Mailing Addresses

All business with the USPTO is transacted in writing and all correspondence relating to patent matters should be addressed to:

Mail Stop _____
Commissioner for Patents
P.O. Box 1450
Alexandria, VA 22313-1450

If a mail stop is appropriate, the mail stop should also be used. Mail addressed to different mail stops should be mailed separately to ensure proper routing. For example, after-final correspondence should be addressed to:

Mail Stop AF
Commissioner for Patents
P.O. Box 1450
Alexandria, VA 22313-1450

and assignments should be mailed to:

Mail Stop Assignment Recordation Services
Director of USPTO
P.O. Box 1450
Alexandria, VA 22313-1450

Any correspondence should include the full return address and zip code. Go to this site for the appropriate mail stops and for more information.

www.uspto.gov/patents/mail.jsp

3.4.1 VERIFICATION - CERTIFICATE OF MAILING

Correspondence will be considered as being timely filed if the correspondence is mailed prior to the expiration of the set period of time by using the following Certificate of Mailing language:

CERTIFICATE OF MAILING

I hereby certify that this correspondence is being deposited with the United States Postal Service with sufficient postage as First Class Mail in an envelope addressed to Mail Stop _____, Commissioner for Patents, P.O. Box 1450, Alexandria, VA 22313-1450, on the date shown below.

Date:_____   (Signature of person mailing the correspondence)

The person signing the certificate should have a reasonable basis to expect that the correspondence will be deposited with the U.S. Postal Service on the date indicated on the certificate.

3.4.2 PRIORITY MAIL EXPRESS

Correspondence can be submitted by Priority Mail Express if the Practitioner desires to have the benefit of the date of deposit in the U.S. Postal Service ("USPS"), e.g., new U.S. patent applications. Correspondence will be stamped with the date of deposit as "Priority Mail Express" with the USPS. The Priority Mail Express label number should appear on the correspondence to show that the correspondence is being sent by Priority Mail Express.

3.5 CENTRALIZED FACSIMILE

All patent application-related correspondence transmitted by facsimile must be directed, with a few exceptions, to:

Central Facsimile Number (571) 273-8300

Any official correspondence transmitted by facsimile in error to prior published facsimile numbers will be either automatically re-routed to the Central Facsimile Number, or manually forwarded to the central facsimile facility for processing but may thereby incur a delay before being processed. The Central Facsimile Number is capable of simultaneous receipt of facsimile transmissions from multiple customers. The following examples are correspondence that may be faxed to the USPTO:

- Amendments
- Petitions for an Extension of Time
- Authorization to charge a Deposit Account
- Information Disclosure Statements (IDS)

* Terminal Disclaimers
* Notices of Appeal and Appeal Briefs
* Continued Prosecution Applications (CPA) under 37 CFR 1.53(d)
* Requests for Continued Examination under 37 CFR 1.114

3.5.1 EXCEPTIONS TO THE CENTRALIZED FACSIMILE

Exceptions to using the centralized facsimile number are set forth below. The correspondence items below may be sent by facsimile to specific facsimile numbers as indicated below as most of these items are for non-patent application related matters.

For each USPTO location listed below, only the particular type of correspondence indicated may be transmitted to the specific facsimile number at that USPTO location. All other types of facsimile transmitted correspondence must be sent to the Central Facsimile Number (571) 273-8300.

1. Application Assistance Unit

The Application Assistance Unit ("AAU") is the call center that serves the Office of Patent Application Processing ("OPAP") and the Office of Data Management ("ODM"). The staff in the AAU is trained to assist with a broad range of questions and issues pertaining to the pre-examination and the post-examination processing of patent applications.

The following is a list of official numbers for AAU:

Facsimile number for Corrected Filing Receipt Requests: (571) 273-8300

Facsimile number for Response to Notice to File Missing
Parts (drawings may NOT be submitted by facsimile):   (703) 308-7751

Telephone number for Customer Service: (888) 786-0101

2. PCT Operations and International Patent Legal Administration

Correspondence subsequent to filing an international application before the U.S. Receiving Office, the U.S. International Searching Authority, or the U.S. International Examining Authority:

Facsimile number for papers in international applications: (571) 273-3201

Facsimile number for response to Decisions on Petition: (571) 273-0459

NOTE: An international application for patent or a copy of the international application and the basic national fee necessary to enter the national stage may NOT be submitted by facsimile. Subsequent correspondence may be transmitted by facsimile in an application before the U.S. Receiving Office, the U.S. International Searching Authority, or the U.S. International Examining Authority, but it will NOT receive the benefit of any certificate of transmission (or mailing). Correspondence during national stage, subsequent to entry, is handled in the same manner as a U.S. national application.

The PCT Help Desk: (571) 273-0419 facsimile number
(571) 272-4300 telephone number

3. Office of Data Management

Payment of an Issue Fee and any required Publication Fee by authorization to charge a Deposit Account or Credit Card may be submitted by facsimile transmission. When drawings are submitted with payment of an Issue Fee, they may be submitted by facsimile, although Applicant or the Applicant's representative is reminded that the facsimile process may reduce the quality of the drawings, and the USPTO will generally print the drawings as received.

The applicable facsimile numbers for payment of the Issue and/or Publication Fee(s) by facsimile are as follows:

Facsimile number for Issue Fee (and any Publication Fee)
Payments: (571) 273-2885

Telephone number to check on receipt of payment: (571) 272-4200
                                                                               or (888) 786-0101

4. Office of Pre-Grant Publication

Petitions for express abandonment to avoid publication, requests to rescind a nonpublication request and notices of foreign filing should be directed to the Pre-Grant Publication Division ("PG-PUB"). Questions regarding publication of patent applications (or rescissions of nonpublication requests) may also be directed by email to pgpub@uspto.gov.

Facsimile number for PG-PUB correspondence: (703) 305-8568

Telephone number for assistance from the PG-PUB: (703) 605-4283

5. *Electronic Business Center ("EBC")*

Request for Customer Number Data Change (PTO/SB/124A) form at *www.uspto.gov/web/ forms/ sb0124-fill.pdf* and **Request for a Customer Number (PTO/SB/125A)** form at *www.uspto.gov/web/forms/ sb0125.pdf* may be facsimile-transmitted to the EBC. The EBC may also be reached by email at ebc@ uspto.gov.

Facsimile number for the EBC:	(571) 273-0177
Telephone number for assistance from the EBC:	(866) 217-9197

6. *Assignment Recordation Branch*

Facsimile transmission to record an assignment or other documents affecting title is permitted. This process allows customers to submit their documents directly into the automated Patent and Trademark Assignment System and receive the resulting recordation notice at their facsimile machine. Credit Card payments to record assignment documents are now accepted. Use of the **Credit Card Form (PTO-2038)** at *www.uspto.gov/forms/2038-fill.pdf* is required for the credit card information and must be separate from the assignment documents. Only documents with an identified patent application or patent number, a single cover sheet to record a single type of transaction, and the fee paid by an authorization to charge a USPTO Deposit Account or Credit Card may be submitted via facsimile:

Facsimile number for the Automated Patent and Trademark Assignment System:	(571) 273-0140
Telephone number for the Assignment Division for Assistance:	(571) 272-3350

7. *Central Reexamination Unit*

Ex parte and *inter partes* reexamination correspondence, except for the initial request:

Facsimile number for the Central Reexamination Unit:	(571) 273-9900
CRU telephone number for customer service and inquiries:	(571) 272-7705

8. Patent Trial and Appeal Board
Correspondence permitted to be transmitted by facsimile related to pending interferences may be transmitted by facsimile to the Patent Trial and Appeal Board at the number below. Correspondence should not be transmitted to this number if interference has not yet been declared.

Facsimile number for pending interference correspondence: (571) 273-0042

9. Office of the General Counsel
Correspondence that is permitted to be transmitted by facsimile to the Office of the General Counsel may be sent to the number below:

Facsimile number for the Office of the General Counsel: (571) 273-0099

10. Office of the Solicitor
Correspondence that is permitted to be transmitted by facsimile may be sent directly to the Office of the Solicitor at the number below:

Facsimile number for the Office of the Solicitor: (571) 273-0373

11. Licensing and Review
Petitions for a foreign filing license pursuant to 37 CFR 5.12(b), including a petition for a foreign filing license where there is no corresponding U.S. application (37 CFR 5.13):

Facsimile number for the Licensing and Review: (571) 273-0185

12. Office of Petitions
Correspondence that is permitted to be transmitted by facsimile may be sent directly to the Office of Petition at the number below:

Facsimile number for Petitions to Withdraw from Issue: (571) 273-0025

NOTE: This is limited to only Petitions to Withdraw. All other types of petitions must be directed to the Central Facsimile Number (571) 273-8300. Any paper other than a Petition to Withdraw from Issue which is sent to the Office of Petitions fax number (instead of the Central Facsimile Number) will be discarded. Petitions sent to the Central Facsimile Number should be marked "Special Processing Submission".

13. Office of Enrollment and Discipline ("OED")
Correspondence permitted to be transmitted to the OED.

Facsimile number for the OED: (571) 273-0074

Customer service and inquiries for the OED: (571) 272-4097

14. Office of Finance
Refund requests, Deposit Account inquiries, and Maintenance Fee payments.

Facsimile number for the Office of Finance: (571) 273-6500

Telephone number for customer service and inquiries: (571) 272-6500

15. Office of Public Records
Requests for certified copies of Office records may be transmitted.

Facsimile number for the Office of Public Records: (571) 273-3250

Telephone number for customer service and inquiries: (571) 272-3150

3.5.2 VERIFICATION - CERTIFICATE OF TRANSMISSION
Correspondence transmitted by facsimile to the USPTO will be accorded a date on which the complete transmission is received in the USPTO, unless that date is a Saturday, Sunday, or Federal holiday within the District of Columbia, in which case the date-stamped will be the next succeeding business day, which is not a Saturday, Sunday, or Federal holiday within the District of Columbia.

Correspondence can be transmitted by facsimile with the following Certificate of Transmission language:

CERTIFICATE OF FACSIMILE TRANSMISSION

I hereby certify that this paper is being transmitted via facsimile to the U.S. Patent and Trademark Office at (571) 273-8300, on the date shown below.

Date:_____   (Signature of person faxing documents)_____

3.5.3 DOCUMENTS/CORRESPONDENCE WHICH CANNOT BE FAXED
The following patent correspondence cannot be faxed to the USPTO:

* Correspondence relating to registration to practice before the USPTO in patent cases, enrollment, or disciplinary matters.
* Documents required by statute to be certified.
* A national patent application specification and drawing (Provisional or Nonprovisional) or other correspondence for the purpose of obtaining an application filing date, other than a continued prosecution application.
* International applications for patents.
* International design applications.
* Third-party submissions.
* A copy of an international application and the basic national fee necessary to enter the national stage.
* Color drawings.
* Request for Reexaminations.
* Request for Supplemental Examinations.
* Correspondence to be filed in a contested case or trial before the Patent Trial and Appeal Board, except as the Board may expressly authorize.
* Correspondence required to be filed in a patent application subject to a Secrecy Order and directly relating to the secrecy order content of the application.

3.6 PAPERS REQUIRING IMMEDIATE ATTENTION
The Applicant and Practitioners should follow the directions below for the listed, and only the listed, document types. Special procedures will be followed for these documents after submission. No special marking of these documents is required.

1. Petitions for express abandonment to avoid publication under 37 CFR 1.138(c)

    a.   The petition may be filed by mail, facsimile, hand-carried or EFS-Web.

Mail: The Applicant must mail the petition or letter to:

> Mail Stop Express Abandonment
> Commissioner for Patents
> P.O. Box 1450
> Alexandria, VA 22313-1450

Facsimile: The Applicant may transmit the petition or letter by facsimile directly to the Pre-Grant Publication Division at (703) 305-8568 during business hours (8:00 a.m. – 5:00 p.m.).

Hand Carried: The Applicant must hand carry the petition or letter to:

> Pre-Grant Publication Division
> U.S. Patent and Trademark Office
> 2900 Crystal Drive
> Arlington, VA 22202

Best practice is to prepare a filing receipt identifying the patent application and documents to be filed so that the receipt can be date-stamped by the clerk at the Customer Service Window.

EFS-Web: The Applicant must file the petition electronically. The document description is "Letter Express Abandonment of the Application". Check the current Fee Schedule at *www.uspto.gov/learning-and-resources/fees-and-payment/uspto-fee-schedule* for the Petition Fee.

    b.   For more information, contact the Pre-Grant Publication Division at (703) 605-4283.

Because a petition under 37 CFR 1.138(c) will not stop publication of the application unless it is recognized and acted on by the Pre-Grant Publication Division in sufficient time to avoid publication, the Applicant should use either facsimile or hand-carry in all instances where the projected publication date is less than three (3) months from the date of the petition. All submissions should be made at least four (4) weeks prior to the projected publication date.

2. Petition to withdraw from issue under 37 CFR 1.313

The petition may be filed by mailing, facsimile, hand-carried or EFS-Web.

Mail: The Applicant must mail the petition or letter to:

> Mail Stop Petitions
> Commissioner for Patents
> P.O. Box 1450
> Alexandria, VA 22313-1450

Facsimile: The Applicant must transmit the petition or letter by facsimile to the Central Facsimile Number (571) 273-8300 and should indicate "Special Processing Submission" or if urgent, the petition may be facsimile transmitted directly to the Office of Petitions at (571) 273-0025.

Hand-Carried: The Applicant must hand-carry or use non-USPS delivery services and address the petition to:

> Mail Stop Petitions
> U.S. Patent and Trademark Office
> Customer Service Window
> Randolph Building
> 401 Dulany Street
> Alexandria, VA 22314

The Customer Service Window is located on the Ballenger Avenue side of the Randolph Building. Best practice is to prepare a filing receipt identifying the patent application and the petition to be filed so that the receipt can be date-stamped by the clerk at the Customer Service Window.

EFS-Web: The Applicant may file the petition electronically via EFS-Web. The document description is "Petition to Withdraw from Issue".

Any questions should be directed to the Petitions Help Desk at (571) 272-3282. Hours of operation are 8:30 a.m. to 5:00 p.m., EST, Monday through Friday.

3. Request for Expedited Examination of a Design Application (Rocket Docket)

An Applicant seeking expedited examination may file a design application in the USPTO together with a corresponding request by hand-delivering the application papers and the request directly to the Director of the Design Technology Center 2900 ("TC 2900") Office. The telephone number for the customer service of TC 2900 is (571) 272-2900. If an Applicant chooses to file a design application and the corresponding request under 37 CFR 1.155 by mail, the envelope should be addressed to:

Mail Stop Expedited Design
Commissioner for Patents
P.O. Box 1450
Alexandria, VA 22313-1450

These procedures will help assure that these time-critical documents will be considered in time for processing.

3.7 CORRESPONDENCE FOR WHICH CENTRALIZED DELIVERY OF HAND-CARRIED PAPERS IS NOT REQUIRED

Non-patent application related papers and a few exceptions to the general rule for patent application-related correspondence may be delivered to specific non-central locations as set forth below. Thus, the following types of correspondence should be delivered to the specific location where they are processed instead of the Customer Service Window. Any such correspondence carried by error to the Customer Service Window will be accepted and then routed to the appropriate USPTO location, thereby incurring a delay before being processed.

Best practice is to prepare a filing receipt or an itemized postcard identifying the patent application or PTO matters of the document(s) being filed and have the receipt date-stamped by the office to which the document(s) has been delivered.

1. Access Requests

Requests for access to patent application files may continue to be hand-carried to:

File Information Unit
U.S. Patent and Trademark Office
2900 Crystal Drive (South Tower), Room 2E04
Arlington, VA 22202

Requests for access to patent application files that are maintained in the Image File Wrapper system and that have not yet been published may also be hand-carried to:

Public Search Facility
U.S. Patent and Trademark Office
Madison East Building
600 Dulany Street, 1st Floor
Alexandria, VA 22314

2. *Patent Term Extensions under 35 USC 156*

Patent term extension applications under 35 USC 156 (Hatch/Waxman) may be hand-carried to:

Office of Patent Legal Administration
U.S. Patent and Trademark Office
Madison West Building
600 Dulany Street, Room 07D85
Alexandria, VA 22314

At the guard station in Madison West (near the elevators), the security guard should call the Office of Patent Legal Administration at either (571) 272-7744 or (571) 272-7746 for delivery assistance.

3. *Assignments to be recorded*

Assignments may be hand-carried to:

Office of Public Records
Customer Service Window
U.S. Patent and Trademark Office
South Tower Building
2900 Crystal Drive, 2nd Floor
Arlington, VA 22202

4. *Office of General Counsel*

Correspondence for the Office of General Counsel may be hand-carried to:

Office of General Counsel
U.S. Patent and Trademark Office
Madison East Building
600 Dulany Street, Room 10A20
Alexandria, VA 22314

At the guard station in Madison East (near the elevators), the security guard should call the Office of General Counsel at (571) 272-7000 for delivery assistance. Hand-carried papers will be accepted on business days between the hours of 8:30 a.m. until 5:00 p.m.

5. *Office of the Solicitor*

Correspondence for the Solicitor's Office may be hand-carried to:

> Solicitor's Office
> U.S. Patent and Trademark Office
> Madison West Building
> 600 Dulany Street, Room 8C43
> Alexandria, VA 22314

At the guard station in Madison West (near the elevators), the security guard should call the Solicitor's Office at (571) 272-9035 for delivery assistance. Hand-carried papers will be accepted on business days between the hours of 8:30 a.m. until 5:00 p.m.

6. *Interference related correspondence*

Correspondence relating to interferences may be hand-carried to:

> U.S. Patent and Trademark Office
> Madison East Building
> 600 Dulany Street, 1st Floor Lobby
> Alexandria, VA 22314

There is a drop-off box at this location for hand-carried documents to be filed with the Patent Trial and Appeal Board. Customers need to pass through the magnetometer and have the materials passed through the x-ray sensors before placing them in the drop-off box. The drop-off box is for Interference-related correspondence only. Boxes are not permitted in the drop-off box. Boxed materials must be hand-carried to Madison East, Room 9B55-A using the following procedures. At the first floor guard station in Madison East (near the elevators), the security guard should call the Patent Trial and Appeal Board at (571) 272-9797 to obtain authorization to allow entry into the building for delivery to Room 9B55-A. Access to Room 9B55-A is available on business days from 8:30 a.m. to 4:45 p.m. only. Documents/boxes hand-carried to the drop-off box or to Room 9B55-A after 4:45 p.m. (EST) will receive the next business day's filing date.

Customers desiring a stamped return receipt for their filing need to personally bring their filing and the return receipt to Room 9B55-A during the hours stated above, or leave a postcard with the filing (postcard must include correct postage mail stamp and the address where the postcard is to be mailed). The Board will stamp the filing date on the postcard and mail the postcard to the customer. The postcard or return receipt must identify the documents to be filed, the patent application number and the proceeding number.

7. *Secrecy Order*

Applications subject to a secrecy order pursuant to 35 USC 181, or which are national security classified, and correspondence related thereto, may be hand-carried to the Licensing and Review location. The Licensing and Review location is:

> Technology Center 3600
> U.S. Patent and Trademark Office
> Knox Building
> 501 Dulany Street, Room 4B31
> Alexandria VA 22314

At the guard station in Knox (near the elevators), the security guard should call Licensing and Review at (571) 272-8203 for delivery assistance.

8. *Expedited Foreign Filing License Petitions*

Petitions for a foreign filing license for which expedited handling is requested and petitions for a retroactive license may be hand-carried to the drop box located at the guard station in the Knox building. Upon approaching the guard station, the delivery personnel should state their desire to drop off the request. Correspondence packages will be inspected/scanned before being placed in the drop box. All requests should identify a facsimile number, telephone number, and mailing address. All responses to the request will be sent by facsimile, followed by a mailed copy. If a facsimile number is not available, a hard copy will be mailed to the mailing address provided.

9. *Documents requested by the Office of Patent Publication*

Documents requested by the Office of Patent Publication may be hand-carried to:

> Office of Patent Publication
> U.S. Patent and Trademark Office

South Tower Building
2900 Crystal Drive, Room 8A24
Arlington VA 22202

For any questions, the Office of Patent Publication phone number is (571) 272-4200. Hand-carried papers will be accepted on business days between the hours of 8:30 a.m. until 5:00 p.m.

10. *Office of Enrollment and Discipline ("OED")*
Correspondence for the OED may be hand-carried to the receptionist at:

Office of Enrollment and Discipline
U.S. Patent and Trademark Office
Madison West Building
600 Dulany Street, 8th Floor
Alexandria VA 22314

At the guard station in Madison East (near the elevators), the security guard should call the OED at (571) 272-4097 for delivery assistance. Hand-carried papers will be accepted on business days between the hours of 8:30 a.m. until 5:00 p.m.

11. *Office of Finance*
Refund requests, Deposit Account replenishments, and Maintenance Fee payments may be hand-carried to the receptionist at:

Office of Finance
U.S. Patent and Trademark Office
Carlyle Place Building
2051 Jamieson Avenue, Suite 300
Alexandria, VA 22314

Hand-carried correspondence will only be accepted and not processed. Although the receptionist will not process any correspondence, if the correspondence is delivered with a postcard identifying the correspondence to be filed and the Deposit Account number, the receptionist will provide a delivery receipt by date-stamping the postcard. Depending on whether the correspondence is a refund request, Deposit Account related (e.g., a Deposit Account replenishment), or Maintenance Fee related (e.g., a Maintenance Fee

Payment), the correspondence should be placed in an envelope with REFUND, DEPOSIT ACCOUNT, or MAINTENANCE FEE written in dark ink across the envelope.

12. *Best Practice for Hand-Carried Documents*

Notwithstanding references to postcard requirements set forth above, with any hand-carried documents to be addressed to a specific office, best practice is always to prepare a filing receipt or postcard identifying the patent application or PTO matter and the document(s) being filed and have the receipt date-stamped by the office to which the document(s) has been delivered.

3.8 PATENT ELECTRONIC BUSINESS CENTER

Patent Electronic Business Center Contact Information:

Hours: Monday – Friday, 6:00 a.m. to 12:00 midnight (Eastern Time)

Phone: (866) 217-9197 (toll-free) or (571) 272-4100 (local)

Email: ebc@uspto.gov

Fax: (571) 273-0177

Mail: Mail Stop EBC
Commissioner for Patents
P.O. Box 1450
Alexandria, VA 22313-1450

PTO: Madison East Building
600 Dulany Street, 8th Floor, Room C53
Alexandria, VA 22314

Website: www.uspto.gov/patents/ebc/index.jsp

The Patent Electronic Business Center ("EBC") is the e-commerce home for conducting business with the USPTO. The following activities will enable the Paralegal to do business with the USPTO electronically:

- Initial filing of a patent application for unregistered and registered eFilers.
- After initial filing of a patent application, submitting follow-on documents for registered eFilers.
- Checking the status of a patent application for registered eFilers.
- Checking the status of a published patent application for unregistered eFilers.
- Help.

3.8.1 eFILING
Unregistered and registered eFilers can file patent applications and documents electronically.

3.8.1.1 eFiling as an Unregistered eFiler
An unregistered eFiler is a person who does not have a Digital PKI Certificate issued by the USPTO. Anyone (patent attorneys, patent agents, legal secretaries, pro se filers) who visits EFS-Web can submit patent applications and documents. However, an unregistered eFiler must provide contact information and select the type of application being filed before proceeding through the application process.

An unregistered eFiler may file the following applications and documents:

- Accelerated Examination Requests
- Design Application
- Design Reissue Application
- International Application for filing in the U.S. Receiving Office
- Provisional Application
- Requests for Reexamination
- Utility Patent Application
- Utility Reissue Patent Application
- U.S. National Stage Patent Application Under 35 USC 371
- Petition to Accept Intentionally Delayed Payment of Maintenance Fee in an Expired Patent (37 CFR 1.378(c)).
- Petition to Make Special based on Age.

3.8.1.2 eFiling as a Registered eFiler
A registered eFiler has both an assigned Practitioner and a Digital PKI Certificate for secure communication with the USPTO.

NOTE: A Paralegal may be working under the authority of the Practitioner who is a certificate holder; however, such authority does not imply that the Paralegal is a registered eFiler.

User Authentication is required for registered eFiler user.

User authentication is safe and secure which grants access to authorized eFilers for application submissions. Authentication is only successful if both the encrypted Digital PKI Certificate and password are valid.

A Paralegal working under the authority of the certificate holder must:

- Certify his or her status.
- Provide his or her name and email address.
- Indicate if the filing is a new or existing application.

A registered eFiler may file the following applications and documents:

- Utility Track I Prioritized Examination (Nonprovisional Application under 35 USC 111(a))
- Utility Accelerated Examination
- Design (Nonprovisional Application under 35 USC 171)
- Design Reexamination Request
- Design Reissue Application
- International Application for filing in the U.S. Receiving Office (PCT)
- Utility Provisional Application
- Utility Reexamination Request
- Utility Supplemental Examination Request
- Utility (Nonprovisional Application under 35 USC 111(a))
- Utility Reissue Application
- U.S. National Stage Application Under 35 USC 371
- Petition to Accept Unintentionally Delayed Payment of Maintenance Fee in an Expired Patent (37 CFR 1.378(c))
- Petition to Make Special Based on Age
- Pre-Grant Publication Under 37 CFR 1.211 to 37 CFR 1.221

3.9 EFS-WEB
The USPTO electronic filing system is called EFS-Web. It is the web-based patent application and document submission to upload patent applications and documents in PDF format to the USPTO. Using EFS-Web, anyone with a web-enabled computer can file patent applications and documents without downloading special software or changing document preparation tools and processes.

EFS-Web utilizes standard web-based screens and prompts to enable the eFiler to submit patent application documents in PDF format directly to the USPTO within minutes. When creating the PDF documents choose the tool, process, and workflow of the documents; convert them to standard PDF files and then submit them to USPTO's secure servers. EFS-Web is safe, simple, and secure and gives all of the same benefits as paper filings, including an electronic receipt that acknowledges the submission date.

EFS-Web offers the ability to file patent applications and other patent documents electronically in a fraction of the time and at substantially less cost than paper filings. No more printing, postage, and courier costs. The EFS user will receive immediate notification that the submission has been received. Unlike paper filings, most new applications submitted electronically can be viewed in Private PAIR within minutes.

3.9.1 ACCESSING EFS-WEB
Go to *www.uspto.gov*, under "Patents" tab, click "Filing Online" (under Application Process), then onto the "File Online" page, click "EFS-Web", then on the "About EFS-Web" page, click "Launch EFS-Web Registered eFiler", then "User Authentication" pops up on the screen.

3.9.2 TYPES OF APPLICATIONS LIMITED TO EFS-WEB FILING ONLY
The following types of applications must be submitted via EFS-Web only:

* Track One Priority Examination requests
* Applications under the Accelerated Examination Program
* Pre-Grant Publication requests

3.9.3 RULES FOR DOCUMENT INDEXING
The rules for indexing documents for filing documents by EFS-Web are as follows:

1. New Applications:
New applications must be divided or (separated) into appropriate sections under the category "Application Part":

- Specification
- Claims
- Abstract
- Drawings

2. *Response to Rejection:*

A response to a Non-Final Office Action called an "Amendment" or "Request for Reconsideration" must be divided (or separated) into its appropriate sections under the category "Amendment":

- Amendment/Req. Reconsideration – After Non-Final Reject
- Specification
- Claims
- Applicant Arguments/Remarks Made in an Amendment
- Abstract
- Drawings – only black and white line drawings or
  Drawings – other than black and white line drawings

3. *Information Disclosure Statement ("IDS"):*

A paper associated with an IDS must be divided (or separated) into its appropriate sections under the category "IDS/References":

- Transmittal Letter
- Information Disclosure Statement (IDS) Form (SB08)
- Foreign Reference
- NPL Documents (Non-Patent Literature, e.g., articles, publications)

4. *Appeal Briefs:*

Appeal Briefs do not have to have the "Claims" section separated out.

5. *Petitions:*

Petitions that are accompanied with Amendments must have separate application part document descriptions as mentioned above, but if the petition cites the application part, that part should be separated out.

3.9.4 APPLICATION FILING PROCESS

Once the eFiler has signed on and the application filing process has begun, the tab structure at the top of the screen expands to show you the components of the application process. The first tab indicates whether the person is filing as a registered or unregistered eFiler. The white tab indicates that the eFiler is within the application process.

> NOTE: Tabs allow the eFiler to move forward and backward within EFS-Web pages. If, for some reason, the eFiler has to make changes on the previous page, do not use the browser back button; only navigate by clicking on the tabs. If the eFiler clicks on the browser back button, the data may be lost, and the application process will have to start again.

3.9.5 ENTERING APPLICATION DATA

The eFiler must specify the title of the invention, the first named inventor, and a correspondence address.

> NOTE: If a Customer Number is not entered, then the submitted application will not be associated with the Practitioner's Digital PKI Certificate. If this relationship is not made, then a registered eFiler will not be able to view the application in Private PAIR.

3.9.6 UPLOADING DOCUMENTS

After the eFiler clicks "Continue", the bibliographic data entered by the eFiler is echoed back. If any errors are found, the eFiler can go back and correct them by clicking "Application Data". The next step is to upload a PDF file. The steps are as follows:

1. Browse and select the file (in PDF format) to be submitted.
2. Indicate whether the file (in PDF format) has multiple documents by clicking "Yes" or "No".
3. Enter the document description for the file or its parts.
4. If additional files (in PDF format) need to be uploaded, click "Add File" and repeat steps 1 to 3.
5. If any one of the uploaded files needs to be deleted, click "Delete" corresponding to that file row.
6. Click "Upload & Validate" to automatically check for compliance and to be notified of errors and warnings before submission.

> NOTE: EFS-Web can validate a maximum of 20 files uploaded at one time. Up to 60 documents can be uploaded per submission.

EFS-Web can upload one sequence listing (txt) file up to 100 MB per submission. The sequence listing file must be uploaded separately from other types of files. If the sequence listing does not conform to the ST.24 or ST.25 format, a warning will display.

IMPORTANT: Click "Upload and Validate" prior to "Review" or the uploaded files will be deleted.

Any errors can be corrected by clicking the "Attach Files" button.

3.9.7 FILING MULTIPLE PDF DOCUMENTS

PDF files that contain multiple documents must be separately indexed to be labeled properly in the USPTO Image File Wrapper ("IFW"). For example, a patent application PDF file may contain a specification, claims, abstract, and drawings that should be listed as separate documents in the IFW. Enter the page ranges for each section so that the documents are properly displayed in the IFW. Amendments should be separated as well.

At this point, additional sections of documents can be added by clicking "Add File" or "Upload & Validate" these documents.

NOTE: For new submissions, there must be at least one attachment other than the EFS-Web generated fee sheet.

3.9.8 CALCULATION OF FEES

Fees are dynamically generated based on the values entered by the eFiler.

* Indicate the business size - regular (undiscounted) or small entity (50% discount).
* Select all applicable fees.

NOTE: The application may be submitted without generating fees at this time by clicking the "Confirm/Submit" link or the "Continue" button. However, be aware that extra fees may be incurred.

Click "Calculate to see fees" and "Continue" to proceed to the next section.

WARNING: If "Cancel" is clicked on any screen during the process, a message will inform the eFiler that entered information will be deleted and request confirmation that the eFiler intends to cancel. Upon clicking "OK" to cancel, the information is deleted. The eFiler will be returned to the login screen to start the process again.

3.9.9 SUBMITTING THE APPLICATION

"Confirm/Submit" tab marks the last time before submission that the eFiler will be able to:

- Review and confirm or edit application data.
- Edit fees associated with the application.
- Remove or edit the documents associated with the application.

Once the application has been successfully submitted, EFS-Web will display a "Congratulations" screen that provides the following:

- The Application Number
- The Confirmation Number associated with the Application Number
- EFS ID

The eFiler will have the opportunity to either pay the required fees at this time or indicate that the fees will be paid later. If the latter, there will be an acknowledgement that additional charges may be incurred.

> **TIP:** The confirmation number is tied to the application. The application number and the confirmation number decrease the mismatching of submissions with their existing applications. This pair of numbers is required for submitting documents and/or fees to existing applications.

3.9.10 EFS-WEB RECEIPTS
eFilers are able to launch email programs by clicking the "Email Receipt Info" link to send information about Acknowledgement Receipts and Pre-Acknowledgement Receipts. eFilers must specify and include an email address for each recipient.

3.9.11 PAYMENT OF FEES
Fees may be paid to the USPTO via one of 3 ways:

- Charging the eFiler's USPTO Deposit Account.
- Charging by Credit Card.
- Electronic Funds Transfer.

USPTO Deposit Account:
Once the payment type is selected, click "Start online payment process", and follow the steps forth below:

1. Enter Deposit Account Number.
2. Enter Deposit Account Access Code.

3. Click "Choose an Authorized User for this Deposit Account".
4. Choose an authorized user of the Deposit Account from the drop-down menu.
5. Click "Yes" to certify eFiler has the right to use the account.
6. Check if any additional fees are required.
7. Click "Yes - charge Deposit Account now".

Credit Card Payment:

Filing fees may be charged to a VISA, MasterCard, American Express, or Discover credit card by providing and confirming credit card and billing information.

Electronic Funds Transfer ("EFT"):

Enter the Practitioner's User ID and password. If the Practitioner does not have a User ID and password, click "please create a USPTO EFT account now".

3.9.12 ACKNOWLEDGEMENT RECEIPT

Once the PTO fees have been paid, if any, the next screen will provide an Acknowledgement Receipt which provides the time (ET) and the date the submission was received as well as displaying the bibliographic information and uploaded files of the documents filed.

The Acknowledgement Receipt screen provides the following options:

* Email Receipt Info
* Print Receipt
* Save Receipt
* File Another Application
* File an Assignment of Ownership
* Pay Maintenance Fees
* Access Private PAIR

For more information regarding EFS-Web, go to *www.uspto.gov/ebc/efs_help.html*.

3.9.13 DOCUMENT DESCRIPTIONS

A document description is a USPTO-defined description of forms and documents that are received and processed in the USPTO. These document descriptions have corresponding document codes that are established and managed in the IFW. A document submitted via EFS-Web must be assigned to a USPTO document description.

The below site is the document descriptions spreadsheet which contains USPTO-defined descriptions of forms and documents that are received and processed in the USPTO. The eFiler must select from the list of pre-approved document descriptions to describe any files submitted via EFS-Web.

www.uspto.gov/ebc/portal/efs/efsweb_document_descriptions.xls

The below site has the general rules for document description indexing.

www.uspto.gov/ebc/portal/efs/rules_doc_codes.htm

3.9.14 Filing Documents in an Existing Application
In order to file follow-on documents in EFS-Web, the eFiler must have the application number and confirmation number handy.

> **Tip:** Avoid use of Miscellaneous Incoming Letter in EFS-Web when submitting documents such as Change of Address or Power of Attorney as this will take longer to process and be indexed properly at the USPTO.

3.10 Global Dossier Initiative
The Global Dossier Initiative is a set of business services being developed by the IP5 Offices aimed at modernizing the global patent system and delivering benefits to the IP community through a single portal/user interface. Global Dossier provides a single, secure point of access for the management of dossier and examination information, enabling and encouraging streamlining of office procedures among different IP Offices. This will lead to improved efficiency and predictability of global patent family prosecution with increased cost savings provided to patent applicants.

The members of IP5 are the following offices:

1. United States Patent and Trademark Office (USPTO)
2. European Patent Office (EPO)
3. Japan Patent Office (JPO)
4. Korean Intellectual Property Office (KIPO)

5. State Intellectual Property Office of the People's Republic of China (SIPO)

The IP5 Offices together handle about 80% of the world's patent applications, and 95% of all work carried out under the Patent Cooperation Treaty (PCT).

The first service being provided by the Global Dossier Initiative is a secure online access to the file histories of related applications from the IP5 Offices.

By using this service, users can see the patent family for a specific application, containing all related applications filed at participating IP Offices, along with the dossier, classification, and citation data for these applications. This service also provides Office Action Indicators to help users identify applications that contain office actions, a Collections View for saving documents and applications for review later on in the session, and the ability to download the documents in an application.

The Global Dossier can be found at *www.globaldossier.uspto.gov* and there is also a link to access Global Dossier in Private and Public PAIR above the Image File Wrapper tab in the application record.

3.11 FREE PUBLIC DATABASES

3.11.1 GOOGLE PATENTS
Google Patents provides image-based version, as well as PDF downloadable copies of most U.S. Patents, but only a portion of U.S. Pre-Grant Publications are available. Go to *www.google.com/patents* for accessing this site.

3.11.2 FREE PATENTS ONLINE
Go to *www.freepatentsonline.com* in order to download U.S. Patents (in PDF). Freepatentsonline provides text-based information of most U.S. Patents and Pre-Grant Publications, as well as some foreign documents. PDF copies of the U.S. Patents/Publications are available to registered users (registration is free).

3.11.3 PAT2PDF
Go to *www.pat2pdf.org* in order to download U.S. Patents or U.S. Application Publications (in PDF). Pat2PDF has become the industry standard for quickly obtaining PDF versions of U.S. Patents or Pre-Grant Publications.

The steps for using *www.pat2pdf.org* are set forth below:

1. Enter Document Number and then click "Fetch Patent".

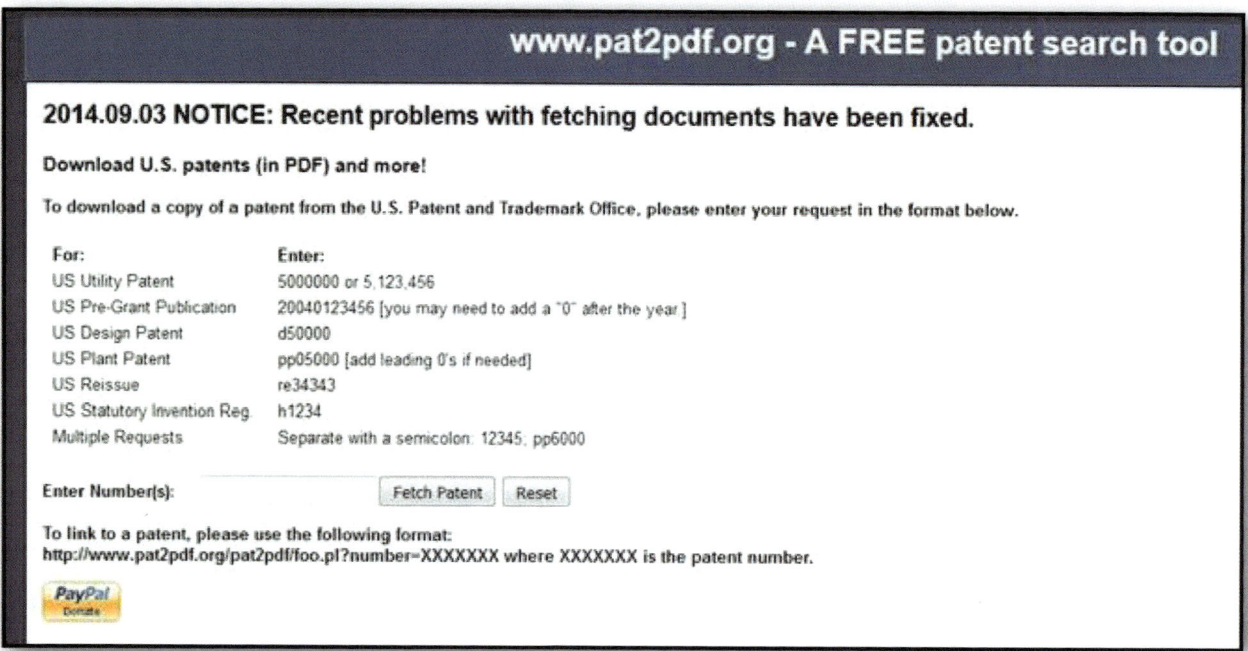

2. Click on the highlighted blue link.

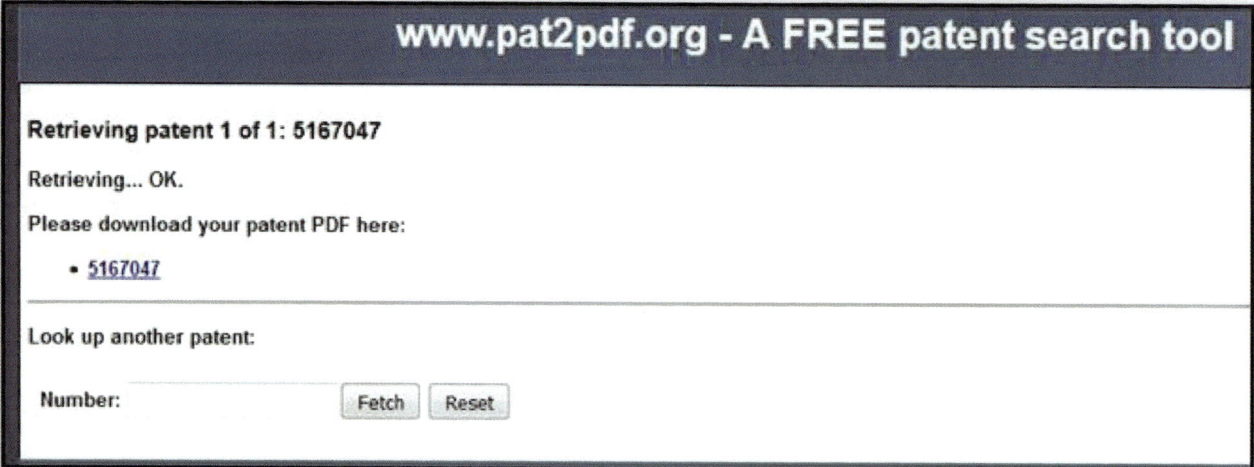

3. The document will be in PDF format on the screen.
4. The entire document can be printed at this point or save it to your computer if a copy is to be forwarded electronically.

3.11.4 PATENT RETRIEVER

Go to *www.patentretriever.com* in order to download most U.S. Patents and some U.S. Application Publications (in PDF). While downloads tend to be quicker through *www.patentretriever.com* as compared to *www.pat2pdf.org*, the site has issues with some U.S. Application Publications.

With respect to Patent Retriever, the USPTO prefix, i.e., "US", must precede the patent number. For example, enter US9999999 with the patent number. Click "Download" to view or print the patent.

3.12 POWER OF ATTORNEY PRACTICE

The Applicant for patent may give Power of Attorney. Use of Transmittal for **Power of Attorney to One or More Registered Practitioners (PTO/AIA/82)** form at *www.uspto.gov/forms/aia0082.pdf* is recommended for use by Applicants, including individual inventors, to appoint one or more Practitioners as having Power of Attorney in the application file.

Form PTO/AIA/82 has two parts, A and B. Part A is used to identify the application to which the Power of Attorney is directed and must be signed in accordance with 37 CFR 1.33(b) (e.g., a Practitioner). Part B is the Power of Attorney. The correspondence address may also be specified on this form. Where there are multiple Applicants, a Power of Attorney must be signed by each Applicant. Power of Attorney may only be given by the Applicant for patent (e.g., if the Applicant for patent is the Assignee, the inventors may not give Power of Attorney).

For example, where the Applicant is the Assignee, the Assignee (e.g., the President of a company) may execute the Power of Attorney (PTO/AIA/82B) or an equivalent) without need to resort to 37 CFR 3.71 and 37 CFR 3.73. The Practitioner may complete and assign the accompanying transmittal letter (PTO/AIA/82A) and submit a copy of the Power of Attorney into each respective application.

An Assignee who was not named as the Applicant and who wishes to appoint a Practitioner must proceed under 37 CFR 3.71 and 37 CFR 3.73 and file a **Statement Under 37 CFR 3.73(c) (PTO/AIA/96)** form at *www.uspto.gov/forms/aia0096.pdf* and a **Power of Attorney (PTO/AIA/80)** form at *www.uspto.gov/forms/aia0080.pdf*. The Power of Attorney must be signed by someone who is authorized to act on behalf of the assignee-Applicant (i.c., a person with a title that carries apparent authority, or a person who includes a statement of authorization to act).

> **NOTE:** A Power of Attorney to a Practitioner does not empower the Practitioner to sign the submission on behalf of the Assignee/Applicant.

Pro se inventors (i.e., prosecuting the application without a Practitioner) who are the Applicant may give Power of Attorney by using the **Power of Attorney to One or More of the Joint Inventors**

and Change of Correspondence Address (PTO/AIA/81) form at *www.uspto.gov/forms/aia0081.pdf.* This Power of Attorney permits the appointed inventor(s) to sign all correspondence on behalf of all of the inventors. If no power of attorney is given to one or more of the joint inventors, then all of the joint inventors who are the Applicant must sign patent application correspondence being filed with the USPTO.

A copy of a power of attorney may not be used if a new Applicant is being named in a continuing application, e.g., in the parent application the Power of Attorney was given by the inventors and the continuing application is filed by a juristic entity.

The filing receipt reflects the Power of Attorney that has been entered for the application. If the Power of Attorney has been rejected, the Practitioner will receive a separate notice that the Power of Attorney was rejected or denied due to improper submission.

If the Assignee is the Applicant on the ADS, then the Power of Attorney can be signed by the Assignee, not by the inventors.

If the original ADS does not establish an Applicant, the Power of Attorney must be signed by the inventors, not by the Assignee.

The Applicant must be added or changed before a Power of Attorney by Applicant will be accepted.

The Applicant or the patent owner must sign the Power of Attorney.

Inventors who are not the Applicant may not sign the Power of Attorney.

The USPTO discourages using a combined Declaration and Power of Attorney.

Under AIA, there are 3 Power of Attorney forms for use in patent applications:

* PTO/AIA/82 (Power of Attorney by Applicant) - **Recommended**
* PTO/AIA/81 (Power of Attorney to one or more joint inventors)
* PTO/AIA/80 (Power of Attorney by Assignee who is being the Applicant under § 1.46(c))

More information about the Power of Attorney forms can be found at

www.uspto.gov/forms/guid_aia-poa.pdf.

3.13 WITHDRAWAL FROM REPRESENTATION

In the event that a Notice of Withdrawal is filed by the Practitioner of record, the Practitioner must certify that he or she has:

- Given reasonable notice to the client, prior to the expiration of the reply period that the Practitioner intends to withdraw from employment.
- Delivered to the client or a duly authorized representative of the client all papers and property (including funds) to which the client is entitled.
- Notified the client of any replies that may be due and the time frame within which the client must respond, including any fees that may be due with a reply.
- Advised the client of the consequences of failing to comply with any reply which is due.

To expedite the handling of requests for permission to withdraw, the Practitioner should use this form to **Request for Withdrawal as Attorney or Agent and Change of Correspondence Address (PTO/ SB/83)** at *www.uspto.gov/web/forms/sb0083.pdf*. This form provides a section where Practitioners may certify the completion of the above-listed activities necessary for the request to withdraw from representation to be granted.

CHAPTER 4

Private and Public Pair

● ● ●

4.1 PRIVATE AND PUBLIC PAIR

PAIR IS AN ACRONYM FOR the USPTO Patent Application Information Retrieval system. Public PAIR displays only issued or published applications. To access Public PAIR, one needs only to enter a patent number, application number, or publication number to begin a search. Private PAIR allows Practitioners having Digital PKI Certificates to view patent applications prior to publication as a patent or view current patent application status electronically via the Internet before the application becomes published.

4.2 PRIVATE PAIR

Private PAIR provides secure real-time access to pending patent application status and history using digital certificates issued from the USPTO's Public Key Infrastructure ("PKI"). It also provides real-time status information for all actions taken by the USPTO for a given application and allows the certificate holder to have access to the USPTO's internal database (PALM). Therefore, the certificate holder can view the information as soon as it is posted. To access Private PAIR, one must:

- Be a registered Patent Practitioner/Agent or an Independent Inventor.
- Have a Customer Number.
- Have a Digital PKI Certificate to secure the transmission of the application to the USPTO.

4.2.1 CUSTOMER NUMBER

In order to apply for a Customer Number, download and complete the **Request for Customer Number (PTO/SB/125A)** form at *www.uspto.gov/sites/default/files/web/forms/sb0125.pdf*.

Fax the form to (571) 273-0177, or mail it to:

Mail Stop Customer Number
Commissioner of Patents
P.O. Box 1450
Alexandria, VA 22313

NOTE: The Patent Practitioner/Agent's registration number must be associated with the Customer Number. This can be accomplished by adding the registration number to the Customer Number Request form.

4.2.1.1 How to Associate Existing Application(s) with New Customer Number
Once the Customer Number is known, the current patent application(s) must be associated with it.

Download and complete the Customer Number Upload Spreadsheet at *www.uspto.gov/ebc/documents/cust_req_instructions.xls* in MS Excel.

This information can be sent on a CD or USB memory stick to:

Mail Stop EBC Customer Number
Commissioner of Patents
P.O. Box 1450
Alexandria, VA 22313

This spreadsheet can be used to change the correspondence address, and/or maintenance fee address, which will show a legal record of change. This spreadsheet MUST be accompanied by a cover letter, signed by someone who, for each application or patent listed on the attached spreadsheet, is one of the following:

- Pro Se applicant
- Sole Inventor (where there is not a registered Patent Attorney, or Agent of Record)
- Attorney or Agent of Record

4.2.1.2 How to Update a Customer Number
Customer Number updates can be made electronically in Private PAIR via the Customer Number Details option.

Other options would be to download and complete the **Customer Number Data Change (PTO/SB/124A)** form at *www.uspto.gov/sites/default/files/web/forms/sb0124-fill.pdf*.

Fax the form to (571) 273-0177, or mail it to:

Mail Stop EBC Customer Number
Commissioner of Patents
P.O. Box 1450
Alexandria, VA 22313

4.2.2 DIGITAL CERTIFICATE

After the Practitioner has read the Subscriber Agreement at *www.uspto.gov/ebc/documents/subscribersagreement.pdf* and obtained his/her Customer Number, a Certificate Action Form at *www.uspto.gov/ebc/documents/certificateactionform.pdf* must be completed for the Practitioner.

When completed, the Certificate Action Form must be signed by the Practitioner and notarized. The original form (no faxes or copies) must be mailed to:

Mail Stop EBC
Commissioner for Patents
P.O. Box 1450
Alexandria, VA 22313-1450

The information on the form will be used to generate a Digital PKI Certificate for the Practitioner that will be used to uniquely identify the Practitioner and allow the Practitioner to have secure access to the patent application data. To assure the security of the data, follow the policy described in the Subscriber Agreement.

4.2.2.1 Obtaining Access Codes

After the Digital PKI Certificate has been approved and issued by the USPTO, the Practitioner will receive two codes:

1. Authorization Code
2. Reference Number

The Authorization Code will be sent to the Practitioner via email. Once the Practitioner receives his/her Authorization Code via email, the Paralegal can call the EBC at (866) 217-9197 to receive the Practitioner's Reference Number. Once the Authorization Code and Reference Number have been received, the Digital PKI Certificate can be created.

4.2.2.2 Recovery of Access Codes

The Authorization Code expires in ninety (90) days from the date of issuance. If the Practitioner's Code expires or has been lost, contact the EBC at (866) 217-9197 to request reactivation. A new Authorization Code will be sent to the Practitioner via email. Call the EBC to receive the Reference Number. The EBC will help the Practitioner to ensure that he/she is reactivated again.

4.2.3 DIGITAL CERTIFICATE MANAGEMENT

The Digital Certificate Management website allows certificate holders to create and manage the digital certificate contact information, create a set of seven (7) recovery codes, and recover lost or damaged digital certificates online. The following features are available in Private PAIR.

4.2.3.1 Steps to Create a Digital PKI Certificate

1. Upon receipt of the access codes, go to the Digital Certificate Management home page via the UPSTO portal at *https://dcm.uspto.gov/UserRegistration/do/Home*.
2. Click on "New User" link or recover by clicking "Patent EBC Assisted Recovery" and enter the codes received from the EBC.
3. Choose a location to save the .epf file and create a username (i.e., hjones) and enter a unique password twice, then click the "Submit" button.

Once the Digital PKI Certificate has been successfully created, the Practitioner and/or Paralegal on behalf of the Practitioner will be able to access Private PAIR and take advantage of electronic filings of patent applications and patent application status checks via the Internet.

> **TIP:** Save the .epf file on your desktop or under C:/Program Files/USPTO on your hard drive so you can easily access it when you authenticate the Practitioner's number in Private PAIR. Every time you go into Private PAIR, you will have to authenticate the Practitioner's number by using the .epf file.

4.2.3.2 Register for Recovery Codes

Certificate holders will be able to register a set of seven (7) recovery codes for use in the event the .epf file becomes expired or corrupt. In order to register for these codes:

1. Go to the Digital Certificate Management home page via the UPSTO portal at *https://dcm.uspto.gov/UserRegistration/do/Home*.
2. Click "Register for Recovery Codes".

3. "User Login – Entrust Desktop Security Store" – Enter your security store name (.epf file), check box and click "Authenticate".
4. Assign the certificate holder a unique email address and re-enter the password.
5. A set of seven (7) recovery codes will be generated and assigned to the Practitioner's account.

Print or save these codes and keep them in a secure location for future use.

4.2.3.3 Recover with Recovery Codes

If, for some reason, the .epf file becomes expired or corrupted, and the certificate holder has already registered for recovery codes, there is no need to call the EBC. Follow these steps:

1. Go to the Digital Certificate Management home page via the UPSTO portal at *https://dcm.uspto.gov/UserRegistration/do/Home*.
2. Click "Recover with Codes".
3. 3Enter the user's registered email address, click "Submit".
4. Enter one of the recovery codes that have not been used, click "Submit".
5. Enter user name to be saved and a unique password twice, click "Submit".
6. The next screen pops up: "Your digital ID has been recovered successfully".

Each of these codes can only be used once. Once the seventh (7th) recovery code has been used, call the EBC for assistance.

4.2.4 PRIVATE PAIR ACCESS

To access Private PAIR, go to *https://ppair.uspto.gov/epatent/portal/home* and click on the "Private PAIR" link.

The system displays the Private PAIR login screen:

1. Browse to the location of the user's PKI certificate file (ending in ".epf").
2. Enter the Digital PKI certificate
3. Agree to the disclaimer
4. Press the "Authenticate" button

Once in Private PAIR, the user can search for applications by Customer Number, applications with status changes, view outgoing correspondence, and view or update Customer Number details.

4.2.4.1 Description of Tabs in Private Pair

Once an application has been selected, detailed information will be displayed by various tabs. Tabs appear only if data exists for that item. The following are descriptions for each tab that may be displayed in a specific application.

"Select New Case" - Select the Application Number, Control Number, Patent Number, PCT Number, Publication Number, International Design Registration Number, or Search by Attorney Docket Number.

"Application Data" - Bibliographic data of the application.

"Transaction History" - Listing in date order of the documents filed that are associated with the application.

"Image File Wrapper" – Listing of PDF copies of documents filed in the application that can be downloaded and printed from your computer.

"Continuity Data" - Listing of prior patent applications to which the patent applicant is claiming priority.

"Foreign Priority" – Listing of foreign patent applications to which the patent applicant is claiming foreign priority.

"Fees" – Listing of the fees paid in the application, including maintenance fee payments.

"Published Documents" - The application will be published at eighteen (18) months from filing date, and will be made public.

"Address & Attorney/Agent" - Displays Correspondence Address, along with the Attorney/Agent information.

"Supplemental Content" – Lists any supplemental documents in the image file wrapper, e.g., sequences, megatables, computer program listings, color drawings, chemical formulas and appendices are some examples.

"Assignments" - Assignment information if an assignment has been filed.

"Display References" - All information cited in an IDS cited by the Applicant and/or cited by the Examiner and considered by Examiner are displayed.

"First Action Prediction" – Information estimating when first action on the merits can be expected.

"Publication Review" - The application can be reviewed prior to the publication date of the application, and if needed, the application can be amended before the application publishes.

When a Practitioner is set up to participate in Private PAIR, he/she can grant authorization to a Paralegal to look up status on the applications associated with the Practitioner's Customer Number. Any new applications filed with the USPTO must be filed with the Customer Number in order to access information on the applications in Private PAIR.

> TIP: Private PAIR cannot be bookmarked into online favorites. In order to access Private PAIR, go to the USPTO website at *www.uspto.gov*. The reason for this is that Private PAIR is updated periodically and if Private PAIR is saved in favorites, it may not be updated to the latest version and, therefore, may not work.

4.3 PUBLIC PAIR

Public PAIR may be used without having a Digital PKI Certificate to search for specific patent numbers or publicly-available application numbers.

Go to *portal.uspto.gov/pair/PublicPair* to access Public PAIR.

Enter the verification code as shown in the box. The reason for the verification is to prevent disruptive use by automated programs. You will need to have both cookies and JavaScript enabled on your browser to use Public PAIR.

4.3.1 DESCRIPTION OF TABS IN PUBLIC PAIR

Except for "First Action Prediction" and "Publication Review" tabs, Public PAIR has the same tabs as Private PAIR. However, Public PAIR includes the following tabs not found in Private PAIR.

"Patent Term Adjustments" - Displays total patent term adjustments, including adjustments for USPTO and Applicant delays.

4.3.2 HOW TO ACCESS PATENT APPLICATION PDF IMAGES OF DOCUMENTS FILED IN APPLICATIONS USING PUBLIC PAIR

In order to access patent application full-page images in Public PAIR, follow these steps:

1. Go to *https://uspto.gov/learning-and-resources/portal-applications*.
2. Click on "Public Pair".
3. Both cookies and JavaScript need to be enabled on your browser. Enter the "RECAPTCHA" text as shown in the box. Then click "Continue".

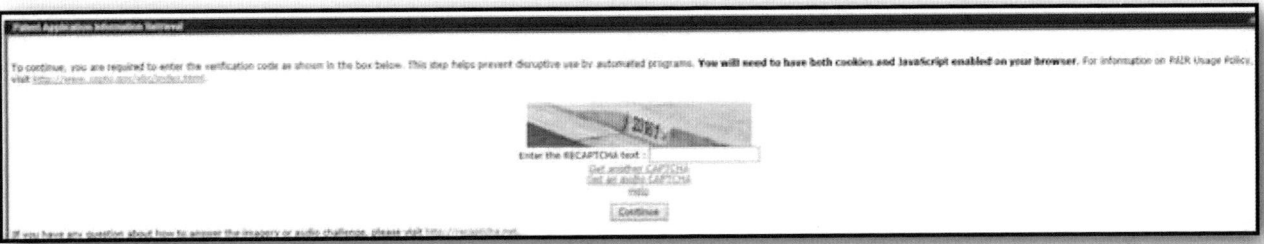

4. Search for Application and click "SEARCH" button.

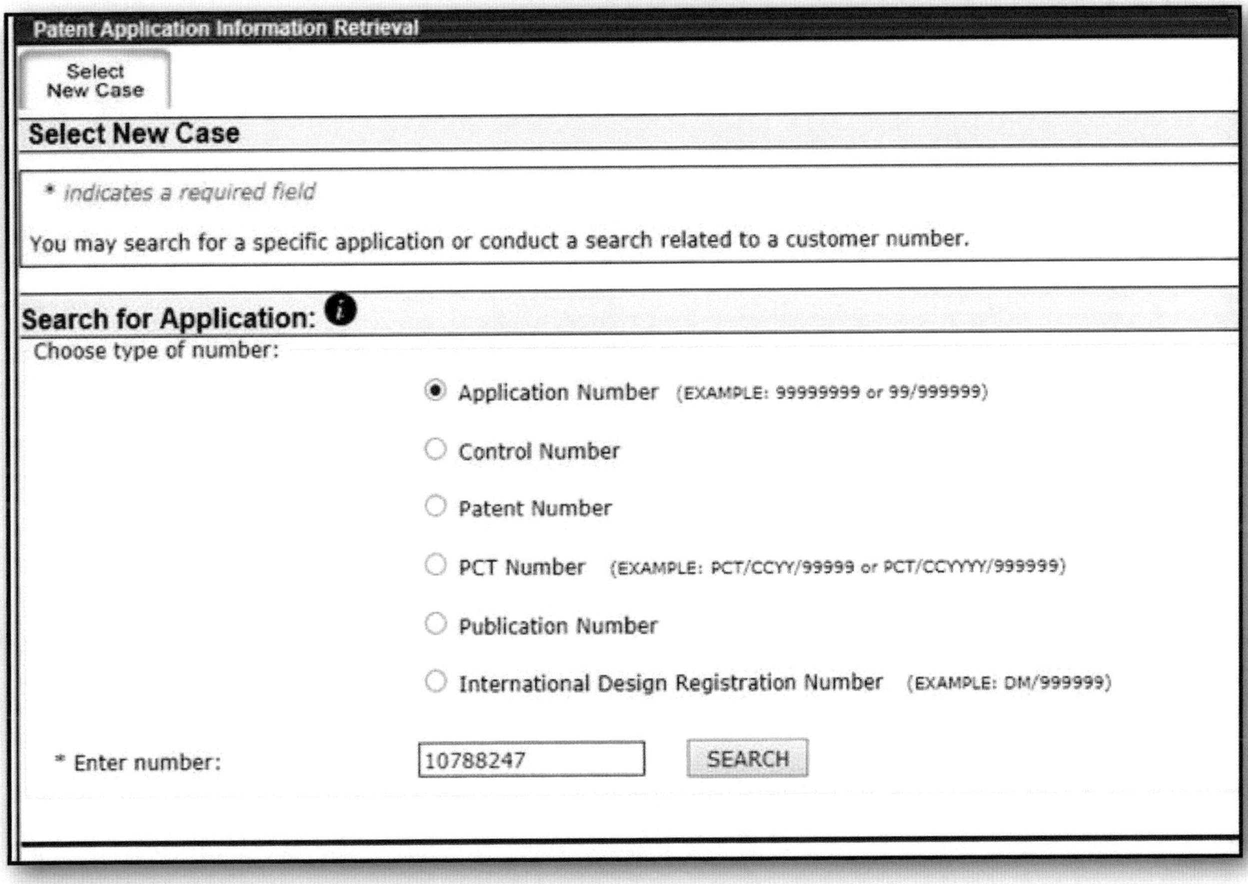

Patent Application Information Retrieval

Select New Case

Select New Case

* indicates a required field

You may search for a specific application or conduct a search related to a customer number.

Search for Application: ⓘ

Choose type of number:

- ● Application Number (EXAMPLE: 99999999 or 99/999999)
- ○ Control Number
- ○ Patent Number
- ○ PCT Number (EXAMPLE: PCT/CCYY/99999 or PCT/CCYYYY/999999)
- ○ Publication Number
- ○ International Design Registration Number (EXAMPLE: DM/999999)

* Enter number: `10788247` **SEARCH**

5. Click on the tab "Published Documents".

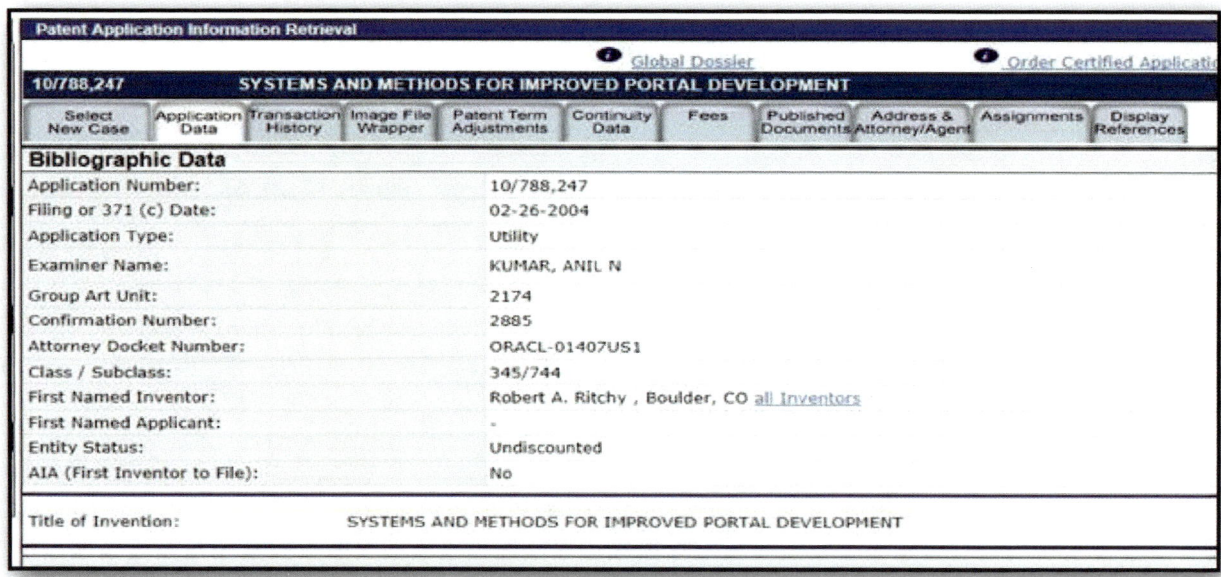

6. Click "View" under "Full Text and Image".

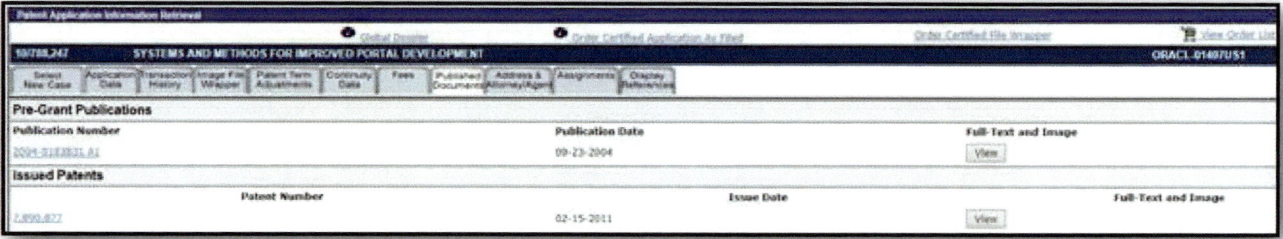

7. Click "Images".

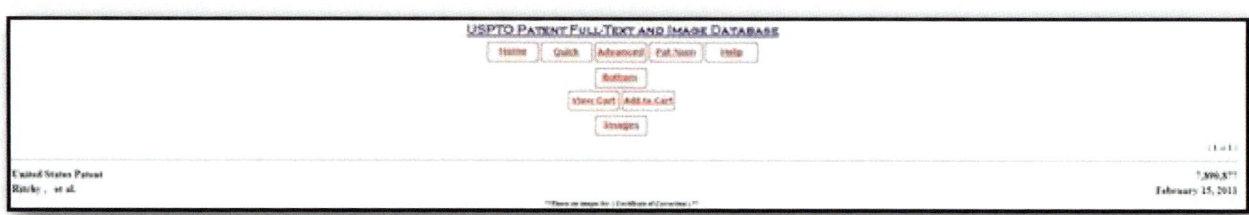

8. Click "Activate Adobe Acrobat" and the first page of the patent appear on the screen.

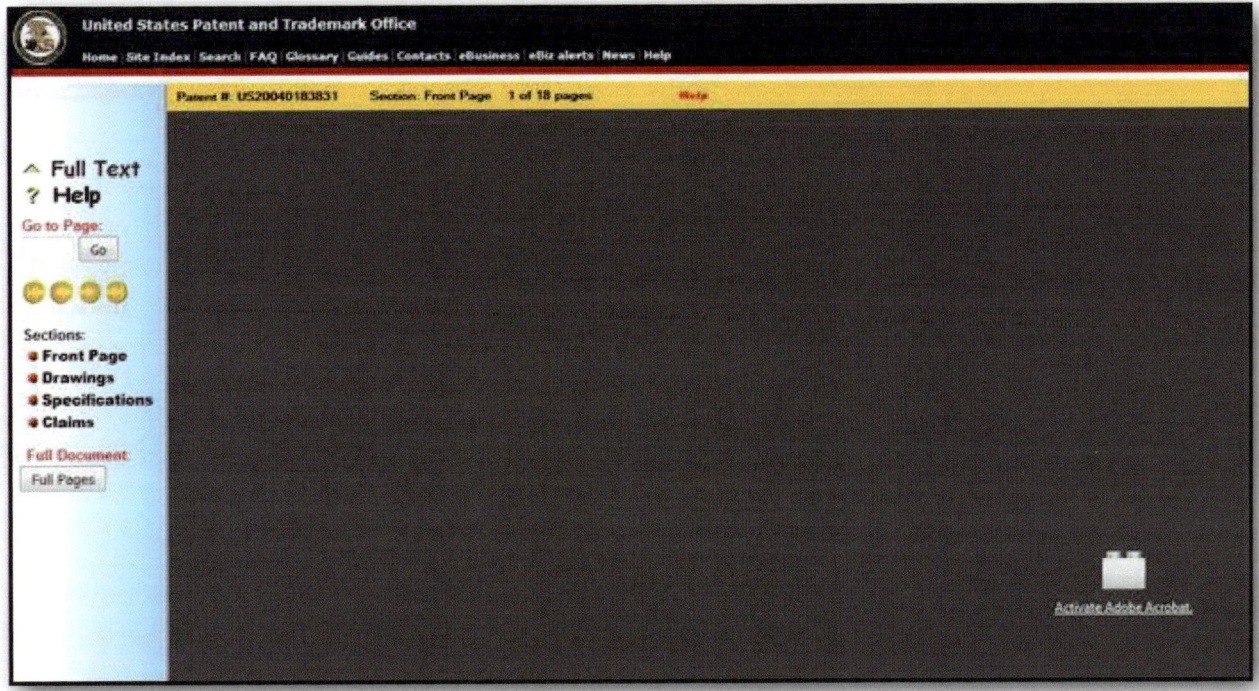

CHAPTER 5

Preparing New Patent Applications

● ● ●

5.1 PATENT APPLICATION TYPES

THERE ARE FIVE PATENT APPLICATION types: Provisional Application, Nonprovisional Application, Design Application, Plant Application, and PCT International Application, which are described below.

5.1.1 PROVISIONAL APPLICATION

A Provisional Application for patent is a U.S. national application that does not require a formal patent claim, Inventor's Oath or Declaration, or any Information Disclosure (prior art) Statement. The application is not examined by the Patent Examiner.

The Provisional Application is used to establish an early effective filing date for a later-filed Nonprovisional Application.

The Provisional Application has a pendency lasting twelve (12) months from the date the Provisional Application was filed. If the delay was unintentional to file the Nonprovisional Application at twelve (12) months from the Provisional Application's filing date, the Applicant or Applicant's representative must file a petition and payment of applicable fee within two (2) months from the expiration of the Provisional Application in order to claim the benefit of the Provisional Application in a Nonprovisional Application.

The Provisional Application must comply with three requirements for Nonprovisional Applications - **written description, best mode, and enablement**. It is the responsibility of the Practitioner drafting the application to ensure these requirements are met. Care should be taken by the Paralegal to ensure that the disclosure filed as the Provisional Application contains all of the pages that the Practitioner intends to file. Missing pages of written description or drawings may prevent the Provisional Application from meeting one (or more) of the three requirements mentioned above.

5.1.2 NONPROVISIONAL APPLICATION

In order for a Nonprovisional Application to claim priority to a Provisional Application, the Nonprovisional Application must contain a specific reference to the Provisional Application. A Nonprovisional Application initiates the examination process. A Nonprovisional Application must include a Specification, including a Claim or Claims, Drawings (when necessary), an Inventor's Oath or Declaration, Application Data Sheet, and the filing fee.

5.1.3 DESIGN APPLICATION

A Design Application is an application for a design that consists of the visual ornamental characteristics embodied in, or applied to, an article of manufacture. Since the design is manifested in its appearance, the subject matter of a Design Application may relate to the configuration or shape of an article, to the surface ornamentation applied to an article, or to the combination of configuration and surface ornamentation. The specification of a Design Application simply refers to its attached drawings. It is article illustrated in the drawings that undergo examination for patentability.

5.1.4 PLANT APPLICATION

A Plant Application is to protect invented or discovered, asexually reproduced plant varieties. The drawings are normally color drawings.

5.1.5 PCT INTERNATIONAL APPLICATION

The Patent Cooperation Treaty ("PCT") enables the U.S. Applicant to file one application, "an international application," in a standardized format in English in the U.S. Receiving Office, and have that application acknowledged as a regular national or regional filing in any State or region that is party to the PCT. See ***Chapter 27 – Patent Cooperation Treaty***.

5.2 CONTINUING APPLICATIONS

There are three types of utility and design continuing applications: Divisional Application, Continuation Application, and Continuation-in-Part Application, each of which claims the benefit of the filing date of the prior application. In addition, a Substitute Application may be filed, but without a benefit of the filing date of the prior application, all of which are described below.

5.2.1 DIVISIONAL APPLICATION

A Divisional Application ("DIV") is a subsequent application for an independent or distinct invention, carved out of a pending application and disclosing and claiming only subject matter disclosed in the earlier or parent application. A Divisional Application is often filed as a result of a restriction requirement made by the Examiner. The Divisional Application must claim the benefit of the prior Nonprovisional Application.

5.2.2 CONTINUATION APPLICATION

A Continuation Application ("CON") is a subsequent application for the same invention claimed in a prior Nonprovisional Application and filed before the original parent application becomes abandoned or is patented. The Continuation Application must include at least one inventor named in the prior Nonprovisional Application. The disclosure presented in the Continuation Application must be the same as that of the original application, e.g., the Continuation Application should not include anything which would constitute new matter if inserted in the original application. The Continuation Application must claim the benefit of the prior Nonprovisional Application.

5.2.3 CONTINUATION-IN-PART APPLICATION

A Continuation-In-Part Application ("CIP") is filed during the lifetime of an earlier Nonprovisional Application, repeating some substantial portion or all of the earlier Nonprovisional Application and *adding subject matter not disclosed* in the earlier Nonprovisional Application.

> NOTE: An application can also be a CIP if subject matter is deleted from the earlier Nonprovisional application. In addition, a CIP can file in a foreign country within one (1) year of the filing date.

5.2.4 SUBSTITUTE APPLICATION

A Substitute Application is a duplicate of an application by the same Applicant abandoned before the filing of the later application.

> NOTE: A Substitute Application does not obtain the benefit of the filing date of the prior application. The filing of a Substitute Application is rare.

5.3 PROVISIONAL APPLICATIONS

Provisional Application Quick Reference

Parts Required for a Complete Provisional Application (See *Section 5.3.2*)

Application Data Sheet
Filing Fee
Description of Invention
Provisional Application Checklist (See *Appendix A.4*)
eFiling a Provisional Application via EFS-Web (See *Section 6.1.2*)

5.3.1 MINIMUM PROVISIONAL APPLICATION PARTS TO OBTAIN A FILING DATE

The Provisional Application must be made in the name(s) of all of the inventor(s). It can be filed up to one (1) year following the date of first sale, offer for sale, public use, or publication of the invention. These disclosures are commonly referred to as "statutory bars" or "bar dates".

In order to receive a filing date, a Provisional Application must contain:

* A written description of the invention.
* Any drawings necessary to understand the invention.

If either of these items is missing or incomplete, no filing date will be accorded to the Provisional Application. Claims are not required for the Provisional Application to be accorded a filing date.

5.3.2 PARTS REQUIRED FOR A COMPLETE PROVISIONAL APPLICATION

To be complete, a Provisional Application **must** include:

* **Application Data Sheet 37 CFR 1.76 (PTO/AIA/14)** form at *www.uspto.gov/forms/aia0014.pdf* for Practitioner's signature.
* Written Description of the Invention.
* Drawings (if any).
* Filing fee.

5.3.3 PROVISIONAL APPLICATION FEES

Fees are subject to change annually. The current fee for a Provisional Application for Patent can be found on the USPTO fee page at *www.uspto.gov/learning-and-resources/fees-and-payment/uspto-fee-schedule*.

Three sets of fees exist, one for regular undiscounted (large entity with no discount), one for small entity (50% discount), and one for micro entity. A small entity is an independent inventor, a small business concern, or a nonprofit organization eligible for reduced patent fees. If an Inventor or Assignee qualifies as a small entity for patent fee purposes, no special form is required to claim entitlement to reduced fees (a box on the transmittal form may be checked).

To qualify as a Micro entity, an Applicant must (i) qualify as a small entity, and (ii) not have been named as an inventor on more than four (4) previously filed patent applications, other than applications filed in another country. Institutions of higher education may qualify under the micro entity status. There is a 75% reduction of fees for filing, searching, examining, issuing, appealing, and maintaining patent applications if the Applicant qualifies as a micro entity.

5.3.4 What if a Part is Missing
If a part of the Provisional Application is missing when the Provisional Application is filed, the USPTO will send a Notice to File Missing Parts. The Notice to File Missing Parts gives notice to the Applicant as to what part is missing and a time frame (usually two (2) months) to reply to the Notice. Failure to reply to the Notice will result in abandonment of the Provisional Application.

5.3.5 Limited Time to File Nonprovisional Application Claiming Benefit to Provisional Application
Benefit to a Provisional Application cannot be claimed if a Nonprovisional Application is not filed within twelve (12)-months from the filing date of the Provisional Application. However, if the Nonprovisional Application is filed after the twelve (12)-month period, the benefit of the Provisional Application may be restored by filing a petition under 37 CFR 1.78.

A Provisional Application is not examined and cannot issue as a U.S. patent. However, if one of the following two events occurs within twelve (12) months of the Provisional Application filing date, a patent application which can be examined will result:

1. Filing a corresponding Nonprovisional Application for patent. The Nonprovisional Application may be entitled to a filing date of the Provisional Application if the Nonprovisional Application includes a claim for the benefit of the earlier filed provisional application (unless the benefit of the Provisional Application was restored under 37 CFR 1.78, in which case the Nonprovisional Application may be filed within fourteen (14) months from Provisional Application filing date); or
2. A petition under 37 CFR 1.53(c)(3) is filed and granted to convert the Provisional Application into a Nonprovisional Application.

Notes: The following are limitations with respect to Provisional Applications:

- Provisional Applications may not be filed for design inventions.
- Provisional Applications are not examined on their merits.
- Provisional Applications for patent cannot claim the benefit of a previously-filed application, either foreign or domestic.
- The disclosure of the invention in the Provisional Application should be as complete as possible.
- If there are multiple inventors, each inventor must be named in the Provisional Application.
- The Nonprovisional Application must have at least one inventor in common with the inventor(s) named in the Provisional Application in order to claim benefit of the Provisional Application filing date.
- A Provisional Application must be entitled to a filing date and include the basic filing fee in order for a Nonprovisional Application to claim benefit of that Provisional Application.
- There is a surcharge for filing the basic filing fee or the cover sheet on a date later than filing the Provisional Application.
- Amendments are not permitted in Provisional Applications after filing, other than those to make the Provisional Application comply with applicable regulations.
- No Information Disclosure Statement may be filed in a Provisional Application.
- In order to obtain the benefit of the filing date of a Provisional Application, the claimed subject matter in the later filed Nonprovisional Application must have support in the Provisional Application.

5.3.6 DELAYED FILING OF THE SUBSEQUENT NONPROVISIONAL APPLICATION

If the subsequent nonprovisional application has a filing date which is after the expiration of the twelve (12)-month period of the provisional application but within two (2) months from the expiration of the fourteen (14) month period, the benefit of the provisional application may be restored if the delay in filing the subsequent nonprovisional application was unintentional. In this situation, a petition to restore the benefit of a provisional application on or after May 13, 2015, must be filed in the subsequent application, and any petition to restore the benefit of a provisional application must include the following items:

1. The reference required by 35 U.S.C. 119(e) to the prior-filed provisional application in an application data sheet identifying it by provisional application number (consisting of the series code and serial number), unless previously submitted.
2. The petition fee.
3. A statement that the delay in filing the subsequent nonprovisional application within the twelve (12)-month period was unintentional. The Director may require additional information where there is a question whether the delay was unintentional.

NOTE: **Petition for Revival of an Application for Patent Abandoned Unintentionally Under 37 CFR 1.137(b) (PTO/SB/64)** form or an e-Petition cannot be used as the request to restore the right of priority to a provisional application as it needs to be written out in an amendment style format. For example, the Practitioner may need to petition the Director under 37 CFR 1.78(b) for restoration of the right of priority to a provisional application and state the reasons why the delay in filing the subsequent nonprovisional application was unintentional. Also, the Applicant may need to sign a Declaration Under 37 CFR 1.132 certifying that the delay in filing a subsequent nonprovisional application was unintentional.

5.4 NONPROVISIONAL APPLICATIONS

Nonprovisional Application Quick Reference

Parts Required for a Complete Nonprovisional Application (See *Section 5.4.2*)
    Application Data Sheet (PTO/AIA/14)
    Specification (with at least one claim)
    Drawings (if any)
    Executed "new language" Oath or Declaration (for any patent application filed after 9/16/2012)
    Executed Power of Attorney
    Appropriate Fees
Nonprovisional Application Checklist (See *Appendix A.5*)
eFiling a Nonprovisional Application via EFS-Web (See *Section 6.2.2*)

5.4.1 MINIMUM REQUIREMENTS FOR FILING NONPROVISIONAL APPLICATION

A Nonprovisional Application must be in the English language or be accompanied by a translation in the English language, a statement that the translation is accurate, and a fee.

The USPTO requires that all papers, which are to become part of the permanent record of the application, must be typewritten or produced by a mechanical (or computer) printer. The text must be in permanent black ink or its equivalent; on a single side of the paper; in portrait orientation; on white paper that is all of the same size, flexible, strong, smooth, non-shiny, durable, and without holes. The paper size must be either:

- 8 ½" by 11" (U.S. letter size)
- A4 (European letter size)

There must be a left margin of at least 1 inch and the top, right, and bottom margins must be at least ¾ inch. The drawing requirements are explained further in *Section 5.4.13*.

NOTE: Effective **December 18, 2013**, a Nonprovisional Application (other than a design) may be filed without claims and/or drawings or may be filed by a reference to a previously filed application. However, an application will not be placed on an Examiner's docket until the application is complete, i.e., the application includes at least one claim. If the application is filed without claims, the USPTO will issue a Notice to File Missing Parts giving the Applicant a time period in which to submit at least one claim in order to avoid abandonment.

5.4.2 PARTS REQUIRED FOR A COMPLETE NONPROVISIONAL APPLICATION
A complete Nonprovisional Application should contain the elements listed below, arranged in the order shown:

1. **Application Data Sheet 37 CFR 1.76 (PTO/AIA/14)** form at *www.uspto.gov/forms/aia0014.pdf* signed by the Practitioner. See *Chapter 8 – Application Data Sheet.*
2. Specification (with at least one claim) and Abstract (responsibility of Practitioner).
3. Drawings (when necessary) (responsibility of Practitioner).
4. A "New language" Oath or Declaration. See *Section 5.4.14 - Inventor's Oath or Declaration*.
5. A Power of Attorney. See *Section 3.11 – Power of Attorney Practice*.
6. Application Fees.

5.4.3 APPLICATION FEES
Before the Application is forwarded to the Examining Corps for examination, Application fees are required to be paid. The required fees are filing, search, and examination fees. These fees may be paid electronically via EFS-Web by using a credit card, electronic funds transfer, or USPTO Deposit Account. If the fees are not paid at the time of initial filing of the Application, there will be a late or surcharge fee for payment of any of the fees after the filing date of the Application.

Also, the Nonprovisional Application may be filed by mail or hand-delivery. However, there is an additional fee to the regular filing, search, and examination fees for not filing an Application through the EFS-Web. If the filing is by paper, always include the **Fee Transmittal (PTO/SB/17)** form (in duplicate) at *www.uspto.gov/forms/sb0017.pdf* to calculate the required filing, examination, and search fees, any excess claim fees or application size fee, and indicate the method of payment (by check, money order, USPTO Deposit Account, or credit card).

NOTE: Fees are subject to change. Before fees are paid, it is best practice to check the current Fee Schedule at *www.uspto.gov/learning-and-resources/fees-and-payment/uspto-fee-schedule*. The late or surcharge fee will vary depending on whether the Applicant is a regular undiscounted (large entity), a small entity (50% discount) or a micro entity. There is also a late surcharge fee charge if the required Inventor's oath or declaration is filed on a date later than the application filing date. So it is best to ensure that the required fees and the Inventor's oath or declaration are included with the specification (including claims) and drawings filed via EFS-Web.

If the fees are paid later by check or money order, they must be made payable to the "Director of the USPTO." If an application is filed without the fees, the Applicant will be notified and required to submit the fees plus the late surcharge within the time period set forth in the notice.

> NOTE: If a check is returned to the USPTO for insufficient funds ("NSF"), OED will be notified and an investigation will be initiated to determine if the Practitioner has violated a disciplinary rule.

If the specification and drawings of the Nonprovisional Application filed via EFS-Web exceeds 133 pages, an additional payment for the application size fee, will be required. For applications filed in paper form, the application size fee is due if the total number of pages exceeds 100 pages. Whether filed via EFS-Web or in paper format, if the application has more than 3 independent claims or more than 20 total claims, payment of excess claim fees will be required.

5.4.4 FEE DISCOUNTS

The majority of the Applicants pay regular undiscounted (large entity) fees. However, fees for filing, searching, examining, issuing, appealing, and maintaining patent applications and patents are reduced by 50% for any small entity that qualifies for reduced fees under 37 CFR 1.127(a), and are reduced by 75% for any micro entity that files a certification that the requirements under 37 CFR 1.29(a) or (d) are met.

5.4.5 APPLICATION DATA SHEET

Post-AIA, submission of an ADS is required for all Nonprovisional Applications. Applications filed on or after September 16, 2012, any domestic benefit claim(s) and any foreign priority claim(s) must be made in an ADS within four (4) months from filing or sixteen (16) months from the filing date of the prior-filed application, whichever is later.

An ADS contains bibliographic data: Inventor information, Applicant information, correspondence information, representative information, domestic priority information, foreign priority information and assignment information. The USPTO has an electronic soft copy fillable form for the ADS that can be submitted electronically in **Application Data Sheet 37 CFR 1.76 (PTO/AIA/14)** form at *www.uspto.gov/ forms/aia0014.pdf*. See ***Chapter 8 - Application Data Sheet***.

A corrected ADS may be subsequently supplied prior to payment of Issue Fee to either correct or update information in a previously submitted ADS.

5.4.6 SPECIFICATION

The specification consists of four parts: (i) a written description of the invention and of the manner and process of making and using the invention, (ii) drawings if required to understand the invention, (iii) at least one claim describing scope of the invention the Applicant regards as the invention, and (iv) an abstract of the disclosure. Each part of the specification must begin on a new page. The written description must be in clear, full, concise, and exact terms to enable any person skilled in the art or science to which the invention pertains to make and use the same.

5.4.7 PARAGRAPH NUMBERING AND/OR LINE NUMBERING IN THE WRITTEN DESCRIPTION PART OF THE SPECIFICATION

If the Practitioner wants to insert automatic paragraph numbering after the application has been typed, use the following steps in Microsoft Word:

Go to the Home tab. Highlight all the paragraphs that you want numbered, then click on the down arrow of the Numbering icon, scroll to the bottom and click "Define New Number Format". On the Number format screen do the following:

Select Number style:
01, 02, 03 or 001, 002, 003, depending upon the number of paragraphs.
Number format:
[0001]

Change the font to bold. Click "OK". Indent the first line by .25, and the hanging indent flushed to the left. Note the following with respect to paragraph numbering:

* Do not number the claims as paragraphs.
* The abstract of the disclosure does not have to have a paragraph number.
* To remove old line numbers, go to File, Page Setup, Layout, go to Line Numbers (at the bottom of the screen), at the "add line numbering" click the check mark to remove the line numbering.

* To remove all automatic numbering – highlight the document that you want to remove all line numbering, then click on the 1,2,3 icon a couple of times.

5.4.8 TITLE OF INVENTION

The title of the invention (or an introductory portion stating the name, citizenship, residence of each Applicant, and the title of the invention) should appear as the heading on the first page of the specification. Although a title may have up to 500 characters, the title must be short and concise as possible.

5.4.9 CLAIMS

A claim or claims must particularly point out and distinctly claim the subject matter that the inventor(s) regards as the invention. A Nonprovisional Application for a utility patent must contain at least one claim. The claim or claims section must begin on a separate physical sheet or electronic page. If there are several claims, they must be numbered consecutively in Arabic.

There are three types of claims: independent, dependent, and multiple dependent claim. Each is described below.

5.4.9.1 Independent Claim

An independent claim is a claim that stands alone, and makes no reference back to a preceding claim. An example of an independent claim is as follows:

1. A chair comprising a seat and four legs.

Each independent claim counts as one claim in the claim fee calculation. See ***Section 5.4.10 – Calculating Claims Fees***.

5.4.9.2 Dependent Claim

A dependent claim is a claim that refers back to a single preceding claim by reference to the claim number. An example of a dependent claim is as follows:

2. The chair of claim 1, further comprising a back support connected to the seat.

Each dependent claim counts as one claim in claim fee calculation. See ***Section 5.4.10 – Calculating Claims Fees***.

5.4.9.3 Multiple Dependent Claim

A multiple dependent claim is a claim that refers back in the alternative to more than one, preceding independent or dependent claim. An example of a multiple dependent claim is as follows:

3.   A chair according to claims 1 or 2 wherein the legs are made of wood.

A multiple dependent claim, which serves as a basis for any other multiple dependent claim, is improper and will not be considered by the Examiner. For fee calculation, a multiple dependent claim will be considered to be that number of claims to which direct reference is made therein. Also, for fee calculation, any claim depending from a multiple dependent claim will be considered to be that number to which direct reference is made in the multiple dependent claims. See *Section 5.4.10 – Calculating Claims Fees*.

5.4.10 CALCULATING CLAIM FEES

The basic application filing fee entitles the Inventor or Assignee to twenty (20) claims, including not more than three (3) independent claims. An additional fee is required for more than three (3) independent claims and more than twenty (20) dependent claims. There is a separate, one (1)-time fee, for presenting multiple dependent claims.

   NOTE: When preparing an Amendment, which includes Amendment to Claims, the claims fee must be recalculated to determine if any additional claims fee is required.

5.4.11 ABSTRACT OF THE DISCLOSURE

The purpose of the Abstract is to enable the USPTO and the public to quickly determine the nature of the technical disclosures of the invention. It should be in narrative form and generally limited to a single paragraph, and it must begin on a separate sheet. An Abstract should not be longer than 150 words.

5.4.12 DRAWINGS

A Nonprovisional Application is required to contain drawings if drawings are necessary to understand the subject matter to be patented. The drawings must show every feature of the invention as specified in the claims. A drawing necessary to understand the invention cannot be introduced into an application after the filing date of the application because of the prohibition against new matter.

5.4.13 DRAWING REQUIREMENTS

There are two acceptable categories for presenting drawings in utility patent applications: black ink (black and white) and color.

Except for plant applications, black and white drawings are normally required. India ink, or its equivalent that secures black solid lines, must be used for drawings. Drawings made by computer printer should be originals, not photocopies. On rare occasions, color drawings may be necessary as the only practical medium by which the subject matter sought to be patented in a utility patent application is disclosed. The USPTO will accept color drawings in utility patent applications and statutory invention registrations only after granting a petition explaining why the color drawings are necessary and payment of appropriate fees under 37 CFR 1.17(h).

Photographs are not ordinarily permitted in Nonprovisional Applications. The USPTO will accept black and white photographs in Nonprovisional Applications only in applications in which the invention is not capable of being illustrated in an ink drawing or where the invention is shown more clearly in a photograph. For example, photographs or photomicrographs of electrophoresis gels, blots (e.g., immunological, western, southern, and northern), autoradiographs, cell cultures (stained and unstained), histological tissue cross sections (stained and unstained), animals, plants, in vivo imaging, thin layer chromatography plates, crystalline structures, and ornamental effects continue to be acceptable. Only one set of black and white photographs is required. Furthermore, no additional processing fee is required.

Photographs have the same sheet size requirements as other drawings. The photographs must be of sufficient quality so that all details in the drawing(s) are reproducible in the printed patent or any patent application publication.

Color photographs will be accepted in Nonprovisional Applications if the conditions for accepting color drawings and black and white photographs have been satisfied.

5.4.13.1 Paper Size of Each Sheet of Drawing

All drawing sheets, including sheets containing photographs, in an application must be the same size. One of the shorter sides of the sheet is regarded as its top. The size of the sheets on which drawings are made must be:

8 ½" by 11" (U.S. letter size)

A4 (European letter size)

TIP: If the client is considering foreign filing, preparing everything on A4 paper makes filing easier because it will be acceptable in the U.S. and Europe.

The sheets must not contain frames around the sight (the usable surface), but may have scan tar-get points (cross hairs) printed on two cater-cornered margin corners. The following margins are required:

8 ½" by 11" drawing sheets: each sheet must include a top margin of at least 1 inch, a left side margin of at least 1 inch, a right side margin of at least ⅝ inch, and a bottom margin of at least ⅜ inch from the edges, thereby leaving a sight no greater than $6\,^{15}/_{16}$ by $9\,⅝$ inches.

A4 drawing sheets: each sheet must include a top margin of at least 1 inch, a left side margin of at least 1 inch, a right side margin of at least ⅝ inch, and a bottom margin of at least ⅜ inch from the edges, thereby leaving a sight no greater than $6\,⅝$ by $10\,^{5}/_{16}$ inches.

A simple rule of thumb for margins that will work in the U.S. and most other countries is one (1) inch on all sides.

5.4.13.2 Numbering Sheets of Drawings and Views

Sheets of drawings should be numbered in consecutive Arabic numerals, starting with numeral 1, within the sight (the usable surface). These numbers, if present, must be placed in the middle of the top of the sheet, but not in the margin. The numbers can be placed on the right-hand side if the drawing extends too close to the middle of the top edge of the usable surface. Drawing sheets numbering must be clear and larger than the numbers used as reference characters to avoid confusion. The number of each sheet should be shown by two Arabic numerals placed on either side of an oblique line, with the first being the sheet number and the second being the total number of sheets of drawings, with no other marking, e.g., 1/7, 2/7, etc.

Different views in the drawing must be numbered in consecutive Arabic numerals, starting with numeral 1, independent of the numbering of the sheets and, if possible, in the order in which they appear on the drawing sheet(s). Partial views intended to form one complete view, on one or several sheets, must be identified by the same number followed by a capital letter. View numbers must be preceded by the abbreviation "FIG". Where only a single view is used in an application to illustrate the claimed invention, it must not be numbered and the abbreviation "FIG" must not appear.

Drawings showing prior art are usually not necessary. However, where needed to understand the Applicant's invention, they may be retained if designated by a legend such as "PRIOR ART."

Drawing Margins

8 1/2 x 11 - Margins

Top	- 1"
Left	- 1"
Right	- 5/8"
Bottom	- 3/8"

A4 - Margins

Top	- 1"
Left	- 1"
Right	- 5/8"
Bottom	- 3/8"

5.4.14 INVENTOR'S OATH OR DECLARATION

An oath or declaration is a formal statement that must be made by the inventor in a Nonprovisional Application, including utility, design, plant, and reissue applications.

The USPTO prefers the Applicants use the **Declaration (37 CFR 1.63) for Utility or Design Patent Application Using an Application Data Sheet (37 CFR 1.76) (PTO/AIA/01)** form at *www.uspto.gov/forms/aia0001.pdf.*

Effective September 16, 2012, the Inventor's Oath or Declaration must contain the following 3 statements:

- The application was made by or authorized to be made by the person executing the declaration.
- The individual believes himself or herself to be the original inventor or an original joint inventor of a claimed invention in the application.
- An acknowledgement of penalties clause referring to fine or imprisonment of not more than five (5) years, or both (attestation clause).

Effective September 16, 2012, the following Inventor's Oath or Declaration statements that are no longer required:

- Citizenship
- That the inventor believes himself or herself to be the "first" inventor of the subject matter
- "Duty to disclose"
- "Reviewed and understands"
- "True or believed to be true"

Along with the executed Declaration for each inventor is a signed ADS that should be filed in all patent applications filed on and after September 16, 2012. The sole exception is when a patent application (i) has no claim for foreign priority, (ii) has no claim for the benefit of priority under 35 USC 119(e) or 35 USC 120, and (iii) does not have a non-inventor Applicant. Otherwise, an ADS must be filed.

The Oath must be sworn to by the inventor before a notary public or other officer authorized to administer oaths. A Declaration may be used in lieu of an Oath. The Declaration must include an attestation clause, i.e., acknowledging that any willful false statement made in the declaration is punishable by fine or imprisonment of not more than five (5) years, or both. Oaths or Declarations are required for applications involving designs, plants, utility applications, and reissue applications. A Declaration does not require any witness or notary to verify its signing.

The Inventor's Oath or Declaration must be signed by the inventor in person, or by the person entitled by law to make application on the inventor's behalf. A full first and last name with middle initial or name, if any, and mailing address are required.

Any Inventor's Oath or Declaration must be in a language the inventor understands. If the Inventor's Oath or Declaration used is in a language other than English, and is not in a form provided by the USPTO, an English translation together with a statement that the translation is accurate, is required.

If the person making the Oath or Declaration is not the inventor, the Oath or Declaration shall state the relationship of that person to the inventor, upon information and belief, the facts which the inventor would have been required to state, and the circumstances which render the inventor unable to sign, namely death, insanity or legal incapacity or unavailability/refusal to sign.

If the inventor has refused or cannot be reached after diligent efforts to execute the Declaration, then the Practitioner may file a Substitute Statement found at *www.uspto.gov/forms/aia0002.pdf*. If the sole or all of the inventors have not signed the Oath or Declaration, then the Oath or Declaration must be signed by the party showing proprietary interest in the application.

If the inventor has died or is legally incapacitated, then the legal representative of the deceased or incapacitated must sign the Oath or Declaration on behalf of the inventor. The Substitute Statement can be found at *www.uspto.gov/forms/aia0002.pdf*, and no petition is required to execute the substitute statement.

Effective September 16, 2012, modifications to the application are permissible after the Inventor's Oath or Declaration is signed.

The Oath/Declaration and an Assignment to be recorded can be filed as follows:

1. File the application via EFS-Web and obtain an application number.
2. Submit the assignment-statement for recording through ePAS on same day the application is filed to avoid the late surcharge.
3. Check the box in ePAS that the assignment is being used as the Inventor's Declaration.

More information about the Inventor's Declaration can be found at *www.uspto.gov/aia_implementation/ inventors-oath-or-declaration-quick-reference-guide.pdf*.

5.4.15 SEQUENCE LISTING (IF APPLICABLE)
The disclosure of a nucleotide or amino acid sequence should contain a listing of the sequence complying with 37 CFR 1.821 through 37 CFR 1.825 and may be filed in paper or electronic form.

5.5 DIVISIONAL OR CONTINUATION APPLICATIONS

DIV or CON Application Quick Reference

Parts Required for a Complete DIV or CON Application (See *Section 5.5.1*)
Application Data Sheet (PTO/AIA/14)
Copy of prior Specification and Drawings
Copy of prior Inventor's Oath or Declaration (filed after 9/16/2012)
Copy of prior Power of Attorney
Appropriate Fees
DIV or CON Application Checklist (See *Appendix A.7*)
eFiling a DIV or CON Application via EFS-Web (See *Section 6.3.2*)

5.5.1 Parts Required for a Complete Divisional or Continuation Application

A complete Divisional ("DIV") or Continuation ("CON") Application has six (6) parts arranged as follows:

1. **Application Data Sheet 37 CFR 1.76 (PTO/AIA/14)** form at *www.uspto.gov/forms/aia0014.pdf* signed by the Practitioner.
2. Copy of the specification (with at least one claim) and Abstract from the parent application.
3. Copy of the Drawings (when necessary) from the parent application.
4. Copy of the Inventor's Oath or Declaration from parent application (if filed after September 16, 2012). If a copy of the Inventor's Oath or Declaration from the parent application was filed before September 16, 2012, then a "new language" **Declaration (37 CFR 1.63) for Utility or Design Application Using an Application Data Sheet (37 CFR 1.76) (PTO/AIA/01)** form at *www.uspto.gov/forms/aia0001.pdf* is required and must be signed by each inventor.
   (If the filing fee and/or Oath or Declaration is not filed at the time of initial filing, the USPTO will issue a Notice to File Missing Parts to pay for the filing fees and surcharge or late fee for the Inventor's Oath or Declaration. The Inventor's Oath or Declaration can be filed up to the payment of the Issue Fee.)
5. Copy of the Power of Attorney from the parent application.
6. Appropriate Fees.

5.5.2 Inventor's Oath or Declaration

A copy of a "new language" Oath or Declaration from a prior Nonprovisional Application filed after September 16, 2012, may be submitted with a DIV or CON Application even if the Oath or Declaration identifies the Application Number of the parent application. However, if such a copy of the Oath or Declaration is filed after the filing date of the DIV or CON Application and an Application Number has been assigned to the DIV or CON Application, the cover letter accompanying the Oath or Declaration should identify the Application Number of the DIV or CON Application. The cover letter should also indicate that the Oath or Declaration submitted is a copy of the Oath or Declaration from the parent application filed after September 16, 2012, to avoid the Oath or Declaration being incorrectly matched with the parent application file.

Also, a copy of a "new language" Oath or Declaration from the parent Nonprovisional Application filed after September 16, 2012, may be filed in a DIV or CON Application even if the specification for the DIV or CON Application is different from that of the parent application, in that revisions have been made to clarify the text to incorporate amendments made in the parent application, or to make other changes provided the changes do not constitute new matter relative to the parent application.

5.5.3 SPECIFICATION AND DRAWINGS

A DIV or CON Application may be filed by providing one of the following:

- A copy of the parent application, including a copy of the "new language" Inventor's Oath or Declaration as filed (if application filed after September 16, 2012).
- A new specification and drawings and a copy of the "new language" Inventor's Oath or Declaration as filed in the parent application (if application filed after September 16, 2012), provided the new specification and drawings do not contain any subject matter that would have been new matter in the parent application.
- A new specification and drawings and a newly executed Inventor's Oath or Declaration provided the new specification and drawings do not contain any subject matter That Would Have Been New Matter In The Parent Application.

5.5.4 INCORPORATION BY REFERENCE

An Applicant may incorporate by reference the parent application by including, in the divisional or continuation application-as-filed, an explicit statement that such specifically enumerated parent application or applications are "hereby incorporated by reference." The statement must appear in the specification. The inclusion of this incorporation by reference statement will permit an Applicant to amend the divisional or continuation application to include subject matter from the parent application(s), without the need for a petition provided the DIV or CON application is entitled to a filing date notwithstanding the incorporation by reference.

5.5.5 CROSS-REFERENCE TO RELATED APPLICATIONS

Any DIV or CON Application filed after September 16, 2012, claiming the benefit of one or more prior-filed copending Nonprovisional Applications (or international applications designating the United States of America) under 35 USC 120, 35 USC 121, or 35 USC 365(c), or to a Provisional Application under 35 USC 119(e), must present the reference to an earlier application in an ADS under 37 CFR 1.76. Cross-references to other related patent applications may be made when appropriate.

5.6 CONTINUATION-IN-PART APPLICATIONS

Continuation-In-Part Application Quick Reference

Parts Required for a Complete CIP Application (See *Section 5.6.1*)
    Application Data Sheet (PTO/AIA/14)

> **Specification (with at least one claim)**
> **Drawings (if any)**
> **Executed Inventor's "New Language" Oath or Declaration**
> **Executed Power of Attorney**
> **Appropriate Fees**

Continuation-In-Part Application Checklist (See *Appendix A.8*)
eFiling a CIP Application via EFS-Web (See *Section 6.4.2*)

5.6.1 Parts Required for a Complete Continuation-In-Part Application

When a Continuation-In-Part Application ("CIP") is filed, the parent application is not automatically abandoned, but remains alive when the CIP Application is filed. Like all applications that claim priority from the parent application, the CIP Application must be filed while the parent application is still co-pending.

A CIP Application is a new application that receives a new filing date and Application Number.

Because a CIP Application contains new matter, a new Inventor's Oath or Declaration must be submitted. A new assignment must also be submitted to the USPTO to cover the new matter that is claimed.

A CIP Application must name at least one inventor in the parent application.

An IDS must also be filed citing all relevant references, including those cited in any prior related applications.

A complete CIP Application has six parts arranged as follows:

1. **Application Data Sheet 37 CFR 1.76 (PTO/AIA/14)** form at *www.uspto.gov/forms/0014.pdf* signed by the Practitioner.
2. Specification that contains new matter (with at least one claim) and Abstract.
3. Drawings (when necessary).
4. A "new language" Oath or Declaration. See *Section 5.6.2 - Inventor's Oath or Declaration*.

(If the filing fee and/or Oath or Declaration is not filed at the time of initial filing, the USPTO will issue a Notice to File Missing Parts to pay for the filing fees and surcharge or late fee for the Inventor's Oath or Declaration. The Inventor's Oath or Declaration can be filed up to the payment of the Issue Fee.)

5. A Power of Attorney. See *Section 3.11 – Power of Attorney Practice*.
6. Appropriate Fees.

5.6.2 Inventor's Oath or Declaration
Effective September 16, 2012, a "new language" Inventor's Oath or Declaration is required for any CIP Application filed after the effective date and must be signed by each inventor.

5.6.3 Specification and Drawings
Since new matter is being introduced in the CIP Application, a new specification and drawings can be submitted.

5.7 Design Patent Applications

Design Patent Application Quick Reference

Parts of a Design Patent Application (See *Section 5.7.2*)
> **Application Data Sheet (PTO/AIA/14)**
> **Specification with a single claim**
> **Drawings (if any)**
> **Executed "New Language" Inventor's Oath or Declaration**
> **Executed Power of Attorney**
> **Appropriate Fees**

Design Patent Application Checklist (See *Appendix A.6*)
eFiling a Design Patent Application via EFS-Web (See **Section 6.5.2**)

5.7.1 The Difference between Design and Utility Patents
In general terms, a "utility patent" protects the way an article is used and works, while a "design patent" protects the way an article looks.

5.7.2 Parts of a Design Patent Application
The parts of a design patent application should include the following:

1. **Application Data Sheet 37 CFR 1.76 (PTO/AIA/14)** form at *www.uspto.gov/forms/aia0014.pdf* signed by the Practitioner. See *Chapter 8 – Application Data Sheet*.
2. Specification. See *Section 5.7.3 – Specification*.
3. Drawings or photographs. See *Section 5.7.4 – Drawings: Black and White Photographs*.
4. A "new language" Oath or Declaration. *See Section 5.7.6 – Inventor's Oath or Declaration*.

5. A Power of Attorney. See *Section 3.10 – Power of Attorney Practice*.
6. Appropriate Fees.

5.7.3 SPECIFICATION
The specification should include the following parts in order:

1. Preamble, stating name of the Inventor, title of the design, and a brief description of the nature and intended use of the article in which the design is embodied.
2. Cross-reference to related application(s) (unless included in the ADS).
3. Statement regarding federally sponsored research or development.
4. Description of the figure(s) of the drawing.
5. Feature description.
6. A single claim.

5.7.4 DRAWINGS: BLACK AND WHITE PHOTOGRAPHS
The drawing is the most important element of the design application. Every design patent application must include either a drawing or a black and white photograph of the claimed design. As the drawing or photograph constitutes the entire visual disclosure of the claim, it is of utmost importance that the drawing or photograph be clear and complete, that nothing regarding the design sought to be patented is left to conjecture.

Drawings are normally required to be in black ink on white paper. Black and white photographs, in lieu of drawings, are sometimes permitted. Consult with the Practitioner to be sure.

5.7.5 COLOR DRAWINGS OR COLOR PHOTOGRAPHS
The USPTO will accept color drawings or photographs in design patent applications, but a petition is required to request acceptance of such drawings and the petition must be granted. Consult with the Practitioner regarding procedures requesting the USPTO to accept color drawings or photographs.

5.7.6 INVENTOR'S OATH OR DECLARATION
The Oath or Declaration required of the Inventor must comply with the same requirements as for a utility application.

CHAPTER 6

Filing New Patent Applications

• • •

6.1 PROVISIONAL APPLICATIONS

6.1.1 PARTS IN FILING A PROVISIONAL APPLICATION

THE BASIC PARTS FOR FILING a Provisional Application are the following:

1. Provisional Application for Patent Cover Sheet (optional).

Provisional Application for Patent Cover Sheet (PTO/SB/16) form at *www.uspto.gov/forms/ ProvisionalSB.pdf* may be used as the cover sheet for a Provisional Application and signed by the Practitioner.

2. Application Data Sheet 37 CFR 1.76 (PTO/AIA/14) form at *www.uspto.gov/forms/aia0014.pdf.*
3. Title Page: On a separate sheet of paper, type the title of the invention and the names and addresses of all inventors.

PROVISIONAL APPLICATION

FOR

(Title of Invention)

Inventors

[Inventor's names and addresses listed here]

4. Description of Invention: This is the substance of the Provisional Application. The description will be prepared by the Practitioner.
5. Filing Fee.

6.1.2 eFiling a Provisional Application via EFS-Web

The basic steps to efile a Provisional Application via EFS-Web are as follows:

1. Go to *www.uspto.gov*.
2. Under "Patents" tab, click "Filing Online" under "Application Process" section.
3. On the "File Online" page, click "EFS-Web".
4. On the "About EFS-Web" page, click "Launch EFS-Web Registered eFiler".
5. Security Warning: "Allow access to the following application from this website?" Click "Allow".
6. When the User Authentication screen appears, browse for the Practitioner's .epf file. (Hint: Save the Practitioner's .epf file on your desktop for easier access.)
7. Enter the Practitioner's password.
8. Check box at left side of screen in order to proceed to next screen.
9. Under "*Main Functions", click "New application/proceeding".
10. Click "Utility" under "Select Type of New Application/Proceeding".
11. Click "Provisional".
12. Click "Continue" for the next screen.
13. Enter the following information:
    * Title of Invention
    * Attorney Docket Number
    * First Named Inventor
    * Correspondence Address (select the Practitioner's Customer Number with the drop down arrow)
14. After all this information has been entered, click "Continue". This step saves the filing up to this point.
15. Browse for the file (PDF format) and upload it to this filing.

NOTE: When naming the PDF file, make sure that there are no spaces or the PDF file attachment will be rejected.

16. Underneath the uploaded document, it states: "Does your PDF file contain multiple documents?" Click "Yes".
17. The following basic document descriptions are used for filing a Provisional Application:

Category	Document Description
General Transmittal	Provisional Cover Sheet (SB-16)
or	
Application Part	Application Data Sheet
Application Part	Specification

Application Part	Claims
Application Part	Abstract
Application Part	Drawings-only black and white line drawings

18. Click "Upload & Validate" to make sure that there are no validation errors. If there is a validation error, there will be a prompt on the screen of an error or a warning! If there is an error, the error must be corrected at this point. If there is a warning, click "Continue" to go to the next screen.

For the remainder of the steps, see **Section 6.2.2** to complete the efiling of the Provisional Application via EFS-Web.

6.2 Nonprovisional Applications

6.2.1 Parts in Filing a Nonprovisional Application

The basic parts needed to file a Nonprovisional Application are as follows:

1. Calculate the claims fee on the **Multiple Dependent Claim Calculation Sheet (PTO/SB/07)** form at *www.uspto.gov/forms/sb0007.pdf*.
2. Specification, Claims, and Abstract.
3. Drawings.
4. "New language" Declaration executed by each inventor.
5. Executed Power of Attorney.
6. An Application Data Sheet signed by the Practitioner.
7. Preliminary Amendment signed by the Practitioner, if any.
8. Information Disclosure Statement signed by the Practitioner, if any.
    * Cited References, if any: Use Form PTO/SB/08a, available on the fillable forms page of the USPTO website at *www.uspto.gov/web/forms/sb0008a.pdf* and *www.uspto.gov/web/forms/sb0008b.pdf*.
    * Copies of foreign references, non-patent literature, and unpublished applications, if any. (Note: It is not necessary to submit copies of U.S. published applications or U.S. Patents.)

6.2.2 eFiling a Nonprovisional Application via EFS-Web

The basic steps to efile a Nonprovisional Application via EFS-Web are as follows:

1. Go to *www.uspto.gov*.
2. Under "Patents" tab, click "Filing Online" under "Application Process" section.
3. On the "File Online" page, click "EFS-Web".
4. On the "About EFS-Web" page, click "Launch EFS-Web Registered eFiler".
5. Security Warning: "Allow access to the following application from this website?" Click "Allow".
6. When the User Authentication screen appears, browse for the Practitioner's .epf file. (Hint: Save the Practitioner's .epf file on your desktop for easier access.)
7. Enter the Practitioner's password.
8. Check box at left side of screen in order to proceed to the next screen.
9. Under "*Main Functions", click "New application/procceding".
10. Under "Select Type of New Application/Proceeding", click "Utility".
11. Click "Nonprovisional Application under 35 USC 111(a)".
12. Click "Continue" for the next screen.
13. Enter the following information:
    * Title of Invention
    * Attorney Docket Number
    * First Named Inventor
    * Correspondence Address (select the Practitioner's Customer Number using the drop down arrow).
14. After all the foregoing information has been entered, click "Continue". This saves the filing up to this point.
15. Browse for the file (in PDF format) and upload it to this filing.

(**NOTE:** When naming the PDF file, make sure that there are no spaces or the PDF file attachment will be rejected.)

16. Underneath the uploaded document, it states: "Does your PDF file contain multiple documents?" Click "Yes".
17. The following basic document descriptions are used for filing a Nonprovisional Application:

Category	Document Description
General Transmittal	Transmittal of New Application (optional)
Application Part	Application Data Sheet
Application Part	Specification
Application Part	Claims
Application Part	Abstract

Application Part	Drawings-only black and white line drawings
Application Part	Oath or Declaration Filed
Change Requests	Power of Attorney
Amendment	Preliminary Amendment (if any)

NOTE: The Preliminary Amendment does not have to be broken down into document descriptions. The USPTO will accept both ways via EFS-Web.

Category	Document Description
Amendment	Preliminary Amendment (Transmittal)
Amendment	Specification (Amendments to the Specification)
Amendment	Claims (Amendments to the Claims)
Amendment	Applicant Arguments/Remarks Made in an Amendment (Amendments to the Drawings)
Amendment	Applicant Arguments/Remarks Made in an Amendment (Remarks)
Amendment	Abstract
Amendment	Drawings – only black and white line drawings

If filing an Information Disclosure Statement, use the following document descriptions:

Category	Document Description
IDS/References	Transmittal Letter
IDS/References	Information Disclosure Statement (IDS) Form (SB08)
IDS/References	Foreign Reference
IDS/References	Non-Patent Literature

18. "Upload & Validate" to make sure that there are no validation errors. If there is a validation error, there will be a prompt on the screen of an error or a warning! If there is an error, the error must be

corrected at this point. If there is a warning, click "Continue" to go to the next screen. (Since some of the USPTO forms used may not be compatible, a warning instead is displayed of an error message.)

19. If there are no errors, the screen will state "No validation errors found", click "Continue". This will save documents submitted up to this point.

20. The next page is "Calculate Fees". Check to see if this application is a small or undiscounted regular entity and select the appropriate status. Select the appropriate fee for filing the Nonprovisional Application. Click "Continue" to save the documents submitted up to this point.

21. If not paying fees for this filing, continue to "Confirm/Submit", which is located at the top of the Calculate Fees screen.

NOTE: If fees are not paid with the filing, the UPSTO will issue a Notice to File Missing Parts, which will include fees due as well as a late or surcharge fee. The Notice will also set a due date to respond to the Notice.

22. On the next screen, check to make sure that all of the information is correct before clicking "Submit". Also, at this point, the submission can be saved by clicking "Save for Later Submission". The submission can be saved up to seven (7) calendar days. This feature is very useful if there is a need to save this filing for the Practitioner to review and submit later.

23. If paying fees at the time of filing, click "Submit". There is a prompt to either pay fees due by USPTO Deposit Account, Charge Credit Card, or Electronic Funds Transfer. Follow the screen instructions to pay the fees. After the fees are paid, there is a prompt to do one of the following actions:
    * Email Receipt Information
    * Print Receipt
    * Save Receipt
    * File Another Application
    * File an Assignment of Ownership
    * Pay Maintenance Fees
    * Access Private PAIR

24. When application filing is complete, and a receipt is requested, email a copy of the Acknowledgement Receipt to Docketing and print/save one copy for the record.

NOTE: The Acknowledgement Receipt will include the assigned Application Number and a Confirmation Number. Both of these numbers are very important if efiling again with follow-on documents, e.g., Amendments, etc.

TIP: Save the executed Assignment onto your desktop and click "File an Assignment of Ownership". This link will take you to ePAS. See ***Chapter 10 - Assignments***.

6.3 DIV or CON Applications

6.3.1 Parts in Filing a DIV or CON Application
The basic parts to file a DIV or CON Application are the following:

1. Calculate the claims fee on the **Multiple Dependent Claim Calculation Sheet (PTO/SB/07)** form at *www.uspto.gov/forms/sb0007.pdf*.
2. Copy of Specification, Claims, and Abstract from the parent application filed after September 16, 2012.
3. Copy of Drawings from the parent application filed after September 16, 2012.
4. Copy of "new language" Declaration from the parent application filed after September 16, 2012.
5. Copy of Power of Attorney from the parent application.
6. Application Data Sheet signed by the Practitioner.
7. Preliminary Amendment, if any, signed by the Practitioner. This is to be used only if there are any amendments to the claims from the original specification.
8. Information Disclosure Statement, if any, signed by the Practitioner and includes the following:
   * Cited References, if any: Use Form PTO/SB/08a, available on the fillable forms page of the USPTO website at *www.uspto.gov/web/forms/sb0008a.pdf* and *www.uspto.gov/web/forms/sb0008b.pdf*.
   * Copies of foreign references, non-patent literature, and unpublished applications, if any. (**Note:** It is not necessary to submit copies of U.S. published applications or U.S. Patents.)

6.3.2 eFiling a DIV or CON Application via EFS-Web
See *Section 6.2.2* for steps for efiling of the DIV or CON via EFS-Web.

DIV or CON applications -- The document descriptions are the same as the Nonprovisional Application.

6.4 CIP Applications

6.4.1 Parts in Filing a CIP Application
The basic parts to file with a CIP Application are as follows:

1. Calculate the claims fee on the **Multiple Dependent Claim Calculation Sheet (PTO/SB/07)** form at *www.uspto.gov/forms/sb0007.pdf*.
2. New Specification, Claims, and Abstract.

3. Drawings.
4. "New language" Declaration executed by each inventor.
5. Copy of Power of Attorney from the parent application.
6. Application Data Sheet signed by the Practitioner.
7. Preliminary Amendment, if any, signed by the Practitioner. This is to be used only if there are any amendments to the claims from the original specification.
8. Information Disclosure Statement, if any, signed by the Practitioner and includes the following:
   - Cited References, if any: Use Form PTO/SB/08a, available on the fillable forms page of the USPTO website at *www.uspto.gov/web/forms/ sb0008a.pdf* and *www.uspto.gov/web/forms/sb0008b.pdf*.
   - Copies of foreign references, non-patent literature, and unpublished applications, if any. (**NOTE**: It is not necessary to submit copies of U.S. published applications or U.S. Patents.)

6.4.2 eFILING A CIP APPLICATION VIA EFS-WEB
See *Section 6.2.2* for steps for efiling a CIP Application via EFS-Web.

The document descriptions are the same as the Nonprovisional Application.

6.5 DESIGN PATENT APPLICATIONS

6.5.1 PARTS IN FILING A DESIGN PATENT APPLICATION
The basic parts to file a Design Patent Application are as follows:

1. Specification and Claim.
2. Drawing(s).
3. Declaration executed by each inventor.
4. Executed Power of Attorney.
5. Application Data Sheet signed by the Practitioner.
6. Information Disclosure Statement, if any, signed by the Practitioner and includes the following:
   - Cited References, if any: Use Form PTO/SB/08a, available on the fillable forms page of the USPTO website at *www.uspto.gov/web/forms/ sb0008a.pdf* and *www.uspto.gov/web/forms/ sb0008b.pdf*.
   - Copies of foreign references, non-patent literature, and unpublished applications, if any. (**NOTE**: It is not necessary to submit copies of U.S. published applications or U.S. Patents.)

6.5.2 eFiling a Design Patent Application via EFS-Web

The basic steps to efile a Design Patent Application via EFS-Web are as follows:

1. After EFS-Web certification, under "*Main Functions", click "New application/proceeding".
2. Click "Design" button under the "Select Type of New Application/Proceeding".
3. Click "Nonprovisional Application under 35 USC 171".
4. Click "Continue" for the next screen.
5. Enter the following information:
   * Title of Invention
   * Attorney Docket Number
   * First Named Inventor
   * Correspondence Address (select the Practitioner's Customer Number using the drop down arrow)
6. After all the aforementioned information has been entered, click "Continue". This saves the filing up to this point.
7. Files to be Submitted: Browse for the file (in PDF format) and upload it to this filing. (**Note:** When naming the PDF file, make sure that there are no spaces or the PDF file attachment will be rejected.)
8. Underneath the uploaded document, it states: "Does your PDF file contain multiple documents?" Click "Yes".
9. The following basic document descriptions are used for filing a Design Patent Application:

Category	Document Description
General Transmittal	Transmittal of New Application (optional)
Application Part	Application Data Sheet
Application Part	Specification
Application Part	Claims
Application Part	Drawings-only black and white line drawings
Application Part	Oath or Declaration Filed
Change Requests	Power of Attorney

If filing an Information Disclosure Statement, use the following document descriptions:

Category	Document Description
IDS/References	Transmittal Letter
IDS/References	Information Disclosure Statement (IDS) Form (SB08)

| IDS/References | Foreign Reference |
| IDS/References | Non-Patent Literature |

10. Click "Upload & Validate" to make sure that there are no validation errors. If there is a validation error, there will be a prompt on the screen of an error or a warning! If there is an error, the error must be corrected at this point. If there is a warning, click "Continue" to go to the next screen.

For the remainder of the steps, see **Section 6.2.2** to complete the efiling of the Design Application via EFS-Web.

CHAPTER 7

Filing Fees and Methods of Payments

● ● ●

7.1 FINANCIAL MANAGER

As of APRIL 9, 2016, Financial Manager is the USPTO's new online fee payment management tool. It allows the user to store and manage electronic payment methods, including credit/debit cards, Deposit Accounts, and EFT accounts, assign user permissions to allow others to access stored payment methods, and create and export a variety of reports in Excel, PDF, or CSV, including recent transaction activity and monthly statements.

Before access to the Financial Manager, the user needs to create an account.

NOTE: The first user will receive all user permissions by default.

7.1.1 CREATE A NEW USPTO.GOV ACCOUNT

In order to access Financial Manager, each user will need to create a USPTO.gov account. The USPTO.gov account will be the primary means of accessing USPTO services and applications online. After creating a USPTO.gov account, the user will be ready to sign into Financial Manager and begin migrating existing payment methods.

7.1.2 STEPS TO CREATE A NEW USPTO.GOV ACCOUNT

1. Navigate to the USPTO.gov account welcome page at *https://my.uspto.gov*.
2. Select the "Create an account" button and follow the instructions to create a new USPTO.gov account.
3. Complete the "reCaptcha" verification and check the box indicating that the user understands and agrees to the USPTO's terms of Use and Privacy Policy. The user is required to enter:
   * First name
   * Last name
   * Email address

4. Check your email and follow the link provided to navigate to the "Activate your account form" page.
5. Complete the "Activate your account form", creating a new password and three (3) security questions.
6. Select the "Activate your account" button to complete the account activation process and return to the USPTO.gov account "Sign in" page.

7.1.3 STEPS TO SIGN INTO FINANCIAL MANAGER

1. Navigate to the Financial Manager homepage at *https://fees.uspto.gov/FinancialManager* or the Fees Self-Service Portal at *https://fees.uspto.gov*.
2. Complete the "Sign in" form, entering the email address and password associated with the user's USPTO.gov account.
3. Select the "Sign in" button, which will go to the "My Payment Methods" page.

7.1.4 STORE OR MIGRATE PAYMENT METHODS
If multiple individuals need access to the store payment method(s), it is recommended that one individual be designated as Administrator to migrate or store the payment method(s) in Financial Manager. The first user will receive user permissions by default.

Follow these steps to store or migrate payment methods:

1. After signing into Financial Manager, select the button to navigate to the "Add a Payment Method" page.
2. On the "Add a Payment Method" page, migrate to the existing payment method(s) using one of the three (3) migration options and/or add new payment method(s).
   * Migrate store payment methods from Financial Profile.
   * Create/add a new credit card, Deposit Account, or electronic funds transfer (EFT) account.
   * Store an existing deposit account or EFT.

7.1.5 ADD USERS AND ASSIGN USER PERMISSIONS
When an Administrator adds someone to a payment method using the Users tab in Financial Manager, he/she will assign customizable user permissions.

The permission levels are as follows:

Administrators: An Administrator will be able to view and modify the administrative details of the Stored Payment Method; delete or close a Stored Payment Method; grant and remove other users' permission and access to the Stored Payment Method; and, for Deposit Accounts, manage the withdrawal options.

Funds Manager: A Funds Manager will be able to view the basic administrative details of a Deposit Account; add funds to the Deposit Account; transfer funds between two (2) Deposit Accounts; and withdraw funds from a Deposit Account (if allowed by the Administrator). This permission is available for Deposit Accounts only.

Fee Payers: A Fee Payer will be able to view the basic administrative details of the Stored Payment Method and make payments to the USPTO using the Stored Payment Method.

Reporters: A Reporter will be able to view the basic administrative details of the Stored Payment Method and develop, view, and share reports about the transactions associated with the Stored Payment Method.

7.1.6 STEPS TO ADD USERS AND ASSIGN USER PERMISSION

1. From user's stored payment method's Summary page, navigate to the "Users" tab and select the "Add Users to this Payment Method" button.
2. Enter the user's email address and select the "Find User" button. The search will generate a "Results" box that lists the matching user's email address, full name, and available permissions. The exact email address must be associated with the user's uspto.gov account.
3. Select the checkboxes to assign appropriate permissions for the user.
4. Select the "Add User" button to add the individual to the payment method.

Each individual in an organization will need his or her own USPTO.gov account to access or help manage a stored payment method.

NOTE: Repeat this process for each of the selected payment methods. There is no limit to the number of users that can be added to a stored payment method. Multiple users can have the same permissions for a payment method. It is recommended to assign at least two (2) Administrators to each payment method for back-up purposes.

7.1.7 SELF-ASSOCIATING WITH EXISTING PAYMENT METHODS

As an alternative to the Administrator-initiated method of adding users described in *Section 7.1.5* above (Add Users and Assign User Permissions), Financial Manager also allows users to self-associate with existing Financial Profiles, Deposit Accounts, and EFTs using any of the migration options outlined in *Section 7.1.4 - Store or Migrate Payment Methods*.

The first user to migrate will receive all user permissions for that payment method by default. User permissions assigned to subsequent users to self-associate vary based on payment method type:

- For EFTs, subsequent users will be granted Fee Payer permission when the EFT profile name and password are provided. The Administrator will be notified via email each time a new user self-associates with an EFT.
- For Deposit Accounts, subsequent users will be granted Fee Payer permission when the Deposit Account access code is provided. Fee Payer and Reporter permissions will be granted when the Deposit Account access code and authorization code are provided. The Administrator will be notified via email each time a user self-associates with a Deposit Account.
- For credit/debit cards, every user will be granted all permissions. An attempt by a user to self-associate with a card migrated previously from Financial Profile will result in an independent profile that will not be linked to other users who have previously migrated to the same card. For this reason, it is recommended using the Administrator-initiated method of added users described in the Add Users and Assign User Permissions section.

Self-association reduces the time it may take to add all users to a payment method, yet limits control of the user permissions initially assigned to those users. A user with Administrator permissions for the payment method can modify permissions for other users at any time.

7.1.8 POST MIGRATION RECOMMENDED ACTIONS FOR ADMINISTRATORS

Once the existing payment methods are migrated to Financial Manager, make sure that the information is accurate and secure by taking the following steps:

1. Add a back-up Administrator to help manage each payment method.
2. Verify the correspondence/billing address associated with each payment method.
3. Confirm that user permissions are assigned in a manner that best suits the business needs of the company.

4. For Deposit Accounts, set up the withdrawal and replenishment options. One option is to allow Funds Managers to withdraw via check, EFT, or not at all. To enable online replenishments, ensure Funds Managers are assigned Fee Payer permission on an EFT.

5. For EFTs, ensure each Fee Payer creates his/her own unique EFT profile and password prior to attempting payment during the temporary transition period.

7.2 PATENT MAINTENANCE FEES STOREFRONT

As of April 9, 2016, Patent Maintenance Fees Storefront is USPTO's new online storefront for looking up and paying patent maintenance fees. In the storefront, users will have the option to upload a bulk file to pay many maintenance fees at once.

7.2.1 BULK FILE PAYMENTS

The user must first create a USPTO.gov account to upload and submit bulk file payments in the Patent Maintenance Fees Storefront.

The steps for bulk file payments are as follows:

1. Create the bulk file by downloading USPTO's formatted template or follow the examples below:

Patent No.:	7 Characters (e.g., 7807783)
Application No.:	8 Digits (e.g., 08443982)
Attorney Docket No. (Optional):	Up to 25 Characters (e.g., Client ABC)
Fee Code:	4 Digits (e.g., 1551)
Fee Amount:	US Dollar Value (e.g., 1600.00)

2. Save the file as a Comma Separated Value (.csv) file.
3. Go to *https://fees.uspto.gov/MaintenanceFees* and sign in.
4. Upload the bulk file to the Patent Maintenance Fees Storefront.
5. Check out using a Deposit Account stored in Financial Manager.
6. Once the bulk mail payment has been processed, the USPTO will email the user a downloadable receipt.
7. Navigate to the Bulk Payment History page to view and download previously uploaded bulk files, receipts, and consolidated PDF statements.

7.3 CURRENT FEE SCHEDULE

The current Fee Schedule is at *www.uspto.gov/learning-and-resources/fees-and-payment/uspto-fee-schedule*.

7.4 METHODS OF PAYMENTS

USPTO fees may be paid by Check, Cashier's Check, Money Order, Credit Card, by Electronic Funds Transfer ("EFT"), or an authorization to charge a Deposit Account if a Deposit Account has been established with the USPTO. EFT payments can only be processed from U.S. bank accounts.

Payment from foreign countries must be payable and immediately negotiable in the United States for the full amount of the fee required.

7.4.1 CHECKS, CASHIER'S CHECKS, OR MONEY ORDERS

All Checks, Cashier's Checks, or Money Orders must be made payable to "Director of the USPTO".

> NOTE: If a check is returned to the USPTO for insufficient funds ("NSF"), the matter will be referred to OED which may open an investigation against the Practitioner to determine if there has been a violation of a disciplinary rule.

7.4.2 CREDIT CARDS

The **credit card payment form (PTO-2038)** is not required (and should not be used) when making a credit card payment via EFS-Web. If not efiling via EFS-Web, use Form **PTO-2038** which can be downloaded at *www.uspto.gov/sites/default/files/documents/PTO-2038.pdf.*

7.4.3 ELECTRONIC FUNDS TRANSFER

The Electronic Funds Transfer ("EFT") payment method allows the eFiler to send the UPSTO a payment over the Internet as simply as writing a check. The EFT profile must be created first before using EFT. The EFT profile contains a User ID, password, address, and banking information which are stored in Financial Manager. To create an EFT profile, go to *www.uspto.gov/financialmanager* and follow the instructions.

7.4.4 DEPOSIT ACCOUNT

For the convenience of Practitioners and the general public for paying USPTO fees, pre-paid Deposit Accounts may be established with the USPTO. This eliminates the need to submit a check, credit card, or other payment type each time a fee is required. Further, where there has been a miscalculation of a fee due, the balance required may be charged to the account with authorization, thus preserving a filing date of the application being filed or the abandonment of an application.

7.4.4.1 Opening a New Deposit Account

As of April 9, 2016, the only way to open a Deposit Account is through Financial Manager at *www.uspto.gov/financialmanager*. After the Deposit Account has been created, customers have forty-five (45) days to add funds using one of the options listed on the Deposit Account Replenishment Options page. The customer may also add other users to the Deposit Account, granting them specific permissions to use or access the Deposit Account. Setting up a Deposit Account is free.

7.4.4.2 Replenishing and Managing Existing Deposit Accounts

Financial Manager provides an easy and secure way for customers to manage and replenish Deposit Accounts online. Customers can manage Deposit Account funds, view the current balance, generate transaction reports, and download monthly statements all online.

7.4.4.3 Deposit Account Replenishment Options

There is no restriction on the frequency of making payments to the Deposit Account to replenish amounts in the Account. Payments can be made by using one of the following four (4) options:

Replenish Online: Visit Financial Manager to replenish the Deposit Account using a one-time electronic funds transfer (EFT) or Deposit Account transfer. There, the customer may also set up and manage a scheduled auto-replenishment by EFT. Replenishment may be accomplished as follows:

- To initiate Deposit Account replenishments in Financial Manager, the customer will need Funds manager permission to add funds to the Deposit Account. Also, the customer will need Fee Payer permission to transfer funds from the Deposit Account/EFT.
- Before setting up a replenishment via EFT in Financial Manager, verify with the financial institution that EFT payments can be processed through the customer's checking or savings account. If the customer has an ACH/EFT block or filter on his or her account, he or she must provide his/her financial institution with the USPTO's ACH company ID number to have his or her account set up properly before submitting EFT payments. The USPTO's ACH company ID is **1310000101**.

Replenish by Wire: Send the replenishment via EFT through the Federal Reserve Fedwire System by providing the below wire transfer information to the financial institution.

NOTE: The bank may charge a fee, and the financial institution may use an intermediate bank to transfer the funds (and the intermediate bank may withhold their fee from the payment that is transmitted). Ensure the full amount of the fee required in U.S. dollars is transmitted.

The customer must provide the purpose of the wire payment and information that helps identify the transaction (e.g., patent maintenance fee, patent number, application number) in the appropriate field or line to ensure timely processing of the payment. Failure to provide the required information in the correct fields or lines may result in delays or rejection of the wire payment.

Instructions for Sending a Domestic Wire Payment to the USPTO

Fedwire Field Tag	Fedwire Field Name	Required Information
[1510]	Type/Subtype	**1000**
[2000]	Amount	(enter payment amount)
[3400]	Receiver ABA Routing Number	**021030004**
[3400]	Receiver ABA Short Name (account is with the Federal Reserve Bank of New York	**TREAS NY** 33 Liberty Street New York, NY 10045
[3600]	Business Function Code	**CTR** (or CTP)
[4200]	Beneficiary ID Code	**D**
[4200]	Beneficiary Identifier (account number)	**13100001**
[4200]	Beneficiary Name	**USPTO** 2051 Jamieson Avenue Suite 300 Alexandria, VA 22314
[5000]	Originator	(enter your company name)
[6000]	Originator to Beneficiary Information (up to 4 lines of 35 characters each)	(enter the brief purpose of payment and information that helps identify the transaction (e.g., maintenance fee, patent number, application number), and a phone number)

Instructions for Sending an International Wire Payment to the USPTO

Field Name	Required Information
(Beneficiary) Bank Number (Line 57a)	//FW021030004
(Beneficiary) Bank Name	TRES NYC/FUNDS TRANSFER DIVISION
Beneficiary Account Number (Line 59)	13100001
Amount	(enter payment amount) **13100001 USPTO**
Payment Details (Line 70) (up to 4 lines of 35 characters each)	(enter the brief purpose of payment and information that helps identify the transaction (e.g., maintenance fee, patent number, application number), and a phone number)
Details of Charges (Line 71a)	Charge Our

NOTES:

* The above information should be transmitted from the remitter's bank to its U.S. Correspondent bank. The U.S. Correspondent bank will use the Fedwire system to complete the transfer.
* Bank Number (Line 57a) must be in the exact format above.
* Beneficiary Account Number (Line 59) must be the USPTO's ALC of 13100001 or the payment will be returned.
* Details of Charges (Line 71a) must be coded as "Charge Our" to have any banking fees charged to the remitter and not deducted from the payment.

Replenish by Mail: Send the replenishment payment via first class mail to the following address:

> Director of the U.S. Patent and Trademark Office
> Attn: Deposit Accounts
> 2051 Jamieson Avenue, Suite 300
> Alexandria, VA 22314

Make checks payable to the "Director of the USPTO". In order to ensure that replenishment payments are credited to the account accurately and in a timely manner, also include the Deposit Account Number on the check.

NOTE: Checks from a Practitioner or the Practitioner's firm returned to the USPTO for insufficient funds will initiate an investigation by OED against the Practitioner to determine if a disciplinary rule has been violated.

Replenish by IPAC (Federal Agencies Only): Use the Department of the Treasury's Intra-Governmental Payment and Collection (IPAC) system. The customer's accounting office must use due care and ensure that all pertinent account numbers are listed on the IPAC transaction and ensure the Deposit Account number is provided to prevent delays in processing the payment. Funds are generally credited and available in the customer's Deposit Account within two-three (2-3) business days.

ALC	Agency Locator Code	13-10-0001
TAS	Treasury Account Symbol	13X1006
DUNS	Data Universal Numbering Systems number	070921085
CAGE	Commercial and Government Entity number	444P0

7.4.4.4 Fees Establishing and Maintaining Deposit Account

There are different fees associated with establishing and maintaining each type of Deposit Account offered by the USPTO:

- **Unrestricted**: This type of account allows account holders to charge any fee or service offered by the USPTO. Account holders must maintain a minimum balance of $1,000 on the last business day of each month. If the account balance is below that amount, the account will be assessed a $25 service charge for that month. The minimum amount required to establish this account is $1,000.
- **Restricted**: This type of account allows Deposit Account customers to order and charge payment for copies of U.S. patents and trademarks, patent subscriptions, and Electronic Ordering Service orders to their accounts. Account holders must maintain a minimum balance of $300 on the last business day of each month. If the account balance is below that amount, the account will be assessed a $25 service charge for that month. The minimum amount required to establish this account is $300.

Any questions or need for additional information about Deposit Accounts and replenishment options can be obtained by contacting the Deposit Account Branch at:

571-272-6500 - USPTO
571-273-6500 - Facsimile

CHAPTER 8

Application Data Sheet

• • •

8.1 WHAT IS AN APPLICATION DATA SHEET?

AN APPLICATION DATA SHEET ("ADS") must be submitted in each patent application. The ADS contains bibliographic data, arranged in a format specified by the USPTO.

Best practice is to file the ADS on or prior to the date that any Inventor's Oath or Declaration is filed. If the Inventor's Oath or Declaration is filed first, then the USPTO will only capture the Inventor's information from the Inventor's Oath or Declaration and not from the ADS.

The bibliographic data in the ADS must include the following:

* Inventor information (name, address, citizenship, residence)
* Correspondence information
* Applicant information
* Representative information
* Domestic priority information
* Foreign priority information
* Assignee information

The ADS must be signed by the Practitioner either handwritten or by S-signature, e.g., /John Doe/. If the ADS is not signed, then a Notice to File Missing Parts will be mailed from the USPTO.

The ADS must contain foreign priority (except national stage applications) or domestic benefit claims.

A Power of Attorney cannot be established using ADS.

The inventor's address may be where the inventor works, a post office box, or other address where mail is received, even if it is not the main mailing address of the inventor.

The domestic benefit or foreign priority data should be correct and properly formatted under these sections. If this information is incorrect, a Corrected ADS is required.

The ADS includes a new Applicant information section to identify non-inventor Applicants.

> NOTE: Where the Applicant is the Assignee or a person to whom the inventor is under an obligation to assign the invention, documentary evidence of ownership should be recorded in the assignment records no later than payment of the Issue Fee.

If the Applicant is a juristic entity, the ADS may only be signed by a Practitioner. For other Applicants, the ADS may be signed by either the Applicant or the Practitioner.

As of October 27, 2015, Applicants are no longer required to select an opt-in box on the ADS form (PTO/AIA/14) to provide the USPTO with authorization to permit a foreign intellectual property office participating in the priority document exchange ("PDX") program access to a U.S. priority application. Instead, the ADS form contains by default the authorization to permit access to the U.S. priority application via the PDX program. Including a properly signed ADS form will provide Applicant's authorization for the PDX program. Should Applicant wish not to provide authorization for the PDX program, Applicant can select the opt-out check box for this authorization on the ADS form. The revised ADS form also contains by default the authorization to permit access to the search results from a U.S. priority application by the European Patent Office (EPO). Like the PDX program, should Applicant wish not to provide the EPO access to the search results, Applicant can select the opt-out check box for this authorization on the ADS form.

> NOTE: A revised ADS form submitted after the filing of an application cannot be used to provide or revoke any of the authorizations to permit access discussed above. Instead, forms PTO/SB/39 and PTO/SB/69, as applicable, should be used to provide or revoke these authorizations to permit access after the filing of an application.

Updated November 16, 2015, ADS instructions for non-National Stage applications can be found at:

www.uspto.gov/forms/aia_ads_form_inst.doc

Where the international filing date of the international application is on or after September 16, 2012, ADS instructions for National Stage applications can be found at:

www.uspto.gov/forms/aia_ads_371_instructions.pdf

8.2 Submitting a Corrected ADS

Under the AIA, there is no longer a "supplemental" ADS. It is now labeled as a "corrected" ADS.

A corrected ADS in pdf format is sufficient if it shows underlines (to add data) and strikeouts (for deletions).

If an ADS is not filed at initial filing of application, then a corrected ADS must be filed later using underlining to add data. The corrected ADS must be properly signed by the Practitioner and labeled "Corrected ADS" at the top of the first page.

The corrected ADS only contain the information that has changed. Do not repeat the information that is unchanged.

- The corrected ADS shows the changed information with strikethroughs and underscores; and
- The footer information should include the word "Corrected" in place of "Initial" and should also contain the Application Number and Filing Date.

See **Section 8.5 – Corrected Web-Based ADS** for information on correcting an ADS via EFS-Web.

8.3 PDF Fillable Form for ADS

Best practice for filing an ADS is to use the computer-readable Form **PTO/AIA/14** at *www.uspto.gov/forms/aia0014.pdf* and efile it in EFS-Web in the first EFS-Web submission for the application. This allows the bibliographic data to automatically load into PALM without having someone at the USPTO type in the bibliographic data from the scanned copy of the ADS.

> NOTE: If submitting the ADS after the initial filing, i.e., Notice to File Missing Parts, the PDF fillable form of the ADS will not permit the entry of the Application Number associated with the application.

8.4 Web-Based ADS

EFS-Web will automatically generate and attach a PDF version of the WebADS.

Basic Guidelines for Filing a Web-Based ADS:

- eFiler must be able to access EFS-Web.
- Available for new applications under the following submission types: Utility and Design.
- Not permitted in PCT and Supplemental Examination submissions.

- Can be either a Registered or Unregistered eFiler. Only Registered eFilers can save a submission as a work-in-progress for up to 7 days.
- Not permitted in follow-on submissions.
- The ADS must be signed by the Practitioner. If the Applicant is prosecuting the application *pro se*, all of the inventors must sign to comply with the rule, unless a Power of Attorney has been given.
- All required fields must be completed in order to proceed with the submission. The required fields are indicated with an asterisk.
- Can only be submitted with the filing of a new application on or after September 16, 2012, or with a U.S. national stage entry under 37 USC 371 where the Patent Cooperation Treaty (PCT) filing date (international filing date) is on or after September 16, 2012.
- Do not attach an ADS as a PDF if submitting a Web-based ADS.
- Submissions under a Secrecy Order may not be filed electronically.

8.5 Corrected Web-Based ADS
On December 21, 2015, the USPTO implemented the Corrected Web-Based ADS to provide a Corrected/Updated ADS, where changes will be identified with underlining for insertions and strike-through for text removal. EFS-Web will generate and attach the Corrected ADS PDF. See Quick Start Guide for more information at *www.uspto.gov/sites/default/files/documents/Corrected-WebADS-QSG.pdf.*

8.6 Enhanced Initial Web-Based ADS
EFS-Web eFilers who have been granted Power of Attorney may retrieve Inventor Information, Domestic Benefit/National Stage data, and/or Foreign Priority data from a parent application when completing their Web-based ADS submission.

A more comprehensive guide on filing a Web-based ADS is found at *www.uspto.gov/patents/process/file/efs/guidance/WebADS_QSG.pdf.*

CHAPTER 9

Information Disclosure Statements

• • •

9.1 Information Disclosure Statements

THE APPLICANT FOR A PATENT application and the Practitioner are required to notify the USPTO of any information that they believe is material to the patentability of the invention. The means for complying with this duty is to file an Information Disclosure Statement, or what is commonly known as an "IDS".

In general, the IDS will include a listing of all U.S. Patents, U.S. Patent Application Publications (also referred to as Pre-Grant Publications or PG-PUB), Foreign Patents, Foreign Patent Application Publications, and International Patent Applications. However, the information submitted to the USPTO is not limited to these patent-related documents. Information outside the scope of patent-related documents is referred to as non-patent literature ("NPL documents"). These NPL documents may include, but are not limited to, journal or scholarly articles, books, magazines, independent publications, and webpages. The Practitioner will provide the Paralegal with documents to be listed.

The USPTO, in general, only accepts document submissions. However, the information material to patentability may not be in document form (such as a prior use). In such cases, the Practitioner may prepare affidavits or other evidence for submission to the USPTO to convey the relevant information.

9.2 IDS Requirements

The following sections are intended to give an overview of common IDS practice. IDS practice is governed by 37 CFR 1.97-1.98 and MPEP 609. When in doubt, as to any issue related to IDS practice, the Paralegal should consult the Practitioner.

9.2.1 Timing

The USPTO provides various time windows when an IDS may be submitted and considered by the USPTO without a fee. An IDS submitted outside these time windows will, in general, incur a fee and/

or require a certification by the Practitioner. The following chart details the relevant time windows and the supplemental requirements for USPTO consideration of the IDS associated with each time frame.

Time Window for IDS Submission			Requirements
Window	**Start**	**End**	
1.1	Filing of application	Within 3 months of filing date	No additional requirements
1.2	Filing of application	Within 3 months of national stage entry	No additional requirements
1.2	Filing of Application	Before 1st Office Action on the merits	No additional requirements
1.3	Filing of RCE	Before next Office Action on the merits	No additional requirements
2.1	After 1.2 or 1.3	Before Office Action closing prosecution (Final Rejection, Notice of Allowance, Quayle Action)	Fee **OR** Certification Statement
3.1	After 2.1	Prior to abandonment or issue fee payment	Fee and Certification Statement **OR** RCE
4.1	After issue fee payment	Issue of patent	Petition to withdraw from issue **AND** RCE

If a time window is missed, the Practitioner must comply with the requirements for the new time window in order for the submitted IDS to be considered. If the requirements for the new time window cannot be met, the Paralegal should consult with the Practitioner.

> NOTE: After filing of an RCE, a fee or certification for IDS submission is not required as long as the IDS is submitted before the next Office Action.

9.2.2 CERTIFICATIONS

After the Examiner has picked up an application for consideration and has issued an Action on the merits, the USPTO generally requires the Practitioner to pay a fee and/or provide a certification when filing an IDS. The lone exception to this is when the Practitioner files an RCE. On filing of the RCE, the IDS time windows are restarted (see window 1.3) such that the Practitioner can submit an IDS without a corresponding fee or certification. RCE practice with respect to IDS submissions is explained in more detail in *Section 9.2.4 – RCE Practice*.

A Certification Statement is required when Practitioner receives a communication (such as a Search Report or Office Action) from a foreign patent office (e.g., non-U.S. authority, including WIPO) in a counterpart foreign application. In this situation, the following Certification Statement (under 37 CFR 1.97(e)(1)) is used by the Practitioner:

> I hereby state that each item of information contained in the information disclosure statement was first cited in any communication from a foreign patent office in a counterpart foreign application not more than three months prior to the filing of the information disclosure statement.

This statement must be explicit and must be signed by the Practitioner. Submission of the IDS with a foreign communication showing a date less than three (3) months from the IDS submission, absent the explicit statement, is not sufficient for the submission to be considered without paying the fee.

Further, according to the USPTO, "the term counterpart foreign patent application means that a claim for priority has been made in either the U.S. application or a foreign application based on the other, or that the disclosures of the U.S. and foreign patent applications are substantively identical." The Paralegal must confer with Practitioner to confirm that the communication relied upon is actually a counterpart foreign application, and not merely a related foreign application.

It is also important to note that the Certification Statement only applies to the first citation of the relevant information in a foreign counterpart application. If the relevant information is cited a second time in a later communication, the Practitioner cannot then rely on this second communication for the Certification Statement. For example, assume that the European Search Report in a counterpart European application lists references A and B and a European Office Action is issued six (6) months later in the counterpart European application and lists references A, B, and C. Within three (3) months of the European Office Action, the Practitioner in the U.S. application may use the Certification Statement to submit an IDS with reference C, but the Practitioner cannot use the Certification Statement to submit an IDS with references A and B. The Paralegal should check to make sure that information to be cited in an IDS relying on the first Certification Statement is the first citation of the information in the counterpart foreign application, as well as any other foreign or U.S. members of the patent family.

When dealing with communications from foreign patent offices, the communication may include a listing of the patent family associated with references cited in the communication. Although it would appear that this listing is not an official citation by the foreign patent office, the USPTO encourages the inclusion of any corresponding U.S. patent documents or English language equivalents from the patent family listing for the cited references. The U.S. or other English language patent will be considered as cited by the foreign patent office for the purpose of using the first Certification Statement. The Paralegal should indicate this in the IDS Transmittal Letter for the Practitioner's signature by noting that the listed U.S. or other English language patents are English language equivalents for the non-English language documents cited by the foreign patent office, and that the U.S. and English language patents were cited in the family listing from the foreign patent office.

Another situation requiring a Certification Statement is when the Applicant becomes aware of information he/she had no previous knowledge. If, after reasonable inquiry, the Practitioner confirms that no one involved in the preparation and prosecution of the application knew of the information more than three (3) months prior to the filing, the Practitioner can use a Certification Statement to have the information considered by the Examiner. In this situation, the Applicant (through the Practitioner) uses the following Certification Statement (under 37 CFR 1.97(e)(2)):

> I hereby state that no item of information contained in the information disclosure statement filed herewith was cited in a communication from a foreign patent office in a counterpart foreign application, and, to my knowledge after making reasonable inquiry, no item of information contained in the information disclosure statement was known to any individual designated in 37 CFR 1.56(c) more than three months prior to the filing of the information disclosure statement.

This statement must be explicit and signed by the Practitioner.

At the direction of the Practitioner, the Paralegal may be called upon to confirm that the information to be cited in the IDS was not known by anyone involved with the application. The Paralegal should exercise due care in this task. In particular, the Paralegal should check the information to be cited in the IDS to make sure that an Inventor in the present application is not an Inventor or co-Inventor of any of the cited information. If the Inventor is named in the cited information, the Paralegal should consult with the Practitioner.

In either of the situations described above, the Practitioner signs the Certification Statement and is responsible for the content of the IDS. Also, it is required that the information submitted in the IDS be submitted within three (3) months of acquisition of the information. In the first situation described above, the IDS must be submitted to the USPTO within three (3) months of the issuance of the foreign office communication in order to use the first Certification Statement.

Use of one of the Certification Statements does not preclude the use of the other Certification Statement. For example, if certain information was cited in a counterpart foreign application and other information became known to Applicant at the same time, the Practitioner can use the appropriate Certification Statement to submit the information to the USPTO. In such cases, the Paralegal should prepare the information to be cited in two separate IDS documents. The first IDS document should be associated with the first Certification Statement while the second IDS document should be associated with the second Certification Statement. Both statements must be reviewed and signed by the Practitioner.

It should also be further emphasized that a Certification Statement is only necessary when an Office Action has been issued by the USPTO. Prior to first Office Action after initial filing or after filing of an RCE, a Certification Statement or fee is not required. See time windows 1.1-1.3.

9.2.3 FEES

Pursuant to 37 CFR 1.97, in certain time windows, a fee may be required by the USPTO in order to consider an IDS.

For time window 2.1, payment of the fee is required if one of the two Certification Statements cannot be used by the Practitioner. For example, if information was not cited in a counterpart foreign application and was known to the Practitioner more than three (3) months before filing the IDS, the IDS submission fee would be required. For time window 3.1, payment of the fee and one of the two Certification Statements are required.

Each IDS submission within a given time window requires a separate fee. The USPTO considers IDS submissions filed on separate days to be separate submissions. If two IDS submissions are filed in window 2.1 on back to back days, two separate fee payments would be required.

Thus, the Paralegal should exercise due care in ensuring that all information intended to be cited is included on an IDS, to prevent the need for multiple submissions. Furthermore, on the same day of filing the IDS, the Paralegal should confirm that all information intended to be included on the IDS was actually filed. If there is any deficiency, the Paralegal may be able to immediately correct the deficiency. Multiple IDS submissions filed with the USPTO on the same day, but at different times will be considered as a single filing and will only require a single fee.

9.2.4 RCE PRACTICE

Once the Examiner has closed prosecution in an application by issuing an appropriate Office Action, the conditions by which an IDS will be considered become more stringent. Actions closing prosecution include a Final Rejection, a Notice of Allowance, and an E*x parte* Quayle Action. As noted with respect to window 3.1, the USPTO requires both the fee and one of the two Certification Statements in order to have the IDS considered by the Examiner. The filing of the RCE restarts the IDS window (i.e., changes to window 1.3) so that neither the fee nor any Certification Statement is required with the IDS submission.

9.2.5 FORMALITIES AND DOCUMENTS FOR SUBMISSION

By rule, an IDS submission should contain at least the following information, as appropriate:

* A list of all patents, publications, or other information submitted for consideration by the USPTO;
* A legible copy of each reference cited, or the relevant portion of the reference, exclusive of U.S. Patents and U.S. Patent Application Publications; and
* A concise explanation of the relevance of any document not in English.

The list should be separate and clearly indicate that this is an IDS submission. The list should be prepared using one of the standard USPTO forms (e.g., Forms PTO/SB/08a and/or PTO/SB/08b). The Paralegal should be cognizant of the fact that references listed within the specification of an application, but not listed on the IDS, will not be considered by the Examiner as a matter of right. The Examiner may choose to consider these references listed in the specification at his/her discretion. The Paralegal should bring to the attention of the Practitioner references listed in Applicant's specification so it may be determined if they are to be included on an IDS submission.

9.2.6 IDS TRANSMITTAL LETTER (OPTIONAL)

The IDS Transmittal Letter (optional) should include at least an application identification portion, a narrative portion, and a signature line portion. The application identification portion serves to notify the USPTO of the relevant details of the application to which the IDS is directed. Like other papers filed with the USPTO, this includes Application Number, filing date, first named inventor, title, Confirmation Number, Examiner and Art Unit (if known), and Attorney Docket Number (if applicable). The application identification portion can also provide intra-USPTO forwarding details, such as the appropriate Mail Stop. The application identification portion should also include an appropriate heading indicating the type of paper being submitted. For a first IDS submission, the heading should be "Information Disclosure Statement." For any IDS submission after the first, the heading should be "Supplemental Information Disclosure Statement." Alternatively, the Practitioner may request that IDS submissions after the first submission be indicated with the appropriate number, e.g., "Second Information Disclosure Statement." The Paralegal should confer with the Practitioner on his/her preferences for subsequent IDS submissions.

9.2.7 IDS FORMATTING

At a minimum, the listing of U.S. Patents on the IDS should include the first named inventor, the Patent Number, and the date the patent was issued (preferably in MM-DD-YYYY format). U.S. Patent Application Publications have a similar requirement. In particular, U.S. Patent Application Publications on the IDS should include the first named inventor, the Publication Number, and the publication date (preferably in MM-DD-YYYY format). To prevent typographical errors, it is recommended that the Paralegal use the USPTO website to find and copy the relevant information for each U.S. Patent or Patent Application Publication.

The U.S. has adapted to the standard WIPO codes to designate what kind of a document is presented. This is called the "Kind Code" and can be found after the Patent/Application Number on the front page of the Patent/Application. Although not required, there is space for document Kind Codes on the USPTO standard IDS forms. If so, Kind Codes should be used as indicated on the U.S. Patent or U.S. Patent Application Publication. For a complete list of Kind Codes, go to *www.uspto.gov/learning-and-resources/ support-centers/electronic-business-center/kind-codes-included-uspto-patent.*

Note: Assigned codes were usually not provided on the face of published documents prior to January 2, 2001.

A sample of frequently used Kind Codes is included in the following Table:

KIND CODES

Kind Code	Document Description
A1	Patent Application
A2	Patent Application (Republication)
A9	Patent Application (Corrected Publication)

B1	Patent (No Previous Application Publication)
B2	Patent (After Previous Application Publication)
C	Reexamination Certificate
E	Reissue Patent
P1	Plant Patent Application
S	Design Patent

In some cases, U.S. Patent Applications which have not been published are cited. The U.S. Patent Application to be cited may be currently pending, but not yet published as a U.S. Patent Application Publication, or may have been abandoned without being published. In general, if a corresponding U.S. Patent Application Publication exists for a particular U.S. Patent Application, the Publication should be cited on the IDS. If no Publication exists, then the U.S. Patent Application should be listed on the IDS. At a minimum, the listing should include the first named inventor, the Application Number, and the filing date.

For foreign patent documents, such as foreign patents and foreign patent applications, the listing in the IDS should include the country or Patent Office which issued the document. Note that International Application Publications are considered as foreign patent documents. For PCT International Application Publications, the listing would use WO as the Patent Office issuing the document. The listing in the IDS for foreign patent documents should also include the appropriate document number and the publication date of the document. Note that it is not required for the listing to include the Applicant or Inventor name for the foreign patent document. However, the Practitioner may request that the first named inventor or the Applicant be included in the listing in the IDS. The Paralegal should consult with the Practitioner regarding the desired preferences with regard to foreign patent document listings.

When listing NPL documents, each NPL document in the IDS should include sufficient information to fully identify the document. Thus, the listing should include, as relevant, the name of the author (in CAPITAL LETTERS), the title of the document, title of the source (if document is taken from book, magazine, journal, etc.), date of publication, page numbers of the document, volume-issue number(s), publisher of the document or source, and city/country where the document or source was published. Where more than one author is indicated for the NPL document, it may be preferable to use the first named author with "et al." The following table lists example of paper document NPL citation formats that may be used in IDS submissions.

Type of NPL	Appropriate Citation Format
Pages in Book	WINSLOW, C.E.A. *Fresh Air and Ventilation*. N.Y., E. P. Dutton, 1926. p. 97-112.
Section of Book	SMITH, J.F. "Patent Searching." in: SINGER, T.E.R., *Information and Communication Practice in Industry* (New York, Reinhold, 1958), pp.157-165.
Encyclopedia articles	CALVERT, R. "Patents (Patent Law)." in: *Encyclopedia of Chemical Technology* (1952 ed.), vol. 9, pp. 868-890.
Sections of Handbook	*Machinery's Handbook*, 16th ed. New York, International Press, 1959. pp. 1526-27.
Periodical Articles	NOYES, W.A. "A Climate for Basic Chemical Research." *Chemical & Engineering News*, Oct. 17, 1960, 38(42): pp. 91-95.
Withdrawn U.S. Patents	U.S. 6,999,999, 10/2002, Brown et al., 403/155 (withdrawn)
Withdrawn U.S. PG-PUB	U.S. 2002/0009999 A1, 07/2002, Jones et al., 403/155 (withdrawn).

Electronic documents (such as webpages) have become increasing prevalent as reference documents. When appropriate, the Paralegal should prepare electronic documents for IDS submission by printing or saving the relevant electronic document with appropriate headers/footers indicating the date of printing or saving, the page numbers, and the webpage address (if appropriate). For the IDS, the documents should be listed under the NPL section using the format for electronic documents in accordance with WIPO guidelines, which the USPTO has adopted. The listing of electronic documents is similar to the paper NPL document formats listed above with the following additions, as appropriate:

* Type of electronic medium provided in square brackets [ ] after the title of the publication or the designation of the host document, e.g., [online], [CD-ROM], [disk], magnetic tape].
* Date when the document was retrieved from the electronic media in square brackets following after the date of publication, e.g., [retrieved on March 4, 1998], [retrieved on 1998-03-04]. The four-digit year must always be given.
* Identification of the source of the document using the words "Retrieved from" and its address where applicable. This item will precede the citation of the relevant passages.
* Specific passages of the text could be indicated if the format of the document includes pagination or an equivalent internal referencing system, or by the first and last words of the passage cited.

The following are several examples of electronic document NPL citation formats provided by the USPTO that may be used in IDS submissions.

Examples of documents retrieved from online databases outside the Internet:

Example 1:

SU 1511467 A (BRYAN MECH) 1989-09-30 (abstract) World Patents Index [online]. London, U.K.: Derwent Publications, Ltd. [retrieved on 1998-02-24]. Retrieved from: Questel/Orbit, Paris, France. DW9016, Accession No. 90-121923.

Example 2:

DONG, X. R. 'Analysis of patients of multiple injuries with AIS-ISS and its clinical significance in the evaluation of the emergency managements', Chung Hua Wai Ko Tsa Chih, May 1993, Vol. 31, No. 5, pages 301-302. (abstract) Medline [online]. Bethesda, MD, USA: United States National Library of Medicine [retrieved on 24 February 1998]. Retrieved from: Dialog Information Services, Palo Alto, CA, USA. Medline Accession No. 94155687, Dialog Accession No. 07736604.

Example 3:

JENSEN, B. P. 'Multilayer printed circuits: production and application II'. Electronik, June-July 1976, No. 6-7, pages 8, 10,12,14,16. (abstract) INSPEC [online]. London, U.K.: Institute of Electrical Engineers [retrieved on 1998-02-24]. Retrieved from: STN International, Columbus, Ohio, USA. Accession No. 76:956632.

Example 4:

JP 3002404 (TAMURA TORU) 1991-03-13 (abstract). [online] [retrieved on 1998-09-02]. Retrieved from: EPO PAJ Database.

Examples of documents retrieved from the Internet:

Example 5 (Entire Work - Book or Report):

WALLACE, S., and BAGHERZADEH, N. Multiple Branch and Block Prediction. Third International Symposium on High-Performance Computer Architecture [online], February 1997 [retrieved on 1998-05-20]. Retrieved from the Internet:< URL: http://www.eng.uci.edu/comp. arch/ papers-wallace/hpca3-block.ps>.

Example 6 (Part of Work - chapter or equivalent designation):

National Research Council, Board on Agriculture, Committee on Animal Nutrition, Subcommittee on Beef Cattle Nutrition. Nutrient Requirements of Beef Cattle [online]. 7th revised edition. Washington, DC: National Academy Press, 1996 [retrieved on 1998-06-10]. Retrieved from the Internet:< URL: *http://www2.nap.edu/htbin/docpage/title=Nutrient+* Requirements+of+ Beef+Cattle%3A+Seventh+Revised+Edtion%2C+ 1996&dload=0& path=/ext5/ extra&name=054265%2Erdo&docid= 00805F50FE7b% 3A840052612&colid=4%7C6%7C41&st art=38> Chapter 3, page 24, table 3-1.

Example 7 (Electronic Serial - articles or other contributions):

Ajtai. Generating Hard Instances of Lattice Problems. Electronic Colloquium on Computational Complexity, Report TR96-007 [online], [retrieved on 1996-01-30]. Retrieved from the Internet <URL: *ftp://ftp.eccc.uni-trier.de/pub/eccc/reports/ 1996/TR96-007/index.htm*l>.

Example 8 (Electronic bulletin boards, message systems, and discussion lists - Entire System):

BIOMET-L (A forum for the Bureau of Biometrics of New York) [online]. Albany (NY): Bureau of Biometrics, New York State Health Department, July, 1990 [retrieved 1998-02-24]. Retrieved from the Internet: *<listserv@health.state.ny.us>*, message: subscribe BIOMET-L your real name.

Example 9 (Electronic bulletin boards, message systems, and discussion lists - Contributions):

PARKER, Elliott. 'Re: citing electronic journals'. In PACS-L (Public Access Computer Systems Forum) [online]. Houston (TX): University of Houston Libraries, November 24, 1989; 13:29:35 CST [retrieved on 1998-02-24]. Retrieved from the Internet: *<URL:telnet:// bruser@a.cni.org>*.

Example 10 (Electronic mail):

'Plumb design of a visual thesaurus'. The Scout Report [online]. 1998, vol. 5 no. 3 [retrieved on 1998-05-18]. Retrieved from Internet electronic mail: *<listserv@cs.wisc.edu>*, subscribe message: info scout-report. ISSN: 1092-3861\cf15.

Example 11 (Product Datasheet obtained from a website):

Corebuilder 3500 Layer 3 High-function Switch. Datasheet [online]. 3Com Corporation, 1997 [retrieved on 1998-02-24]. Retrieved from the Internet: <URL: www.3com.com/products/ dsheets/400347.html>.

Example 12 (Product Manual/Catalogue or other information obtained from a Web-site):

HU D9900111 Industrial Design Application, (HADJDUTEJ TEJIPARI RT, DEBRECEN) 1999-09-28, [online], [retrieved on 1999-10-26] Retrieved from the Industrial Design Database of the Hungarian Patent Office using Internet <URL: *http:/www.hpo.hu/English/db/indigo/>*.

The Paralegal should always confirm that the information provided on the IDS matches that of the document(s) intended to be cited. As should be readily apparent, a simple typographical error in a Patent Number can result in the citation of a completely different (and potentially irrelevant) document than that intended.

9.3 Documents for Submission

The USPTO requires submission of legible copies of all documents listed on the IDS that the USPTO does not already have. In particular, this requires that copies of all listed foreign patent documents and NPL documents be submitted at the time of filing the IDS submission.

Copies of the U.S. patents and U.S. patent applications need not be submitted when filing an IDS. A special case applies to unpublished U.S. Patent Applications. For U.S. Applications that are maintained by the USPTO in their Image File Wrapper (IFW) system, submission of the unpublished U.S. Application is not necessary. However, for U.S. Applications that are not maintained in the IFW system, copies of the application specification, including claims, and any drawings of the application, or that portion of the application which caused it to be listed (including any claims directed to that portion) must be submitted in order to be considered.

This may occur for older U.S. Applications that have since gone abandoned. As older U.S. Application files were maintained solely by the USPTO in paper format, these files are no longer readily available to the Examiners. Thus, a copy of the U.S. Application must be provided. Newer U.S. Applications maintained in IFW are readily available for review on the Examiner's computer desktop. Whenever citing an unpublished U.S. Application, the Paralegal should confirm that the U.S. Application is in IFW by reviewing the Image File Wrapper contents in Public PAIR. In the event that there are no file contents in the IFW tab in Public PAIR, the Paralegal should prepare copies of the U.S. Application for submission to the USPTO.

9.3.1 Foreign Patent Documents

The Paralegal should prepare copies of foreign patent documents using the best possible source document so as to generate a legible copy. Illegible copies may not be considered by the Examiner. For efiling, the Paralegal may download and save an electronic version (e.g., PDF) of the foreign patent document from the appropriate foreign patent office, thereby obtaining the best available copy. If the document is in English, no explanation of the relevance of the document is necessary.

If the foreign patent document is not in English, the Practitioner is required to provide an English translation of the document, or provide an explanation of the relevance of the document. When providing a translation, the translation column (marked with a T) on the IDS forms should be marked with a check (√) to indicate that a translation accompanies this document. No notation is required in the translation column if the document is already in English.

In many cases, a foreign patent office website or patent database, such as espacenet.com, may include an English language abstract for the foreign patent document. This English language abstract may be relied upon for the explanation of relevance. When presented with a non-English foreign patent document, the Paralegal should research if an English language abstract exists. If so, the Paralegal should include the English language abstract on a separate sheet with the respective foreign patent document. The translation column on the IDS form should be noted with "Abstract" (not √) to indicate that an English language abstract accompanies the foreign patent document.

In some cases, the foreign patent document may have a U.S. or English language International counterpart application (note the definition above for what constitutes a counterpart application). In other cases, a U.S. or English language International application may be considered an equivalent application but not a counterpart, such as when both share the same parent application but are not connected directly to each other by their priority claims. Counterpart and equivalent applications may be noted in the family information listed in a foreign search report, or by performing a family search for the foreign patent document on a foreign patent office website, such as espacenet.com. Alternately, the foreign patent document may directly claim priority from a U.S. or International application.

The English language counterpart and equivalent applications may represent a substantial translation of the foreign patent document. The Paralegal should compare the counterpart or equivalent application with the foreign patent document to make sure there are no substantial discrepancies, such as differences in the drawings, which may indicate that the counterpart or equivalent application does not correspond to the foreign patent document. If there are no substantial discrepancies, the Paralegal should consult with the Practitioner to determine if the English language document should be included. If so, the citation to the counterpart or equivalent application should be listed in the appropriate section of the IDS form (if a U.S. Patent, in the U.S. Patent Document section; if a PCT Publication, in the Foreign Patent Document section). The narrative portion of the IDS Transmittal Letter should also be updated to explain that the counterpart or equivalent application (referenced by citation number) has been cited as an English language equivalent for the foreign patent document (referenced by citation number). For example, "Document A3 on the attached list is the U.S. Patent counterpart of Document B2" or "Document A3 on the attached list is an English language equivalent of Document B2."

In the event that no translation is available, the Applicant or the Practitioner may state the relevance of the document to the present application. When required for a foreign reference, the Transmittal Letter should include the Statement of Relevance, which should be clearly labeled as such and begin on a separate page. The Paralegal should receive instructions from the Practitioner as to the contents of the Statement of Relevance. In some instances, the Statement of Relevance may be composed and executed by the Applicant or a Foreign Associate. By rule, the person involved in the prosecution of the application who is most knowledgeable about the content of the foreign language reference should sign the Statement of Relevance. In either instance, the narrative portion of the Transmittal Letter should indicate that a

Statement of Relevance is being provided for the non-English foreign patent documents (referenced by citation number).

If the foreign patent document was cited in a search report or action by a foreign patent office in a counterpart foreign application, the search report or action can be relied on for the Statement of Relevance. Thus, no explicit statement will be necessary by the Applicant or the Practitioner if the foreign search report or action accompanies the IDS submission. The foreign search report or action should be in English or at least indicate the relevance of the foreign patent document by internationally-accepted relevance indicators, such as an indication of "X", "Y", or "A" on the search report. The narrative section of the Transmittal Letter should indicate that the non-English language was cited in a foreign search report or action for a counterpart application. For example, "Document B3 was cited in a European Search Report (copy attached) for counterpart European Application No. EP-1883031."

The Paralegal should make sure to include a copy of the foreign search report or action with the IDS Submission. The foreign search report or action need not be listed in the IDS, since the purpose of the search report or action is to state the relevance of the cited references, not to serve as an independent reference. When filing via EFS-Web, the foreign search report or action may be categorized as NPL. If English language documents are referenced in the foreign search report or action, it is generally good practice to include the foreign search report with the citation of the English language documents in the IDS. Similar to the non-English language documents, the narrative section of the Transmittal Letter should indicate that the listed documents (referenced by citation number) were cited in a foreign search report or action for a counterpart application.

When a foreign search report or action in a counterpart application lists a number of documents which are already of record in the present application, the foreign search report or action should itself be submitted in an IDS for consideration by the Examiner. The Paralegal should list the IDS in the NPL section of the IDS form. The narrative section of the Transmittal Letter by the Practitioner should indicate that the attached foreign search report or action is from a counterpart application and that the documents are already of record. For example, "Document C1 is a European Search Report for counterpart European Application No. EP-1883031. The references noted in said Search Report have already been made of record in the instant application."

> NOTE: If the IDS is submitted during time windows 2.1-3.1, a Certification Statement may be used to have the IDS with the foreign search report or action considered if the foreign search report or action was issued within three (3) months of the IDS filing.

9.4 Search for Foreign Patent Documents

9.4.1 European Patent Office

In order to get a global patent from the European Patent Office, go to *worldwide.espacenet.com*, and obtain documents using the following steps:

1. Enter number and click "Search".

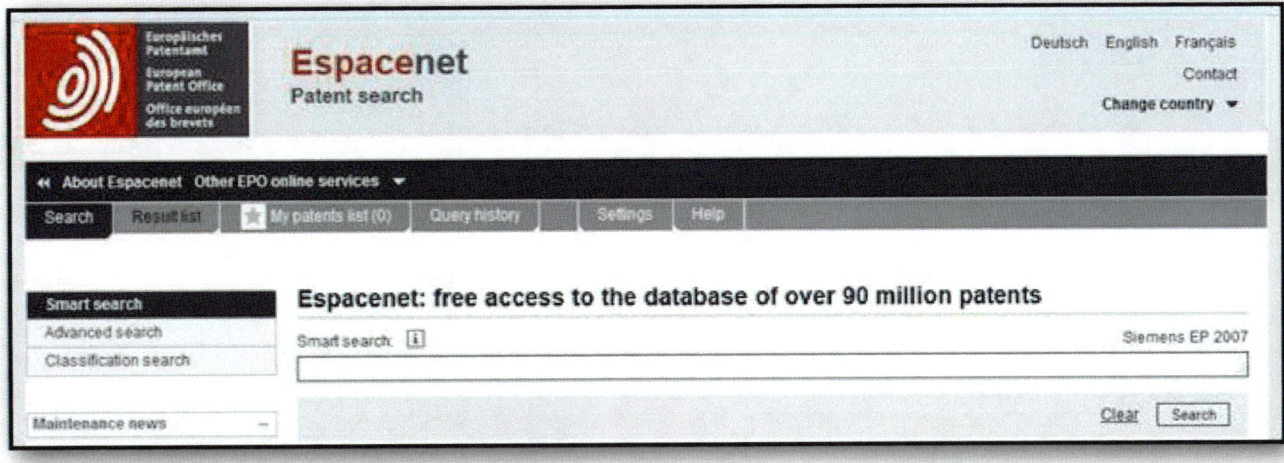

2. Click on the invention's title in order to enter into that patent document.

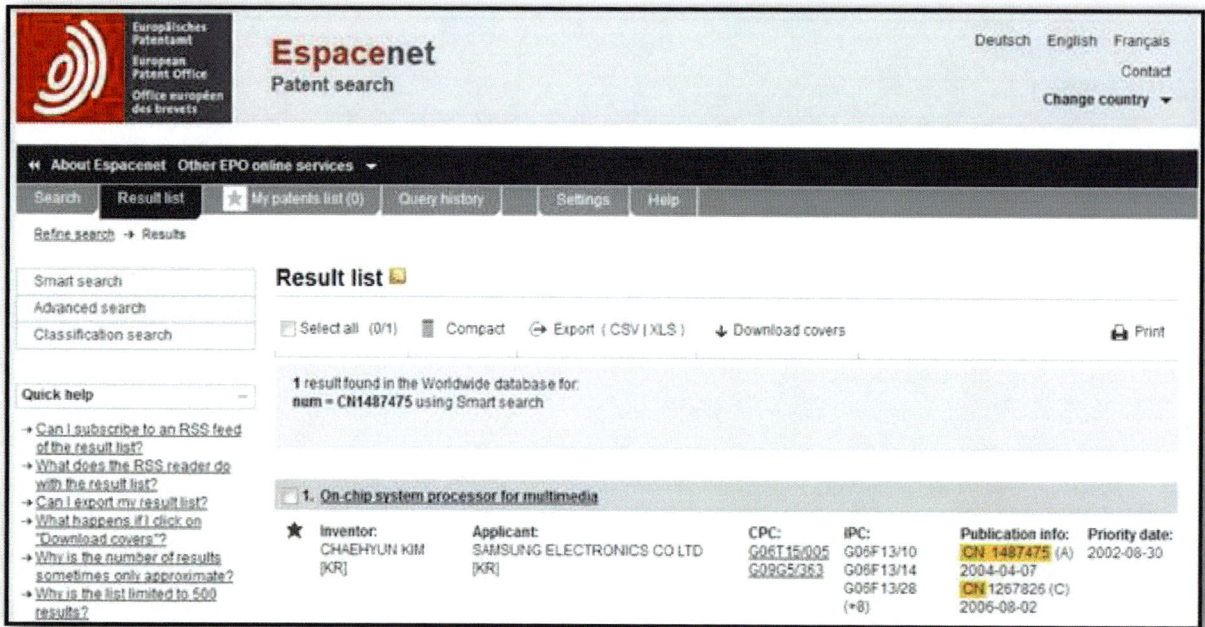

3. Click on the link "Original document".

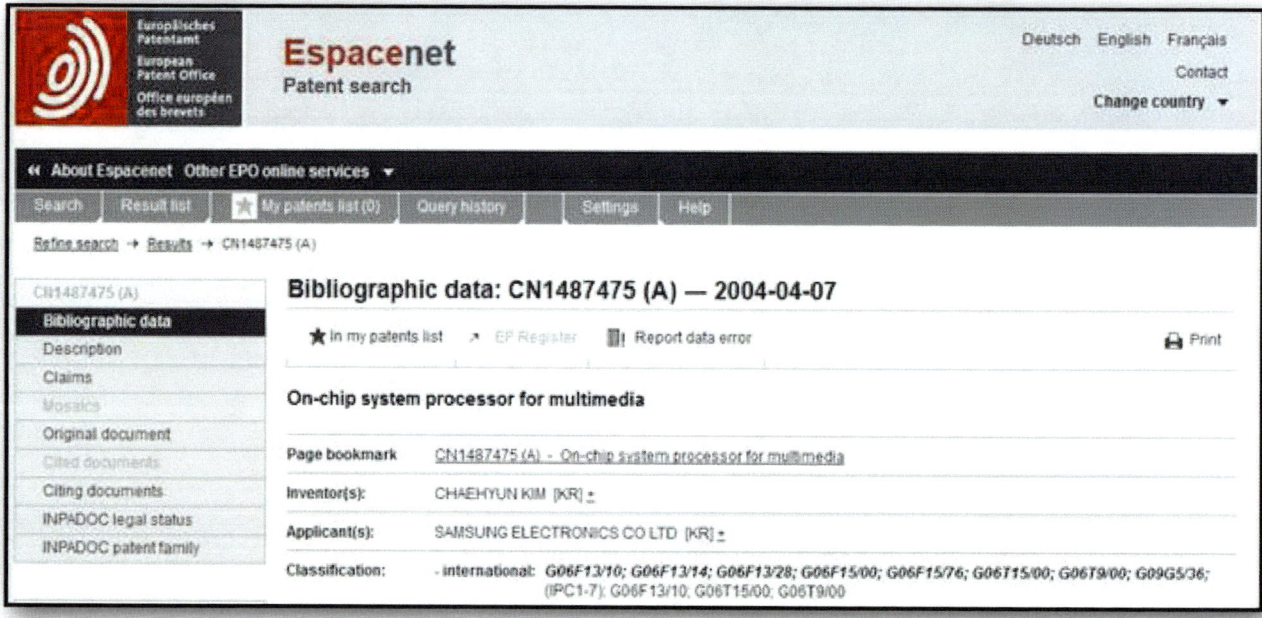

4. After the patent document comes up on the screen, click on "Download".

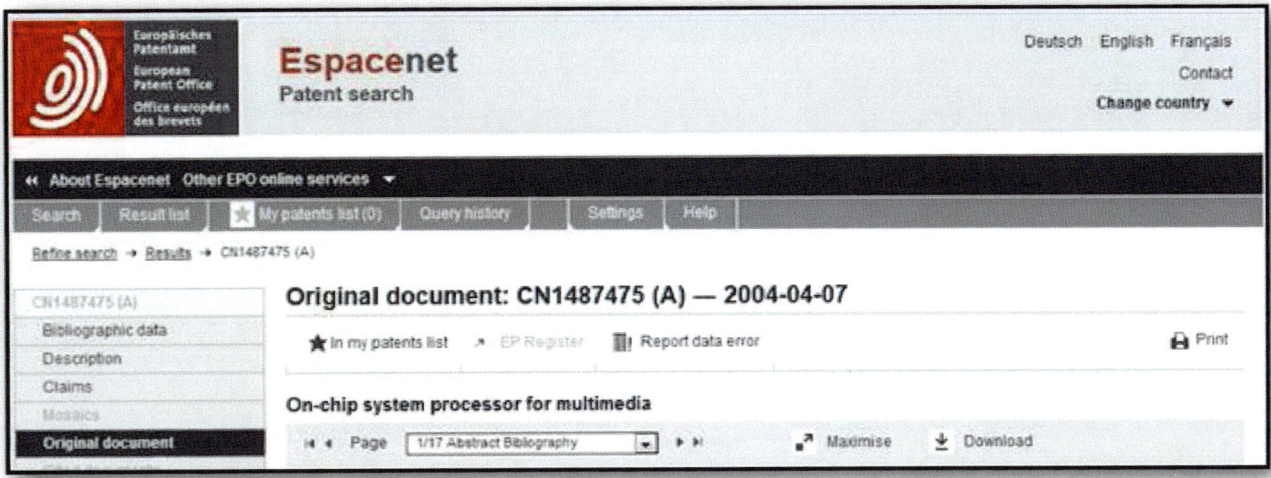

5. Enter the verification number and click "Submit".

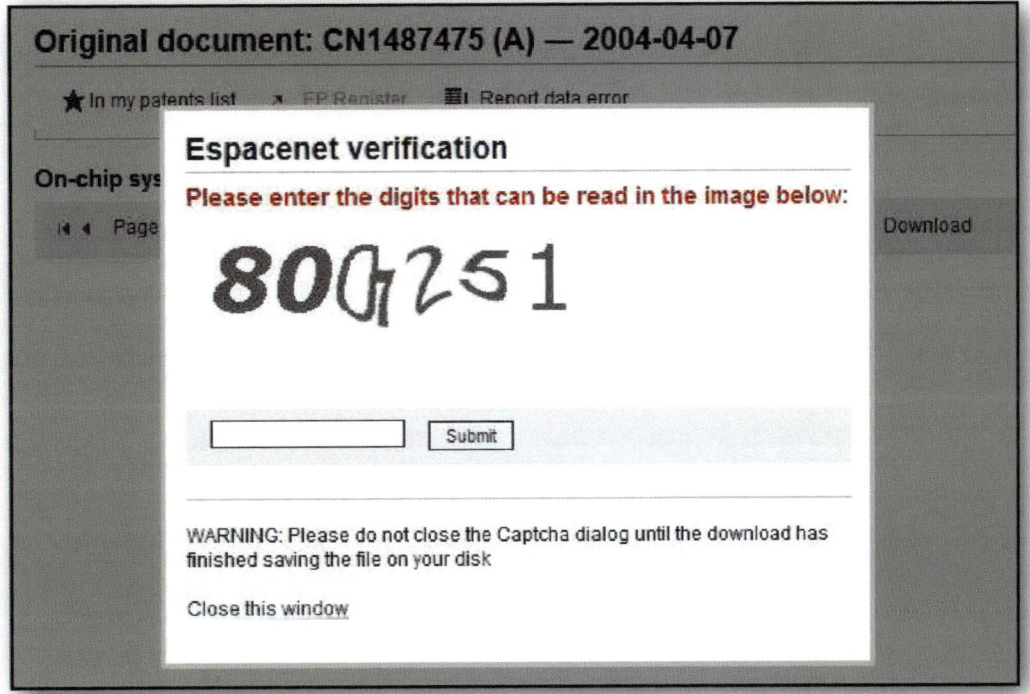

6. Click "OK".

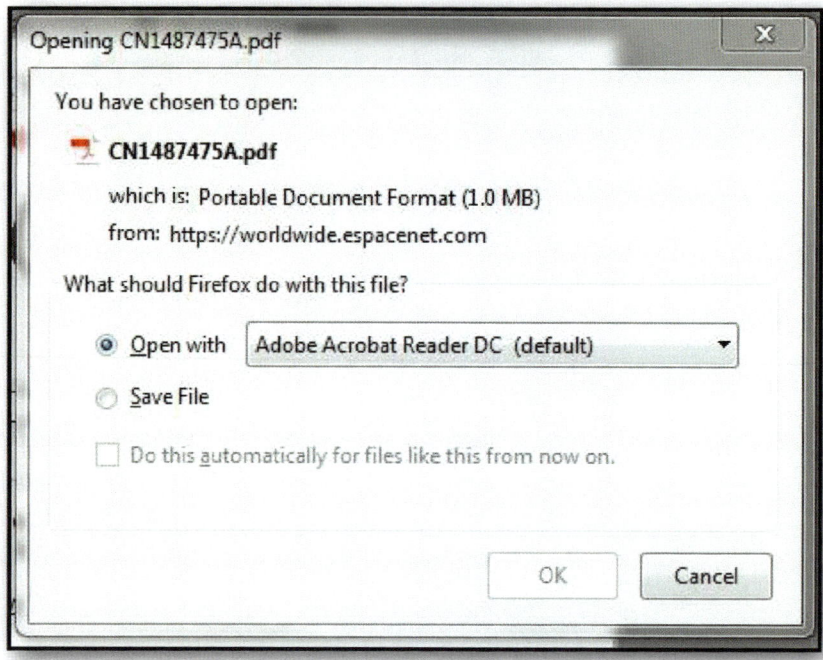

9.4.2 JAPAN PLATFORM FOR PATENT INFORMATION

In order to get a Patent Abstract in English, go to *https://www.j-platpat.inpit.go.jp/web/all/top/BTmTopEnglishPage*, and obtain documents using the following steps.

1. Click "Patent & Utility Model Number Search".

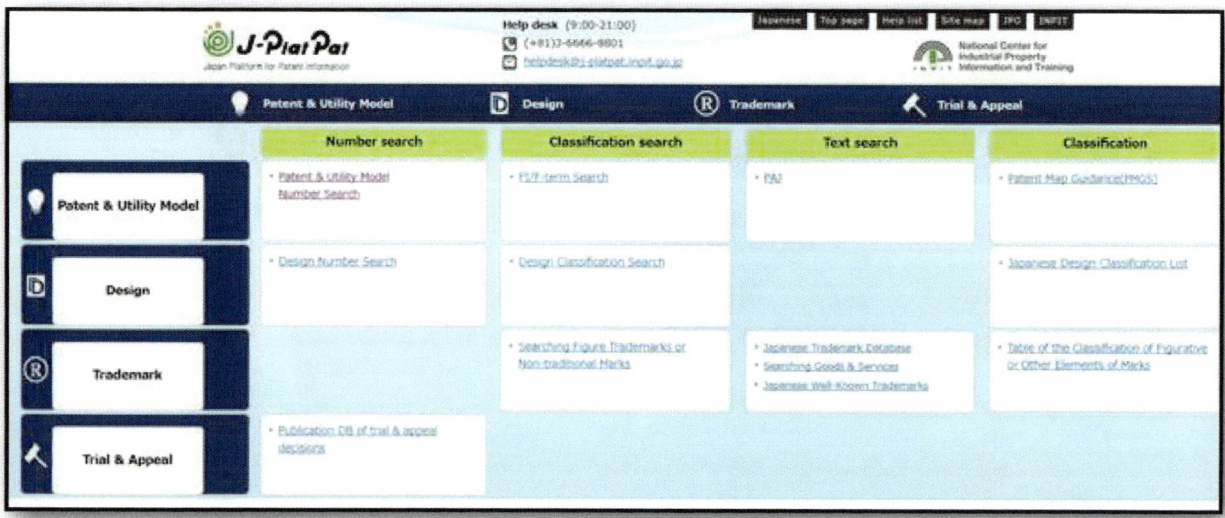

2. Type in the number to be searched and click "Search".

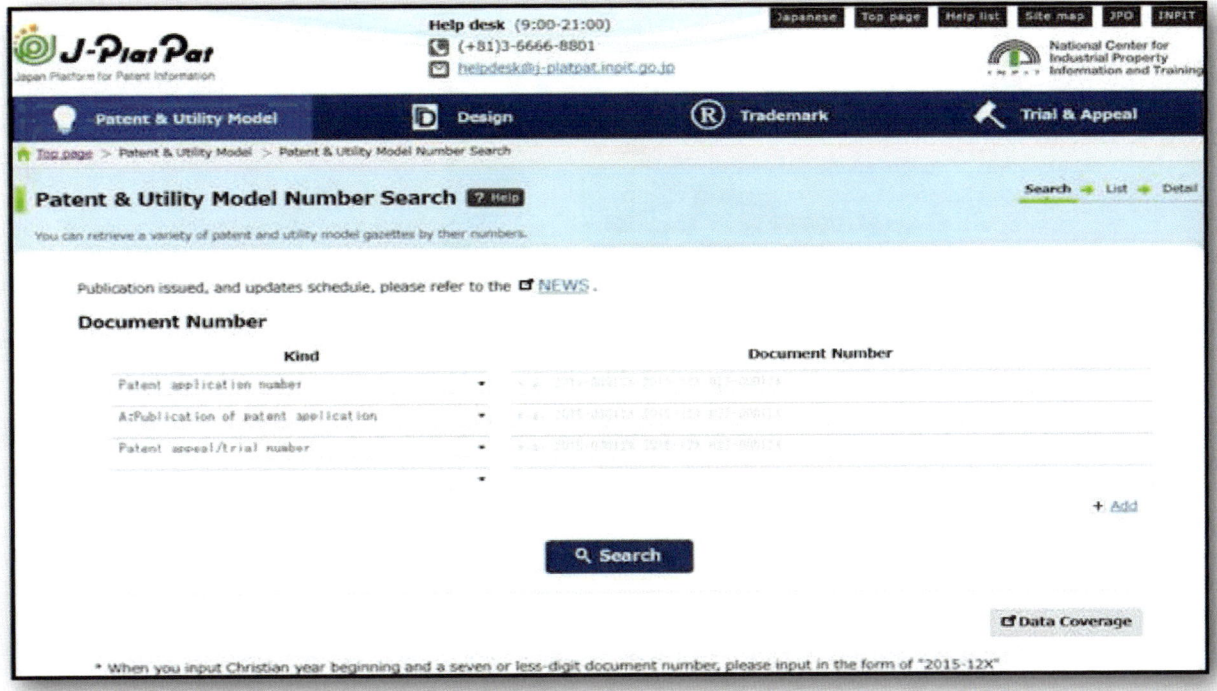

* When you input Christian year beginning and a seven or less-digit document number, please input in the form of "2015-12X"

9.4.3 CANADIAN INTELLECTUAL PROPERTY OFFICE

In order to get a Canadian Patent from the Canadian Intellectual Property Office, go to *www.cipo.ic.gc.ca/patents*, and obtain documents using the following steps:

1. Click on the link "Search patent documents" to search the Canadian Patents Database.

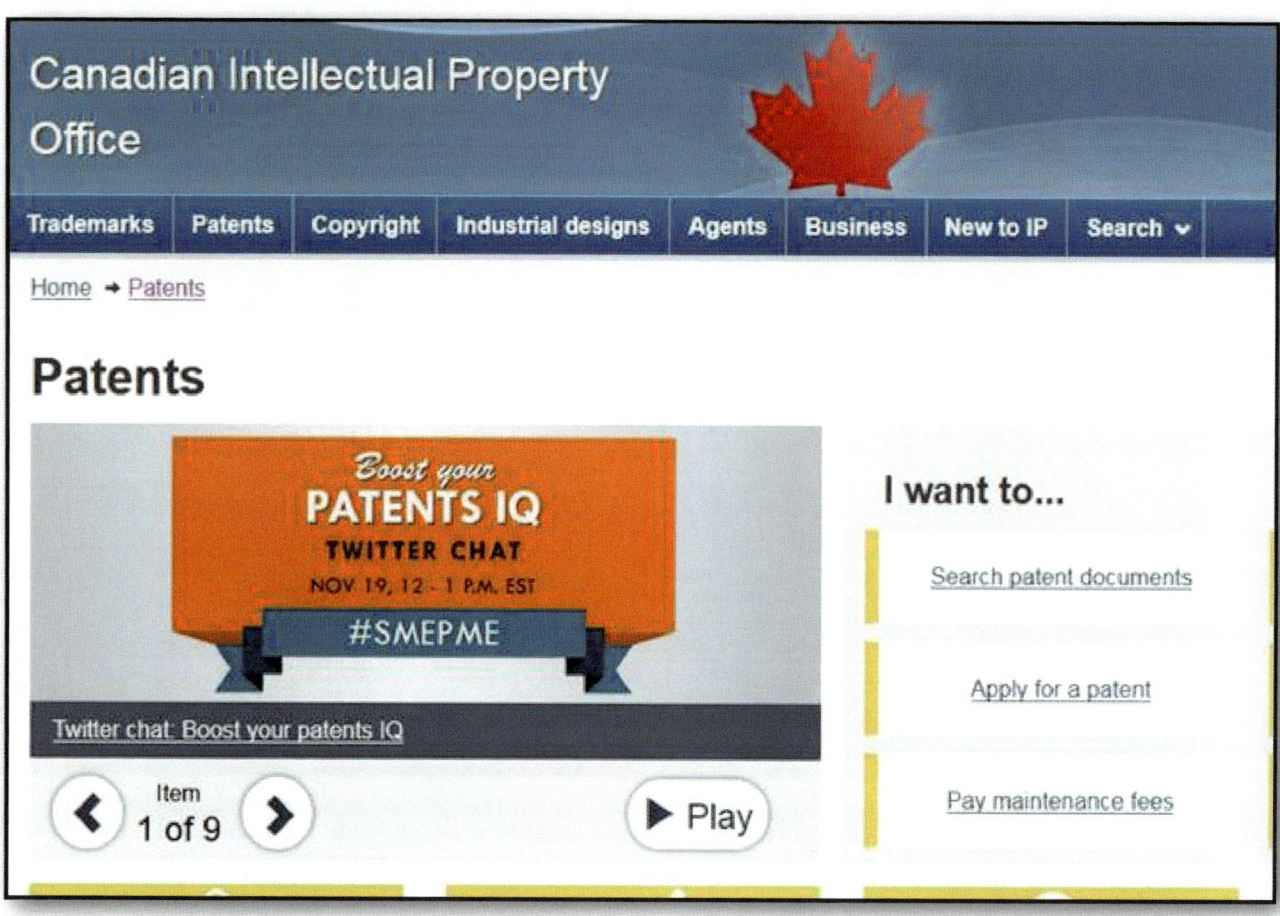

2. Type in the number to be searched and click "Search".

9.4.4 PATENTSCOPE

In order to get a PCT published application and worldwide patent collections, go to *https://patentscope.wipo. int/search/en/search.jsf* and by typing in the number to be searched and click the "Search" button in order to retrieve the documents.

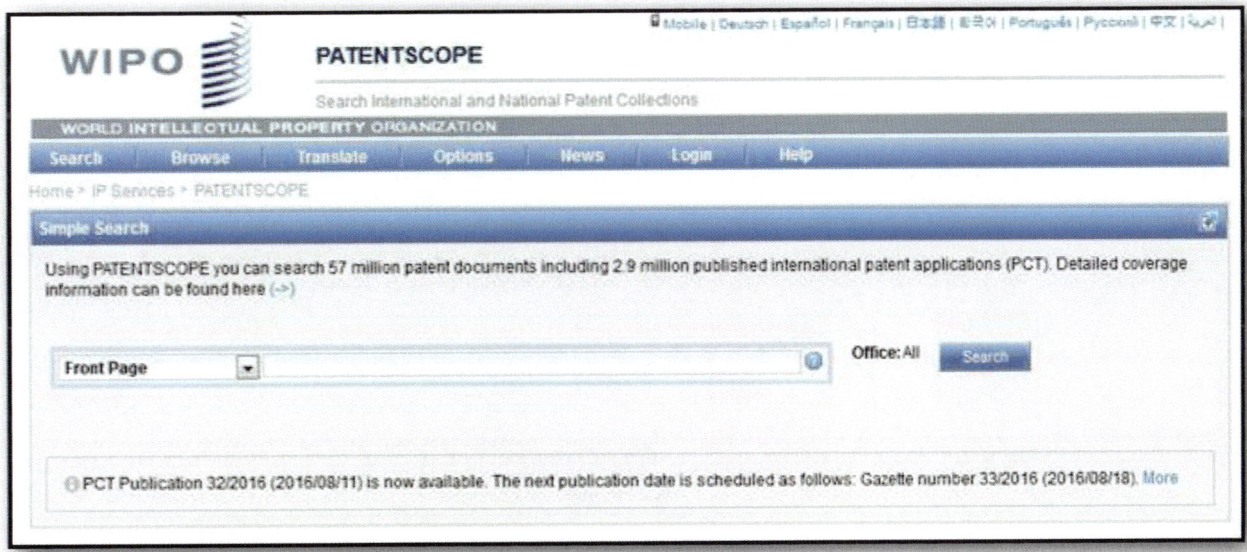

9.4.5 WIPO
Here is another website to get a published PCT application, go to *www.wipo.int/patents/en*. Type in the PCT Application Number or Publication Number in the Search area and click "enter".

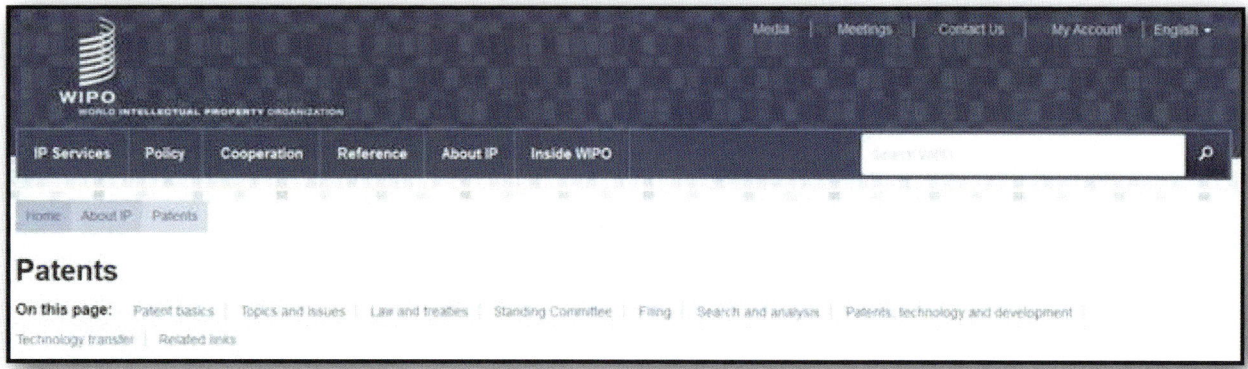

9.4.6 KOREAN INTELLECTUAL PROPERTY OFFICE
In order to get a Patent Abstract in English from the Korean Intellectual Property Office, go to *www.kipo. go.kr/en*, enter number to be searched and click the "Search" button.

9.5 Non-Patent Literature

The Paralegal should prepare copies of Non-Patent Literature ("NPL") documents using the best possible source document so as to generate a legible copy. Illegible copies may not be considered by the Examiner. For efiling, the Paralegal may download and save an electronic version (e.g., PDF) of the NPL document, if available, thereby obtaining the best available copy. If the document is in English, no explanation of the relevance of the document is necessary.

If the NPL document is not in English, Applicant is required to provide an English translation of the document, or provide an explanation of the relevance of the document. When providing a translation, the translation column (marked with a T) on the IDS forms should be marked with a check (√) to indicate that a translation accompanies this document. No notation is required in the translation column if the document is already in English.

> **NOTE: T**he practice described above with non-English language foreign patent documents also applies to non-English language NPL documents. However, it should be noted that NPL documents will not have English language counterparts that can be cited. Thus, the options for explaining the relevance of the document are limited to providing a full translation of the NPL document, providing an English language abstract, relying on a foreign search report, and providing a Statement of Relevance. If an English language abstract is provided, the Examiner will only consider the English language abstract if no other translation of the NPL is provided.

9.6 Exceptions to Document Submissions

Submission of foreign patent documents and NPL documents are required in most cases. However, there are exceptions to this of which the Paralegal should be aware. When in doubt as to whether a copy of a foreign patent document or NPL document should be provided to the USPTO, always err on the side of submitting it to the USPTO. It is never improper to submit copies of foreign patent documents and NPL documents to the USPTO, but it may be improper not to submit them.

When the instant application is a continuing application, the references that were cited in a parent application are automatically considered by the Examiner, but are not listed on any issued patent in the continuing application unless submitted on an IDS. Continuing applications include Continuation, Divisional, or Continuation-In-Part Applications which explicitly claim the benefit under 35 USC 120 to a parent application. It is generally desirable to have all references considered by the Examiner explicitly listed on the issued patent. Thus, a new IDS should normally be filed in a continuing application listing all references cited in the parent application. Copies of an IDS from the parent application should not be used, as the different application numbers on the copied IDS may cause confusion in the USPTO as to which application the IDS is directed. Rather, a new IDS and Transmittal Letter should be prepared for the continuing application.

The Practitioner should update the narrative section to indicate that the cited references are from the parent application. For example, "Applicants wish to make of record in this Divisional application the documents cited in parent U.S. Application No. 99/999,999, whether cited by Applicants or by the USPTO. The documents are listed on the attached Form **PTO/SB/08a**."

However, it is not required to resubmit the copies of the references cited in the parent application, as the USPTO already has copies of the references in the parent application files which the Examiner can easily reference. Accordingly, as long as the IDS submitting the references in the parent application was fully compliant with the relevant provisions of 37 CFR 1.98 and the instant application claims benefit to the parent under 35 USC 120, copies of foreign patent and NPL documents do not need to be resubmitted. The Practitioner should update the narrative section to explicitly note that copies of the foreign patent and NPL documents have not been resubmitted. For example, "Pursuant to 37 CFR 1.98(d), copies of Documents B3-B7 and C1-C5 have been provided in parent U.S. Application No. 99/999,999, which the present application claims the benefit of under 35 USC 120."

9.7 Filing IDS Submissions

As with other papers filed with the USPTO, IDS submissions may be filed in person, by mail, by facsimile, or by electronic filing via EFS-Web. An IDS submission may be filed electronically even if the original application was not filed electronically.

If filing an IDS in person or by mail, it is important to note that the USPTO will only accept hard copies of foreign patent documents and NPL documents. Sending the documents on compact disc (CD) or other storage media to the USPTO is not considered a proper submission, and the USPTO will not consider these documents.

9.8 Consideration by the Examiner

Whenever a new Office Action is received, the Paralegal may be called upon by the Practitioner to review the Office Action with respect to the references cited. In particular, the Paralegal should check to make sure that any IDS submissions in the application have been considered by the Examiner. If the Examiner has considered the IDS, he/she will sign the submitted IDS, initial the references considered, and return the IDS with the Office Action.

If any IDS submission or a particular document in an IDS submission has not been considered by the Examiner, either by omission or by strikethrough, the Paralegal must bring this to the attention of the Practitioner. The Examiner may not overlook consideration of an IDS, in whole or in part. The Practitioner would need to note the omission to the Examiner so that it may be brought to the Examiner's attention by the Practitioner. The Examiner may consider a particular citation in the IDS deficient (e.g., a copy of a foreign patent document is missing) and therefore line through the citation on the IDS to indicate it was not considered. In this event, the Practitioner would need to resubmit the IDS with the deficiency corrected to have the reference considered by the Examiner.

9.9 PATENT FAMILY MONITORING

The Paralegal may be called upon by the Practitioner to monitor pending applications in a particular patent family for references cited by a patent office that need to be cited in another patent office. As this activity is highly dependent upon the practice and resources of the Practitioner, the Paralegal should discuss in detail with the Practitioner the desired scope and strategy for this type of activity.

In general, the Paralegal should monitor all incoming Office Actions throughout the family for any new references cited that are not already of record in the family members. The Paralegal should docket an IDS, as needed, to cite the new references in the pending U.S. Applications of the family. In addition, the Paralegal should docket citation of the new references in any other pending application in countries that require a duty of disclosure, such as Israel. Members of the patent family may include, but are not limited to, parent or child U.S. or foreign applications, U.S. or foreign applications with common benefit or priority claims, and client applications related to the same technology.

9.10 IDS FORMS

The USPTO provides standard forms which the Practitioner can use for preparing and submitting IDS. Use of the forms is not required so long as the IDS document that is prepared complies with the requirements set forth above. However, use of the standard forms is strongly preferred by the USPTO.

The IDS forms can be found in the "forms" section at the USPTO website at *www.uspto.gov/patent/patents-forms*. There are two forms of interest with regard to IDS submissions: Form **PTO/SB/08a** and Form **PTO/SB/08b**. Form **PTO/SB/08a** is used for citing U.S. and foreign patent documents while Form **PTO/SB/08b** is used for citing non-patent literature, such as articles or publications. In general, IDS submissions may include a mixture of one or more of these forms, according to the type and number of references to be cited. The forms provide by the USPTO are PDF forms which can be edited and saved. Instructions for using the PDF form can be found below.

For ease of reference, the Paralegal should associate a reference number in the citation column of the IDS form with each citation. The Paralegal should consult with the Practitioner on the desired manner of citation. For example, the Practitioner may ask that all references be consecutively numbered starting with the U.S. Patent Documents or the Practitioner may ask that each section be assigned a reference letter and then consecutively numbered, such that the U.S. Patent Documents begins with citation number A1, the Foreign Patent Document begins with citation number B1, and so on. In still another example, the Practitioner may ask that citation numbers from previous IDS carry over to the next IDS, such that the first IDS may list citations 1-10 and then the second IDS may list citations 11-20. The Paralegal should confirm the desired convention for each client with the Practitioner and adhere to this convention in all IDS submissions for the client.

Moreover, the Paralegal should consult with the Practitioner on the preferred order of citation of the references on the IDS. Many Practitioners will request that the U.S. patents be sorted in terms of issue date and that the U.S. Patent Application Publications be separately sorted in terms of publication date. The Practitioner may rely on a similar convention with regard to the foreign patent documents and NPL. The Paralegal should confirm the desired convention for each client with the Practitioner and adhere to this convention in all IDS submissions for the client.

9.11 eFiling an IDS via EFS-Web

The following steps are used to file an IDS via EFS-Web:

1. After EFS-Web certification, under "*Main Functions", click "Existing application/patent/ proceeding".
2. Select Type of Submission: Click "Document/Fees for an existing application/proceeding".
3. Type in the Application Number and Confirmation Number of the existing patent application. Click "Continue" for the next screen.
4. Files to be Submitted: Browse for the file (in PDF format) and upload it to this filing.
5. Underneath the uploaded document, it states: "Does your PDF file contain multiple documents?" Click "Yes".

NOTE: The USPTO has PDF fillable forms that can be used for the **Information Disclosure Statement (pg. 1) (PTO/SB/08a)** at *www.uspto.gov/web/forms/sb0008a.pdf* and/or **Information Disclosure Statement (PTO/SB/08b)** at *www.uspto.gov/web/forms/sb0008b.pdf*. Instructions for using these PDF fillable forms are at *www.uspto.gov/ebc/ portal/efs/US_ids_form_inst.doc*.

6. When using the IDS standard forms PTO/SB/08a and PTO/SB/08b, along with an IDS Transmittal Letter (in lieu of the PDF fillable forms), use the following document descriptions:

Category	Document Description
IDS/References	Transmittal Letter
IDS/References	Information Disclosure Statement (IDS) Form (SB08)
IDS/References	Foreign Reference
IDS/References	Non-Patent Literature
IDS/References	Other Reference-Patent/App/Search documents

7. Click "Upload & Validate" to make sure that there are no validation errors. If there is a validation error, there will be a prompt on the screen of an error or a warning! If there is an error, the error must be corrected at this point. If there is a warning, click "Continue" to go to the next screen.

For the remainder of the steps, see ***Section 6.2.2*** to complete the efiling of the IDS via EFS-Web.

9.12 THIRD-PARTY SUBMISSIONS

Effective September 16, 2012, a third party is permitted to submit patents, published patent applications or printed publications along with a concise description of the relevance of each document to the USPTO for consideration during the examination of a patent application.

Third-party submissions must be made (i) before the later of six (6) months after the date the application is first published by the USPTO or the date of a first Office Action on the merits rejecting any claim, and (ii) before the date a notice of allowance is given or mailed.

A third-party submission may be made in any Nonprovisional Utility, Design, or Plant Application, including any continuing application. The application may be pending or abandoned and need not be published. Third-party submissions are not permitted in reissue applications and reexamination proceedings.

The resource page for third-party submissions is located at:

www.uspto.gov/aia_implementation/patents.jsp#heading-7

Look under the head title for "Preissuance Submissions" to receive more information regarding third-party submissions.

The requirements for a third-party submission must include the following:

1. Form **PTO/SB/429** (or equivalent document list), identifying the publications, or portions of publications.
2. A concise description of the asserted relevance of each item identified in the document list.
3. A legible copy of each item identified in the document list, other than U.S. patents and U.S. patent application publications.
4. An English language translation of any non-English language item identified in the document list.
5. Statements by the party making the submission that:
   (i) The party is not an individual who has a duty to disclose information with respect to the application.
   (ii) The submission complies with the requirements of 35 USC 122(e) and 37 CFR 1.290.
6. Any required fee, or the 37 CFR 1.290(g) statement that the fee exemption applies to the submission.

NOTE: There is no fee required if the third party's first submission is up to three (3) references and is accompanied by selecting the appropriate box on *www.uspto.gov/forms/sb0429_preview.pdf.*

9.13 QUICK PATH IDS PILOT PROGRAM

The Quick Path IDS ("QPIDS") pilot program is geared toward eliminating the requirement for processing a request for continued examination of an IDS filed after payment of the Issue Fee in order for the IDS to be considered by the Examiner. If the Examiner determines that no item of information in the IDS necessitates reopening prosecution, the Examiner will issue a corrected notice of allowability.

The QPIDS pilot program has been extended through **September 30, 2017**. All compliant requests for considering the IDS under the QPIDS pilot program filed **on or before September 30, 2017**, will be considered. .

Basic Guidelines for Filing a QPIDS ePetition:

* The user must be a registered eFiler.
* Registered eFilers are strongly advised to transmit their electronic filings sufficiently early in the day to allow time to contact the Patent EBC for assistance when the transmission cannot be initiated or correctly completed.
* The ability to submit a QIPDS ePetition under EFS-Web Contingency is not permitted.

The following steps are used to submit a QPIDS ePetition via EFS-Web:

1. After EFS-Web certification, under "*Main Functions", click "Existing application/patent/proceeding".
2. Type of Submission: Click "Document/Fees for an existing application/proceeding".
3. Click "ePetition" under "Select Type of Submission for Existing Application".
4. File one of the following petitions:
   * Petition to Withdraw from Issue After Payment of the Issue Fee.
   * Petition to Withdraw from Issue After Payment of the Issue Fee with Assigned Patent Number.
5. Enter the application number, confirmation number, and select "Consideration of a Request for Continued Examination" as the reason for withdrawal.
6. After proceeding to the ePetition Request screen, the reason for withdrawal and other information provided on the Certification Screen will be displayed for review purposes, but cannot be changed. If it is necessary to change the application number, the reason for withdrawal, or the petition filer type, click the "Cancel" button to restart the petition.
7. There will be a prompt to indicate whether the required documents and/or fees have been previously filed or will accompany the ePetition. For consideration of QPIDS, you must select: RCE Request, Submission, and Fee are attached.
8. At the bottom of the screen, complete the user information and provide an S-signature.
9. After entering the petition data, the information will be automatically compiled into a petition document (petition-request.pdf), which will be listed on the "attach documents" screen. A reminder will be displayed directing you to attach the mandatory Request for Consideration (RCE) and Information Disclosure Statement (IDS).

NOTE: The QPIDS transmittal (PTO/SB/09) is also a required document and must be attached for QPIDS consideration.

10. The following basic document descriptions are used for filing QPIDS:

Category	Document Description
Petition	Request for Continued Examination (RCE)
Petition	Information Disclosure Statement (IDS) Form (SB08)
Petition	Quick Path Information Disclosure Statement

11. Click "Upload & Validate" to make sure that all the pages match the PDF file(s). If there is an error, there will be a prompt on the screen of an error or a warning! If there is an error, the error

must be corrected at this point. If there is a warning, click "Continue" to go to the next screen. Some USPTO forms may not be compatible. In this event, a warning will be displayed instead of an error.

12. If there are no errors, the screen will state "No validation errors found". Click "Continue". This will save the submission up to this point.

13. The next screen is "Calculate Fees". Check to see if this application is a regular undiscounted (large entity) or small entity and select the appropriate status. Then select the appropriate fee for filing the Petition and RCE. Click "Continue" to save the submission up to this point.

14. On the next screen, check to be sure that all of the information is correct before you click "File ePetition & Pay". Also, the submission at this time can be saved by clicking "Save for Later Submission". The submission can be saved for up to seven (7) calendar days. This feature is very useful if the submission needs to be saved in order for the Practitioner to review and submit later.

15. Click "File ePetition & Pay". There will be a prompt to either pay by Charge USPTO Deposit Account, Charge Credit Card, or Electronic Funds Transfer. Follow the screen instructions to start the online payment process. After the fee is paid, an Acknowledgment Receipt of the filing can be saved. This is the proof of the actual filing. Also, the QPIDS ePetition filing will appear in Private PAIR within minutes.

For additional information regarding this pilot program, visit the following site:

www.uspto.gov/patent/initiatives/quick-path-information-disclosure-statement-qpids

CHAPTER 10

Assignments

● ● ●

USPTO Assignment Services Division Contact Information:

Hours: Monday – Friday, 8:30 a.m. to 5:00 p.m. (Eastern Time)

Mailing Address

Mail Stop Assignment Recordation Services
U.S. Patent and Trademark Office
P.O. Box 1450
Alexandria, VA 22313-1450

Street Address

South Tower Building, Second Floor
2900 Crystal Drive
Arlington, VA 22202

Phone: (571) 272-3350

Fax: (571) 273-0140

Email: *ePAS@uspto.gov* (Online Filing)
          assign@uspto.gov (Paper Filing)

10.1 ASSIGNMENT DOCUMENT

AN ASSIGNMENT IS A LEGAL document that is used to transfer all or part of the rights in a patent or patent application from one party to another. For example, where the inventor is an employee of a corporation and once an assignment is executed (signed) by the inventor (the Assignor), the corporation becomes the owner (or Assignee) of the patent or application, but the employee remains the inventor.

The USPTO Assignment Division provides the service of recording assignments (also called recordation) and maintaining microfilm or electronic image records of assignment documents and a database of assignments for the public to search.

Best practice is to record any Assignment no later than three (3) months after the date that it was executed.

An assignment that contains the information and statements in an oath or declaration ("assignment-statement") may be used as the inventor's oath or declaration.

10.2 IDENTIFYING APPLICATIONS AND PATENTS IN AN ASSIGNMENT DOCUMENT

A patent assignment should contain the following identifying information:

- Patent Number
- Issue Date
- Name of Inventor(s)
- Title of Invention

A patent application assignment should contain the following identifying information:

- Application Number (if available)
- Filing Date
- Name of Inventor(s)
- Title of Invention

10.3 WAYS TO RECORD PATENT OR PATENT APPLICATION ASSIGNMENTS

10.3.1 HAND-DELIVERY/COURIER

A patent or patent application assignment (hereinafter "Assignment"), along with Recordation Form Cover Sheet and fee, may be hand-carried to:

Customer Service Window, Office of Public Records
2nd floor of the South Tower Building
2900 Crystal Drive
Arlington, VA 22202

Best practice is to prepare a filing receipt identifying the patent or patent application and Assignment to be date-stamped by the clerk at the Customer Service Window.

10.3.2 CERTIFICATE OF MAILING
An Assignment, along with Recordation Form Cover Sheet and fee, should be addressed to, unless they are filed together with new applications:

Mail Stop Assignment Recordation Services
Director of the U.S. Patent and Trademark Office
P.O. Box 1450
Alexandria, VA 22313-1450

10.3.3 CERTIFICATE OF TRANSMISSION
The USPTO accepts facsimile transmissions to record an Assignment or other documents affecting title or ownership of a patent. This process allows customers to submit their documents directly into the automated Patent and Trademark Assignment System and receive the resulting recordation notice at their facsimile machine.

The fax number for the USPTO Assignment System is (571) 273-0140.

To fax an Assignment for recordation include the following with any Assignment document:

* An identified patent application number or patent number.
* Assignment Recordation Cover Sheet to record a single type of transaction.

An accurate and complete cover sheet is the key to the recordation process because it is the source of the bibliographic data the Assignment Division enters into the USPTO records.

Assignments submitted concurrently with newly filed patent applications must continue to be sent to OPAP with the application.

The USPTO Assignment System assigns reel and frame numbers and superimposes recordation stampings on the processed and stored electronic images. Accordingly, copies of all recorded documents will have the reel and frame numbers and recordation stampings.

10.3.4 εPAS (FILING AN ASSIGNMENT VIA EFS-WEB)

To electronically file an Assignment, follow these steps:

1. Go to *epas.uspto.gov*.
2. "Electronic Patent Assignment System" ("ePAS") pops up on screen. Scroll to the bottom of screen and click "Please click here to access ePAS forms".
3. "Guidelines" pops up on screen. Scroll to the bottom of screen and click "Start".
4. "Conveyance Type" pops up on screen. Select "nature of conveyance". Select "Assignment".
5. Scroll to the bottom of screen and click "Next Screen".
6. "Correspondence Information" pops up on screen.
   a. Enter your "Phone Number", e.g. 999.999.9999 (optional field).
   b. Enter your "Name" or "Firm Name" (required field) (type in CAPS).
   c. Enter "Street address" (required field) (type in CAPS).
   d. Enter "Internal" (Suite No. or Apt. No., if any) (optional field) (type in CAPS).
   e. Enter "City" (required field) (type in CAPS).
   f. Enter "State" (required field) (type in CAPS).
   g. Enter "Postal code" (required field).
   h. Enter "Email Address" (required field).
   i. Enter "Fax number" (10 digits only, e.g., 7039999999).
   After all of this information has been completed, click "Next Screen".
7. "Conveying Party(ies)" will pop up on screen. Enter "conveying party" data:
   a. Enter either "Individual Name" (First Name, Middle Name/Initial and Last Name) or by *Company Name*.
   b. Enter the "date of execution" (Format: MM/DD/YYYY) of the Individual or Company who executed the Assignment.
   c. If there is more than one Individual or Company, click "Add".
   d. After the Individual(s) or Company(ies) have been entered, click "Add and Go To The Next Screen".
8. "Receiving Party(ies)" will pop up on screen. Enter "receiving party" data:
   a. Enter either the "Individual Name" (First Name, Middle Name/Initial and Last Name) or "Company Name" (required field) (type in CAPS).
   b. Enter "Street Address" (required field) (type in CAPS).
   c. Enter "Internal" (Suite No. or Apt. No., if any) (optional field).
   d. Enter "City" (required field) (type in CAPS).

    e.   Enter "State" (required field).

    f.   Enter "Postal code" (required field).

If more than one Receiving Party is entered, click "Add" to add more Receiving Parties.

If no additional Receiving Party(ies) are being entered, click "Add and Go To The Next Screen".

9.   "Property(ies)" pops up on screen.

    a.   Enter the Application number that is on the Assignment or a new Application has just been efiled, the Application Number will appear automatically. The Application Number should be in digits only with no slashes or commas, e.g., 99999999.

    b.   After entering the Application Number, click "Add and Go To The Next Screen".

10.   "Image Attachments" pops up on screen.

    a.   Click "Browse" to search for the file (in PDF format) of the Assignment.

    b.   Once the file (in PDF format) is uploaded, click "Attach File".

    c.   After confirmation that this is the correct attachment, click "Next Screen".

11.   "Signature" pops up on screen.

    a.   Review all the data that appears to make sure that there are no typos.

    b.   As eFiler, sign your S-signature when submitting the Assignment as **/John J. Doe II/** (S-signature example only) in the Signature Block. This is a required field.

    c.   Enter your name, e.g., **John J. Doe II** (example only). This is a required field.

    d.   The date will automatically pop up on screen.

    e.   After you enter your S-signature and name, click "Next Screen".

14.   "Validate" pops up on screen.

    a.   Review again that the information is correct.

    b.   Scroll to the bottom of the screen and enter the attorney docket number (this is optional).

    c.   Check the box that you acknowledge consent to the above statement.

    d.   Then click "Submit".

Note: As of January 1, 2014, there are no fees required to record an assignment at the USPTO through ePAS.

Tip: Before clicking "Submit", click on "Advanced Operations" to customize a template. This allows the selection of screen data and the data content in the screen from the current submission to be reused in future submissions.

15.   "Confirmation Receipt" pops up on screen. Save the Confirmation Receipt for the record.

16.   An email will be sent by the USPTO with the reel and frame numbers of the Assignment within the next day or so.

NOTES:

- Do not use your browser's "back" and "forward" buttons to navigate. Use only the navigation controls on the ePAS screens.

- PDF attachments: Legal supporting documentation may be of either a TIFF or a PDF file. Documents must be black and white. More than one file in more than one format may be attached.

- Create Template: Data from a submission, namely: correspondence information, conveying party(s), receiving party(s) and property(s) can be downloaded to your workstation as a template to re-use in future submissions. To download a template use the "Advanced" button on the Validation screen and choose the "Customize Template" button on the following screen.

- Using the template: To start a new assignment filing from the downloaded template, use the "Start from Template" button shown below on this screen.

- Once submitted, the filing will not be cancelled unless the request fails to satisfy the minimum filing requirements.

10.4 NATURE OF CONVEYANCE

One of the pre-formatted nature of conveyance types may be selected or the conveyance type "Other" may be selected and text entered that describes the interest conveyed or transaction to be recorded. Data entry is limited to 240 characters.

If the nature of conveyance is an "Assignment", "Change of Name", "Merger", "Nunc Pro Tunc", or Security Agreement, check the appropriate box.

Nature of Conveyance (Definitions)

Assignment	A transfer of ownership of a patent or trademark application, published application, issued patent or trademark registration from one entity to another.
Change of Name	The conversion from one name to another
Merger	A union of two or more commercial interests
Nunc-Pro-Tunc Assignments (Now for Then)	A request for record an assignment, which includes documentation of transactions which occurred in the past that have not been made a matter of record in the USPTO.
Security Agreement	An agreement between two or more parties

10.5 CORRECTIVE ASSIGNMENTS

A request to re-record an assignment due to an error previously made in either the cover sheet data or the supporting legal documentation (of the original submission) previously filed can be made by the customer. Enter the following text "Corrective assignment to re-record assignment previously recorded under Reel and Frame xxxx/xxxx (show the actual values) to correct the <field name> from <previous value> to <correct value>.

10.6 ASSIGNMENT OF DIV, CON, AND CIP APPLICATION

Since the subject matter in the specification of the DIV or CON Application is the same as the parent application, the assignment of the parent application will govern the DIV or CON Application as well. However, an additional assignment can also be filed for the DIV or CON Application, if desired, as long as the Assignee remains the same for both the parent application and the DIV or CON Application.

A CIP Application requires a new Assignment in order for a patent to issue to Assignee.

10.7 ASSIGNMENT OF APPLICATION CLAIMING BENEFIT OF PRIORITY TO A PROVISIONAL APPLICATION

If the Provisional Application is not assigned, then an assignment is needed if the application is to be assigned.

If the Provisional Application was assigned, ask the Practitioner if an additional assignment is needed.

10.8 IDENTIFYING THE ASSIGNEE ON AN ISSUED PATENT

A Notice of Allowance is issued after a Nonprovisional Application is allowed (Form **PTOL-85**) by the Examiner. This form includes a Part B, commonly known as the **Fee(s) Transmittal Form (PTOL-85B)**. The Fee(s) Transmittal Form must be completed and signed by the Practitioner. The signed form is returned to the USPTO with the appropriate fees. See ***Chapter 18 – Appeal of Examiner's Rejection***.

- If the application is assigned and an Assignment has been recorded in the USPTO, enter the Assignee's name along with the address of the Assignee into Part 3 block of the Fee(s) Transmittal Form.
- If the Assignment has not been recorded on the date the Fee(s) Transmittal form is submitted, then the Assignee's name and address can be entered into the Part 3 block of the Fee(s) Transmittal form provided the Assignment was submitted to the USPTO for recording before the date on which the completed Fee(s) Transmittal form is submitted to the USPTO or submitted for recordation on the same date the completed Fee(s) Transmittal Form is submitted to the USPTO. Note that the Part 3 block of the form must have a notation that the Assignment has been filed for recordation.
- If the Assignment is recorded after payment of the Issue Fee, as soon as the patent is granted, a Certificate of Correction under 37 CFR 1.323 along with the appropriate fee and other required

documentation should be submitted to the USPTO. The Practitioner must be consulted for compliance for this procedure.

Unless an Assignee's name and address are identified in the Part 3 block of the Fee(s) Transmittal Form, the patent will issue to the Applicant. Assignment data printed on the patent will be based solely on the information provided on the Fee(s) Transmittal Form.

10.8 SEARCH PATENT ASSIGNMENTS

To search for patent assignments, go to *assignments.uspto.gov/assignments/ q?db=pat*. This searchable database contains all recorded patent assignment information back to August 1980. The Advanced Search will provide more options to search for a patent assignment.

Tip: The actual recorded assignment can be found at the little icon next to the Assignment of Assignors Interest (see document for details).

10.9 REPORTING ASSIGNMENT WITH RECORDATION OF ASSIGNMENT

The following template can be used to report an Assignment recordation to the client:

RE: U.S. Patent Application No. _____
         Title:
         Your Ref:
         Our Ref:
Dear _____:

We are enclosing the Assignment together with a copy of the official Notice of Recordation of Assignment Document. The Assignment was recorded on _____, at Reel/Frame No. ____/____. We have checked the Notice for accuracy and found no errors. Please safeguard this document as evidence of ownership of the above-identified patent application.

We shall advise you as soon as there are any developments to report in this application.

CHAPTER 11

Publication of Patent Applications

● ● ●

11.1 18-MONTH PUBLICATION OF PATENT APPLICATIONS

UTILITY PATENT APPLICATIONS ARE NORMALLY published eighteen (18) months after the earliest filing date. Thus, if the application claims the benefit of an earlier-filed Provisional Application, the 18-month time frame begins from the Provisional Application filing date. Likewise, if the application claims priority under 35 USC 120, the 18-month time frame begins from the earliest effective filing date of the first filed application for which priority is claimed. An application may be published before eighteen (18) months at the request of the Practitioner. The Practitioner may also request that the application not be published.

The Practitioner will be informed on the filing receipt of the projected publication date assigned to the application which was filed. The status of any nonpublication request or early publication request is also shown on the filing receipt. Later, the USPTO will send a Notice of Publication of Application, giving the publication date and publication number for the application. Once the application becomes published, it is available for the public to view and/or obtain a copy of the file history (the "file wrapper") of a published application.

Applications are published in electronic format at the PTO website.

An application will automatically be published unless the Practitioner specifically requests that it not be published. A nonpublication request must be made at the time of filing, and the Practitioner must certify that the invention has not and will not be the subject of an application filed in a foreign country.

11.1.1 REQUIREMENTS FOR 18-MONTH PUBLICATION OF PATENT APPLICATIONS

A Nonprovisional Application must have the content necessary to create the patent application publication:

- Executed Oath or Declaration
- Abstract
- Written description of the invention

* Drawing, if necessary for an understanding of the invention
* English translation, if filed in a language other than English
* At least one claim
* Basic filing fee

For 18-month publication purposes, the Oath or Declaration must have at a minimum:

* Name each inventor at least by a family and given name.
* Signed by each inventor or a party qualified to sign.

11.2 Public PAIR Access

After eighteen (18) months from the initial filing of the U.S. patent application, an application is published and the public can access these documents (unless the Practitioner requests for nonpublication) by accessing Public PAIR.

When the application is published, related patent applications can be viewed in Public PAIR.

NOTE: NPL documents are not accessible in Public PAIR, even if published.

11.3 Change or Update Bibliographic Information

In order to change or update the bibliographic information in Private PAIR, go to *www.uspto.gov* and under the "Patents" tab, click "Checking application status" under "Application Process" and proceed with the following steps.

1. Click "Check the status of a pending application".
2. When the User Authentication screen pops up, browse for the Practitioner's .epf file and enter the Practitioner's password.

NOTE: Save the Practitioner's .epf file on the desktop for easier access.

3. Check box at left side of screen in order for you to proceed.
4. Once the Digital PKI Certificate has been authenticated – please certify your identity.
5. Click "Select New Case" and retrieve the patent application for which the bibliographic information needs to be corrected.
6. Under the far right tab, click "Publication Review". This screen allows the Customer Number user to enter and submit Correction Requests to data shown on the Publication Review screen to match previously filed application papers.

NOTE: This screen cannot accept special characters, e.g., umlauts (e.g., ë, accents (e.g., é).

11.3.1 CORRECTION REQUEST

Where a properly signed ADS is submitted when the application is filed, correction of typographical errors made by the USPTO of information from the ADS can be corrected with the Correction Request screen. The corrections include any typographical error by the USPTO that does not match the data set forth in the ADS submitted on filing, e.g., title, inventor invention, attorney docket number, domestic benefit information, and foreign priority information.

NOTE: Representative information is taken from an actual Power of Attorney document present in the application rather than the ADS and thus cannot be corrected with this screen.

Where no ADS was submitted when the application was filed, typographic corrections of data entry errors made by the USPTO that can be corrected with the Correction Request screen include:

* The title to match the title on the specification as filed;
* The name of the inventor to match the spelling shown on the executed declaration submitted upon filing of the application; and
* The residence and/or mailing address of the inventor to match the spelling shown on the executed declaration submitted upon filing of the application (e.g., Wilmington, Delaware was recorded as Wilmington, Germany).

NOTE: The Correction Request may not be more than 4,000 characters long. If the request is more than 4,000 characters, multiple Correction Requests must be submitted.

11.3.2 CORRECTIONS OR CHANGES **NOT** PERMITTED

* National Stage Applications filed under 35 USC 371.
* Corrections based on papers submitted after the filing date of the application. In such an event, Applicant may submit a Request for Corrected Filing Receipt in the application.
* Changes to applications that are abandoned, allowed, or patented.
* Changes to published applications. Data in a published patent application will not be changed if a change is made to the USPTO's electronic records (e.g., PALM). In order to make a change, Applicant must submit the fully amended application as a Pre-Grant Publication submission via EFS-Web).
* Change data that exists in the written record of an application.

For example, the following information cannot be corrected:

- Addition or deletion of an inventor after inventorship has been set, i.e., a proper ADS was filed before or with the inventor's oath or declaration.
- Requests to change the filing date of an application, Applicant must submit a filing date petition).
- Changes by Applicant to the application information, e.g., (i) change of correspondence address and (ii) changes to domestic benefit or foreign priority data, including additions or deletions of domestic benefit or foreign priority claims not previously submitted or not previously recognized by the USPTO as well as corrections to the domestic benefit or foreign priority information to correct typographical errors made by Applicant (changes to domestic benefit or foreign priority data must be by way of an ADS with corrections or updates shown with markings and may also require a petition under 37 CFR 1.78 or 37 CFR 1.55).
- Changes to Assignee Information including Non-Applicant provided on the ADS (Applicant must submit an ADS with corrections or updates shown with markings).
- Changes to information when the papers submitted by Applicant are inconsistent (e.g., title on the specification is different than the title on the ADS).

11.4 REQUEST FOR NONPUBLICATION OF AN APPLICATION

If the invention disclosed in an application has not been and will not be the subject of an application filed in another country, or under a multilateral international agreement, that requires publication of applications eighteen (18) months after filing, Practitioner can request that the application not be published. A nonpublication request must be submitted with the application upon filing.

The Practitioner may rescind a nonpublication request at any time. A request to rescind a nonpublication request must identify the application to which it is directed and state in a conspicuous manner that the request for nonpublication is rescinded. The Practitioner must sign the request to rescind.

If the Practitioner submitted a nonpublication request and files an application directed to the invention disclosed in the application in which the nonpublication request was submitted in another country, or under a multilateral international agreement, that requires publication of applications eighteen (18) months after filing, the Practitioner must notify the USPTO of such filing within forty-five (45) days after the date of the filing of such foreign or international application. The failure to timely notify the USPTO of the filing of such foreign or international application will result in abandonment of the application in which the nonpublication request was submitted.

If nonpublication is requested, there is no publication fee required to be paid with the Issue Fee.

A nonpublication request is provided in **Nonpublication Request Under 35 U.S.C. 122(b)(2)(B)(i) (PTO/SB/35)** form at *www.uspto.gov/web/forms/sb0035.pdf.* Using the USPTO form can help ensure that the request includes the proper language.

To confirm that the USPTO has recognized the nonpublication request, the filing receipt will not include a projected publication date. If a nonpublication request has been made and the filing receipt reflects a projected publication date, alert the Practitioner to the possibility that the USPTO overlooked the request.

11.5 REQUEST FOR EARLY PUBLICATION

The Practitioner may request early publication of an application with a letter requesting early publication. No special form is required for such a request.

If request for early publication of an application is requested, there is no publication fee required to be paid with the Issue Fee.

Category	Document Description
Pre-Grant Pub	Request for Early Publication

11.6 CORRECTIONS TO A PUBLISHED PATENT APPLICATION

The USPTO will grant a request for correction to a published patent application where the USPTO has made a material mistake which is apparent from USPTO records.

Examples of errors that may be considered to be material errors:

* Missing claims
* Missing pages of the specification
* Missing pages of drawings

Examples of errors that are not material errors:

* Missing assignment information
* Missing section headings
* Minor typographical errors

Requests for a corrected patent application must be filed within two (2) months from the date of the patent application publication.

NOTE: Extensions of time are not permitted.

A request for a corrected patent application publication must be in writing and must include:

- A copy of the patent application publication with the errors clearly marked; and
- Reference to the page and line number of the originally filed application where the information was correctly submitted.

Requests for corrected patent application publications can be faxed to (571) 273-8300 or mailed to:

Mail Stop PGPub
Commissioner for Patents
P.O. Box 1450
Alexandria, VA 22313-1450

11.7 REPORTING NOTICE OF PUBLICATION
The following template can be used to report out a Notice of Publication to the client:

RE: U.S. Patent Application No. _____
        Title:
        Your Ref.:
        Our Ref.:

Dear _____:

We are enclosing a copy of the Notice of Publication of the subject patent application. The application was published on _____, as Publication No. _____ (copy enclosed).

The link for accessing an electronic version of the published application is highlighted on the enclosed Notice.

We shall advise you as soon as there are any developments to report in this application.

CHAPTER 12

Proceedings Following Initial Filing of Provisional and Nonprovisional Applications

• • •

12.1 OFFICIAL FILING RECEIPT

WHEN A PATENT APPLICATION IS filed, it is first sent to the Office of Patent Application Processing for an initial review of completeness. The application will be classified and assigned to an Art Unit for examination. The function of Application Processing is to establish whether the application is "complete" and whether it is entitled to a filing date.

12.2 REQUEST FOR CORRECTED FILING RECEIPT

As soon as the Official Filing Receipt ("OFR") is received, best practice is to review it for accuracy and note any necessary corrections.

If an error is found on the OFR, submit a written Request for Corrected Filing Receipt ("RCFR") along with a copy of the OFR with the changes noted. If a "Notice to File Missing Parts" and an OFR are received together for the application, submit any corrections to the OFR with the Practitioner's reply to the Notice. When the USPTO processes the reply to the Notice, the USPTO will generate a new OFR incorporating the requested corrections. There is no fee for corrections.

12.2.1 EFILING A REQUEST FOR CORRECTED FILING RECEIPT VIA EFS-WEB

The basic steps to efile a Request for Corrected Filing Receipt via EFS-Web are as follows:

1. After EFS-Web certification, under "*Main Functions", click "Existing application/patent/proceeding".
2. Select Type of Submission: Click "Document/Fees for an existing application/proceeding".
3. Type in the Application Number and Confirmation Number of the existing patent application. Click "Continue" for the next screen.

4. Files to be Submitted: Browse for the file (in PDF format) and upload it to this filing.

5. Underneath the uploaded document, it states: "Does your PDF file contain multiple documents?" Click "No".

6. The following basic document description is used for filing a Request for Corrected Filing Receipt ("RCFR") is as follows:

Category	Document Description
Pre-Exam	Request for Corrected Filing Receipt

7. Click "Upload & Validate" to make sure that there are no validation errors. If there is a validation error, there will be a prompt on the screen of an error or a warning! If there is an error, the error must be corrected at this point. If there is a warning, click "Continue" to go to the next screen.

For the remainder of the steps, see **Section 6.2.2** to complete the efiling of the Request for Corrected Filing Receipt via EFS-Web.

12.3 FOREIGN FILING LICENSE

Unless the application is classified by the security group, a Foreign Filing License is normally granted. The Foreign Filing License allows the Practitioner to file the application in a foreign Patent Office. It is sometimes not granted if the invention has national security implications. If granted, the phrase "If Required, Foreign Filing License Granted." will appear on the OFR; if not granted, this statement will be absent.

12.4 ASSIGNMENT

The Assignment information listed on the OFR reflects what is on the ADS and not necessarily from the Assignment Services Division. All of the information from the ADS should reflect what is on the OFR.

12.5 REPORTING OFFICIAL FILING RECEIPT – PROVISIONAL PATENT APPLICATION

The following template can be used to report the OFR for a Provisional Application to the client:

RE: U.S. Patent Application No. _____
       Title:
       Your Ref.:
       Our Ref.:

Dear _____:

We are enclosing a copy of the Official Filing Receipt for the above-identified Provisional Application, which was filed on _____. The U.S. Patent and Trademark Office has assigned Application Number _____ to the application. We have checked the Official Filing Receipt for accuracy and found no errors.

Since the Provisional Application was filed on _____, the due date to convert to a Nonprovisional Application is one year from the filing date, namely, _____. We shall advise you as soon as there are any developments to report in this application.

12.6 Reporting Official Filing Receipt – Nonprovisional Application

The following template can be used to report out the OFR for a Nonprovisional Application to the client:

RE: U.S. Patent Application No. _____
        Title:
        Your Ref.:
        Our Ref.:

Dear _____:

We are enclosing a copy of the Official Filing Receipt for the above-identified patent application, which was filed on _____. The U.S. Patent and Trademark Office has assigned Application Number _____ to the application. We have checked the Official Filing Receipt for accuracy and found no errors.

We shall advise you as soon as there are any developments to report in this application.

12.7 Notice to File Missing Parts of Nonprovisional Application – Filing Date Granted

If the Practitioner did not send in all the required formal documents to make the application complete, but did send enough to get a filing date, the Practitioner should receive from OPAP a Notice to File Missing Parts of Nonprovisional Application -- Filing Date Granted ("Notice") (Form PTO-1533).

As indicated on the Notice, an Application Number and filing date have been accorded to this application. The Practitioner is given two (2) months from the date of the Notice within which to file all required items and pay any fees required to avoid abandonment.

> **NOTE:** Up to five (5) months of extensions of time from the due date of the Notice can be requested to respond to a Notice of Missing Parts. If a response is not filed within seven (7) months after the date of the Notice of Missing Parts, the application will become abandoned.

The item(s) indicated below may be missing from the initial filing of the Nonprovisional Application, but the application will still be accorded a filing date:

* Filing Fees.
* Application Data Sheet.
* An English translation of the application, but without the required fee, and a certification statement that the translation is accurate.
* Replacement drawings, if the drawings do not conform to the USPTO drawing requirements.
* An executed oath or declaration.

12.7.1 eFILING A RESPONSE TO NOTICE TO FILE MISSING PARTS

The basic steps for eFiling a Response to Notice to File Missing Parts via EFS-Web are as follows:

1. After EFS-Web certification, under "*Main Functions", click "Existing application/patent/proceeding".
2. Select Type of Submission: Click "Document/Fees for an existing application/proceeding".
3. Type in the Application Number and Confirmation Number of the existing patent application. Click "Continue" for the next screen.
4. Files to be Submitted: Browse for the file (in PDF format) and upload it to this filing.
5. Underneath the uploaded document, it states: "Does your PDF file contain multiple documents?" Click "Yes".
6. The following basic document descriptions are used for filing the Response to the Notice:

Category	Document Description
Pre-Exam	Applicant Response to Pre-Exam Formalities Notice
Application Part	Oath or Declaration filed
Application Part	Drawings – only black and white line drawings (Replacement Drawings)

7. Click "Upload & Validate" to make sure that there are no validation errors. If there is a validation error, there will be a prompt on the screen of an error or a warning! If there is an error, the error must be corrected at this point. If there is a warning, click "Continue" to go to the next screen.

For the remainder of the steps, see **Section 6.2.2** to complete the efiling of the Response via EFS-Web.

12.8 EXTENDED MISSING PARTS PILOT PROGRAM

The USPTO has implemented the Extended Missing Parts Pilot Program in which an Applicant, under certain conditions, can request a twelve (12)-month time period (not extendible) to pay the search fee, the examination fee, any excess claim fees, and the surcharge (for the late submission of the search and examination fees), in a Nonprovisional Application. The Extended Missing Parts Pilot Program benefits Applicants by permitting additional time to determine if patent protection should be sought, at a relatively low cost, and by permitting Applicants to focus efforts on commercialization during this period. The Extended Missing Parts Pilot Program benefits the USPTO and the public by adding publications to the prior art, and by removing from the USPTO's workload those Nonprovisional Applications for which Applicants later decide not to pursue examination. The USPTO has extended the Extended Missing Parts Pilot Program until **December 31, 2016**, to better gauge whether the Extended Missing Parts Program offers sufficient benefits to the patent community before it becomes permanent. This date may be extended by the USPTO for another year depending upon the effectiveness of the program.

12.8.1 REQUIREMENTS FOR THE EXTENDED MISSING PARTS PILOT PROGRAM

The following requirements must be met to participate in the Extended Missing Parts Pilot Program:

1. Applicant must submit a certification and request to participate in the Extended Missing Parts Pilot Program with the Nonprovisional Application on filing by using the **Certification and Request for Extended Missing Parts Pilot Pro**gram **(PTO/AIA/421)** form at *www.uspto.gov/forms/aia0421.pdf.*

2. The application must be an original Nonprovisional Utility or Plant Application, including at least one claim and drawing(s), if necessary, for an understanding of the invention to be entitled to a filing date and thus be eligible for the pilot program.

3. The Nonprovisional Application must directly claim the benefit of a prior provisional application filed within the previous twelve (12) months; the specific reference to the provisional application must be in an ADS.

4. A nonpublication request must not have been filed.

NOTE: The following are excluded from the program: design applications, provisional applications, national stage applications, PCT international applications, reissue applications, and reexamination proceedings.

12.9 NOTICE TO FILE CORRECTED APPLICATION PAPERS – FILING DATE GRANTED

If a **Notice to File Corrected Application Papers – Filing Date Granted** ("Notice") is received, the application is considered informal because it did not comply with the regulations for the reason(s) given on the Notice.

As indicated on the Notice, an Application Number and filing date have been accorded to this application. The Practitioner is given two (2) months from the date of the Notice within which to file all required items and pay any fees required to avoid abandonment. An extension up to five (5) months extensions of time from the due date of the Notice can be requested with the appropriate extension of time fee to respond to the Notice, otherwise the application will go abandoned if no response is filed.

12.9.1 eFILING A RESPONSE TO NOTICE TO FILE CORRECTED APPLICATION PAPERS

The basic steps to efile a Response to Notice to File Corrected Application Papers via EFS-Web are as follows:

1. After EFS-Web certification, under "*Main Functions", click "Existing application/patent/proceeding".
2. Select Type of Submission: Click "Document/Fees for an existing application/proceeding".
3. Type in the Application Number and Confirmation Number of the existing patent application. Click "Continue" for the next screen.
4. Files to be Submitted: Browse for the file (in PDF format) and upload it to this filing.
5. Underneath the uploaded document, it states: "Does your PDF file contain multiple documents?" Click "Yes".
6. The following basic document descriptions are used for filing the Response to the Notice:

Category	Document Description
Pilot Programs	Certification and Request for Missing Parts (Form PTO/AIA/421)
Pre-Exam	Applicant Response to Pre-Exam Formalities Notice

Application Part

Specification and/or
Claims and/or
Abstract and/or
Drawings – only black and white line drawings

7. Click "Upload & Validate" to make sure that there are no validation errors. If there is a validation error, there will be a prompt on the screen of an error or a warning! If there is an error, the error must be corrected at this point. If there is a warning, click "Continue" to go to the next screen.

For the remainder of the steps, see **Section 6.2.2** to complete the efiling of the Response via EFS-Web.

12.10 Notice of Omitted Item(s) in a Nonprovisional Application

If a Nonprovisional Application is filed without all the pages of the specification, yet the application includes (i) at least one drawing figure if necessary under 35 USC 113 (first sentence), (ii) the specification contains information which can be construed as a written description, and (iii) there is at least one claim, the OPAP will mail a "Notice of Omitted Item(s) in a Nonprovisional Application" ("Notice") indicating that the application papers so deposited have been accorded a filing date, but are lacking some pages of the specification.

The Practitioner is given two (2) months from the date of the Notice within which to file all required items and pay any fees required to avoid abandonment. The Paralegal must advise the Practitioner immediately of the Notice and obtain instructions as to the appropriate action necessary to respond to the Notice.

NOTE: The two (2)-month period is <u>not extendable</u> under 37 CFR 1.136.

12.10.1 eFiling a Response to the Notice of Omitted Items

The basic steps to efile a Response to Notice of Omitted Items via EFS-Web are as follows:

1. After EFS-Web certification, under "*Main Functions", click "Existing application/patent/proceeding".
2. Select Type of Submission: Click "Document/Fees for an existing application/proceeding".
3. Type in the Application Number and Confirmation Number of the existing patent application. Click "Continue" for the next screen.
4. Files to be Submitted: Browse for the file (in PDF format) and upload it to this filing.

5. Underneath the uploaded document, it states: "Does your PDF file contain multiple documents?" Click "Yes".

6. The following basic document descriptions are used for filing the Response to the Notice:

Category	Document Description
Pre-Exam	Applicant Response to Pre-Exam Formalities Notice
Application Part	Specification and/or
	Claims and/or
	Abstract and/or
	Drawings – only black and white line drawings

7. Click "Upload & Validate" to make sure that there are no validation errors. If there is a validation error, there will be a prompt on the screen of an error or a warning! If there is an error, the error must be corrected at this point. If there is a warning, click "Continue" to go to the next screen.

For the remainder of the steps, see **Section 6.2.2** to complete the efiling of the Response via EFS-Web.

12.11 Notice of Incomplete Application – Filing Date Not Granted

If a Notice of Incomplete Application – Filing Date Not Granted ("Notice") is received, the application is considered informal because it did not comply with the regulations for the reason(s) given on the Notice. The Notice advises Applicant that a filing date has not been granted to the application. In such an event, the Practitioner must be notified immediately of the Notice.

The Practitioner is given two (2) months from the date of the Notice within which to file all required items and pay any fees required to avoid abandonment. The Paralegal must obtain instructions as to the appropriate action necessary to respond to the Notice.

NOTE: The two (2)-month period is <u>not extendable</u> under 37 CFR 1.136.

12.12 Times to Respond to the Notice

USPTO Paper	Time to Reply	Extension of Time
Notice to File Missing Parts of Nonprovisional Application – Filing Date Granted	2 months	5 months
Notice to File Corrected Application Papers – Filing Date Granted	2 months	5 months
Notice of Omitted Items in a Nonprovisional Application	2 months	None
Notice of Incomplete Application – Filing Date Not Granted	2 months	None

12.13 Petition for Extension of Time

When the time to respond is extendable, as in the case of a "Notice to File Missing Parts of a Nonprovisional Application" or a "Notice to File Corrected Application Papers" to respond to the Notice, the Practitioner has a maximum of seven (7) months from the mailing date. However, the usual practice is to give the Practitioner a shortened statutory period ("SSP") of two (2) months in which to respond to the Notice without the need for a Petition for Extension of Time. If the response is submitted after the two (2)-month SSP period, the Practitioner must request a Petition for Extension of Time and pay the required fee. Due dates can be extended in one (1)-month increments. As a safety net, if the Practitioner has a Deposit Account, the *Response to the Notice* should include the following paragraph authorizing the USPTO to charge all required fees to the Practitioner's USPTO Deposit Account in case there is a miscalculation of the required fee(s) to be paid:

The Commissioner is hereby authorized to charge to Deposit Account No. _____ any fees that may be required by this paper and to credit any overpayment to that Account. If any extension of time is required in connection with the filing of this paper and has not been separately requested, such extension is hereby requested.

12.14 CHECKING STATUS IN PRIVATE PAIR

Before the eighteen (18)-month publication date, the status of the application can be obtained by accessing Private PAIR.

The following steps can be used in Private PAIR to check the status of the application:

1. Go to *www.uspto.gov*.
2. Under the Quicklinks tab on the right side of screen, click on "Private PAIR".
3. After EFS-Web certification, scroll to "Search for Application" and choose the type of number below:
    * Application Number
    * Control Number
    * Patent Number
    * PCT Number
    * Publication Number
    * International Design Registration Number
    * Search by Attorney Docket Number
4. After entering the Application Number, there will be an "Image File Wrapper" tab at the top of the window. Click on this tab to see all documents submitted so far in this application. Click on the "First Action" tab at the top. The screen will display a first action letter indicating the number of months before this application will be examined by the Examiner. This above information is not available in Public PAIR until the application is published. If a request for nonpublication has been submitted, the above information will not be available until the application issues.

12.15 FULL FIRST ACTION INTERVIEW PILOT PROGRAM

The initial Full First Action Interview Pilot Program was implemented on May 6, 2011, and is still currently available for all utility applications in all technology areas.

Under the Full First Action Interview Pilot Program, an Applicant is entitled to a first action interview, upon request, prior to the first Office Action on the merits. The Examiner will conduct a prior art search and provide Applicant with a condensed pre-interview communication citing relevant prior art and identifying proposed rejections or objections. Within thirty (30) days of receipt, Applicant can schedule an interview and submit proposed amendments and/or arguments. At the interview, the relevant prior art, proposed rejections, amendments and arguments will be discussed. If agreement is not reached, the Applicant will receive a first action interview Office Action that includes an interview summary. The interview summary constitutes a first Office Action on the merits under 35 USC 132.

12.15.1 REQUIREMENTS FOR THE FULL FIRST ACTION INTERVIEW PILOT PROGRAM

The application must meet the following requirements to participate in the Full First Action Interview Pilot Program:

- Must be a non-reissue, nonprovisional utility application under 35 USC 111(a) or a national stage application under 35 USC 371.
- Must contain three (3) or fewer independent claims and twenty (20) or fewer total claims.
- Must not contain any multiple dependent claims.
- Must claim only a single invention.
- Must not have a first Office Action on the merits as of the date Applicant requests participation in program.
- Must include a statement that Applicant agrees not to file a request for a refund of the search fee and any excess claims fees paid in the application after the mailing or notification of the Pre-Interview Communication.

12.15.2 EFILE A FULL FIRST ACTION INTERVIEW PILOT PROGRAM VIA EFS-WEB

The basic steps to efile a Full First Action Interview Pilot Program via EFS-Web are as follows:

- If the above requirements are met, complete the **Request for First Action Interview (Full Pilot Program) (PTO/SB/413C)** form at *www.uspto.gov/forms/sb0413c.pdf*. The form must be signed by the Practitioner. Once the form is signed, then it is ready to be efiled via EFS-Web.
- Save form and upload into EFS-Web.

The following basic document description is used when filing the Request:

Category	Document Description
Pilot Programs	First Action Interview - Enrollment Request

See *Section 6.2.2* to complete the efiling of the Request for First Action Interview via EFS-Web.

For more information, go to www.uspto.gov/patent/initiatives/first-action-interview/full-first-action-interview-pilot-program.

12.16 Cancer Immunotherapy Pilot Program

The Cancer Immunotherapy Pilot Program, also known as Patents 4 Patients, provides a fast-track review for cancer immunotherapy-related patent applications without the need for Applicant to pay a petition fee. Under this program, patent applications pertaining to cancer immunotherapy are advanced out of turn for examination, resulting in their accelerated review.

Patents 4 Patients aims to cut the time it takes to review patent applications pertaining to cancer immunotherapy in half by issuing final decisions in one (1) year or less after they are received.

Patents 4 Patients:

- Applications must contain one or more claims to a method of treating a cancer using immunotherapy.
- Applications must file a grantable petition under this initiative via EFS-Web.
- Open to:
    - Any application that has not received a first Office action,
    - Any application where the petition is filed with a Request for Continued Examination ("RCE"), or
    - Any application not under final rejection where the claimed cancer immunotherapy is the subject of an active Investigational New Drug (IND) application that has entered Phase II or Phase III (FDA) clinical trials.
- No additional fee is required to participate in the program.

12.16.1 eFile a Petition for the Cancer Immunotherapy Pilot Program via EFS-Web

The basic steps to efile a Petition for the Cancer Immunotherapy Pilot Program via EFS-Web are as follows:

- Fill out the **Certification and Petition to Make Special Under the Cancer Immunotherapy Pilot Program (PTO/SB/443)** form at *www.uspto.gov/sites/default/files/documents/sb0443.pdf*. The petition requirements and instructions are included in this form.
- Save form and upload into EFS-Web.

The following basic document description is used when filing the Petition:

Category	Document Description
Petition	Petition for Cancer Immunotherapy Pilot

See *Section 6.2.2* to complete the efiling of the Request for First Action Interview via EFS-Web.

CHAPTER 13

Amendments

• • •

13.1 WHAT IS AN AMENDMENT?

AMENDMENTS ARE CHANGES OR CORRECTIONS made to a patent application. Although normally made after filing the application, Amendments may also accompany an application at its initial filing. For example, a Preliminary Amendment may accompany a foreign-origin application to amend it to conform to U.S. practice.

Amendments generally fall into four broad categories:

- Preliminary Amendment.
- Reply to a Non-Final Office Action.
- Reply to a Final Rejection, commonly known as an After Final Amendment.
- Examiner's Amendments.

Preliminary Amendments are those made before the first Office Action in an application. More than one Preliminary Amendment may be filed. Any additional Preliminary Amendments filed after a first one is called Supplemental Preliminary Amendment.

An Amendment is a common type of reply to a Non-Final Office Action in an application. When appropriate, sometimes Practitioner's reply to the Office Action is without amending the application. The time for responding to the Office Action is illustrated in the "Times to Respond to Office Actions." See *Section 13.9*.

An After Final Amendment is made after the USPTO has issued a Final Rejection in an application.

Amendments can also be made in reply to an Examiner's request.

An Examiner's Amendment is prepared by an Examiner after consulting with and obtaining approval by a Practitioner to amend the specification, abstract, and/or claims of the patent application.

13.2 AMENDMENT FORMAT
Amendments prepared by a Practitioner can contain changes to one or more of the following:

* Specification and Abstract
* Drawing(s)
* Claim(s)

Amendments prepared by a Practitioner should contain a Remarks section in which Applicant describes the changes and support for the changes in the specification, original claims, abstract and/or drawings. The Amendment should also contain arguments if traversing any rejections or objections by the Examiner.

There are four sections to an amendment prepared by a Practitioner: amendments to the Specification, amendments to the Claims, amendments to the Drawings, and Remarks. Each section must be on a separate sheet and must follow a specific format.

13.2.1 AMENDMENTS TO THE SPECIFICATION
Amendments to the specification must be made by presenting a replacement paragraph or section or abstract marked up to show changes made relative to the immediate prior version. An accompanying clean version is not required and should not be presented unless required by the Examiner. Newly added paragraphs or sections, including a new abstract (instead of a replacement abstract), must not be underlined. A replacement or new abstract must be submitted on a separate sheet. If a substitute specification is being submitted to incorporate extensive amendments, both a clean version (which will be entered) and a marked up version must be submitted.

The changes in any replacement paragraph or section, or substitute specification must be shown by underlining (for added matter) or strikethrough (for deleted matter) with two exceptions: (1) for deletion of five characters or fewer, double brackets may be used (e.g., [[eroor]]); and (2) if strikethrough cannot be easily perceived (e.g., deletion of the number "4" or certain punctuation marks), double brackets must be used (e.g., [[4]]). As an alternative to using double brackets, however, extra portions of text may be included before and after text being deleted, all in strikethrough, followed by including and underlining the extra text with the desired change (e.g., ~~number 4 as~~number 14 as).

The location of the paragraph or section to be deleted or replaced, or where a new paragraph or section is to be added, must be unambiguously identified.

The location can be identified by using a few words at the beginning and/or the end of the paragraph or section.

Except for amendments to the specification in reissue application, do not underline the text of a new paragraph or section.

Deletion of a paragraph or section must only include an instruction to delete, and the location of the paragraph or section.

Replacement paragraph or section must be a marked-up version showing the changes.

A clean version of any replacement paragraph or section must <u>not</u> be submitted in addition to a marked up version, except when Applicant submits a substitute specification.

For example, the following template can be used for the amendment:

<u>Amendments to the Specification:</u>

<u>In the Specification:</u>

Page __:

Please substitute the following paragraph for the paragraph [____] beginning at page __, line _:

13.2.2 Amendment by Filing a Substitute Specification
The specification, other than the claims, may also be amended by submitting a substitute specification provided the following requirements are met:

1. A clean version (without markings) of the substitute specification.
2. A specification with markings to show all the changes relative to the immediate previous version.
3. A statement that the substitute specification contains no new matter (typically in the remarks).
4. A specification with markings to show all the changes relative to the immediate prior version.

For example, the following template can be used for the amendment:

<u>Amendments to the Specification:</u>

Please replace the original specification with the accompanying substitute specification.

13.2.3 AMENDMENT OF THE TITLE OF INVENTION
The title of the invention can be amended under amendments to the specification. For example, the following template can be used for the amendment:

Amendments to the Specification:

In the Title:

Please change the title to read as follows:

TITLE OF <s>INVETION</s><u>INVENTION</u>

13.2.4 AMENDMENT TO THE ABSTRACT
An amendment to the abstract is treated like an amendment to the specification.

If the changes are minor in nature, submit a replacement abstract with markings to show all changes relative to the immediate prior version.

If the abstract is being substantially rewritten, submit a new abstract in clean text (no markings) accompanied by an instruction to cancel the previous abstract.

Any new, or replacement, abstract must be submitted on a separate sheet.

For example, the following template can be used for the amendment:

Amendments to the Specification:

In the Abstract:

Please replace the original Abstract with the accompanying amended Abstract provided on a separate sheet.

13.2.5 AMENDMENTS TO THE CLAIMS
Each amendment to the claims or cancellation of a claim must include a complete listing of all claims in the application, including claims canceled or withdrawn from consideration due to a restriction requirement.

After each claim number in the listing, the status must be indicated in a parenthetical expression, and the text of each pending claim (with markings to show current changes) must be presented. The claims in the listing will replace all prior claims in the application.

The current status of all of the claims in the application, including previously canceled, not entered or withdrawn claims, must be given in a parenthetical expression following the claim number using only one of the following seven status identifiers: **"Original"**, **"Currently Amended"**, **"Canceled"**, **"Withdrawn"**, **"New"**, **"Previously Presented"** and **"Not Entered"**. The text of all pending claims, **including "Withdrawn" claims,** must be submitted each time any claim is amended. **"Canceled" and "Not Entered"** claims must be indicated by only the claim number and status, without presenting the text of the claims.

The text of all claims being currently amended must be presented in the claim listing with markings to indicate the changes that have been made relative to the immediate prior version. The changes in any amended claim must be shown by underlining (for added matter) or strikethrough (for deleted matter) with two exceptions:

- For deletion of five characters or fewer, double brackets may be used (e.g., [[eroor]].
- If strikethrough cannot be easily perceived (e.g., deletion of the number "4" or certain punctuation marks), double brackets must be used (e.g., [[4]]) or [[,]]. As an alternative to using double brackets, however, extra portions of text may be included before and after text being deleted, all in strikethrough, followed by including and underlining the extra text with the desired change (e.g., ~~number 4 as~~ number 14 as).

An accompanying clean version is not required and should not be presented. Only claims of the status "currently amended" and "withdrawn" may include markings. If a withdrawn claim is currently amended, its status in the claim listing may be identified as **"Withdrawn-Currently Amended"**.

The text of pending claims not being currently amended, including withdrawn claims, must be presented in the claim listing in a clean version, e.g., without any markings. Any claim text presented in a clean version will constitute an assertion that it has not been changed relative to the immediate prior version except to omit markings that may have been presented in the immediate prior version of the claims.

A claim being canceled must be listed in the claim listing with the status identifier **"Canceled"**; the text of the claim must not be presented. Providing an instruction to cancel is optional.

Any claims added by amendment must be presented in the claim listing with the status identifier **"New"**; the text of the claim must not be underlined.

All of the claims in the claim listing must be presented in ascending numerical order. Consecutive canceled, or not entered, claims may be aggregated into one statement (e.g., Claims 1 – 5 (canceled)).

The following are examples of listing of claims (use of the word "**Claim**" before the claim number is optional):

Claims 1-5 (canceled)

Claim 6 (previously presented): A bucket with a handle.

Claim 7 (withdrawn): A handle comprising an elongated wire.

Claim 8 (withdrawn-currently amended): The handle of claim 7 further comprising a <u>plastic</u> grip.

Claim 9 (currently amended): A bucket with a ~~green~~<u>blue</u> handle.

Claim 10 (original): The bucket of claim 9 wherein the handle is made of wood.

Claim 11 (canceled)

Claim 12 (not entered)

Claim 13 (new): A bucket with plastic sides and bottom.

The seven (7) permissible status identifiers and their definitions are as follows:

Original: Claim filed with original specification (not added by preliminary amendment and not previously amended).

Currently amended: Claim being amended in the current amendment. Currently amended claims must include markings (strikethrough, double brackets, or underlining) to indicate changes.

Canceled: Claim canceled or deleted in current amendment or previously. Do not present the text of a canceled claim. Consecutive canceled claims may be grouped together (e.g., claims 1-5 (canceled)).

Withdrawn: Non-elected claim. The text of a withdrawn claim must be presented. Withdrawn claims that are being currently amended must be presented with markings (strikethrough, double brackets, or underlining) to indicate changes.

Previously presented: This is a generic identifier to cover any claim that was previously added or amended in an earlier amendment paper. The identifiers "previously amended" or "previously added" must not be used.

New: Claim being added in the current amendment paper. The text of the claim must be presented in clean form without underlining.

Not entered: Claim presented in a previous unentered amendment. Do not present the text of a not entered claim. Consecutive not entered claims may be grouped together (e.g., Claims 20-25 (not entered)). If in doubt as to whether a prior amendment was entered, the claim should be presumed to be "not entered".

The listing of claims must comply with the following:

- A status identifier for each claim is required. Multiple status identifiers must not be used for any single claim.
- The text of all claims being currently amended must be presented with markings to show changes relative to immediate prior version.
- Only claims of the status "currently amended" and "withdrawn" (if the withdrawn claims are being currently amended) may include markings.

All other pending claims (including withdrawn claims that are not being currently amended) must be presented in clean text (without markings).

Any claim presented in clean text (no markings) constitutes an assertion that it has not been changed relative to the immediate prior version, <u>except</u> omitting markings (e.g., underlining, strikethrough, and double brackets) and deleted text. For example:

If the immediate prior version of the claim as amended was:

"Claim 1 (currently amended) A bucket with a ~~blue~~<u>red</u> handle."

then the listing of claims in the current amendment must read as follows:

"Claim 1 (previously presented) A bucket with a red handle."

"Canceled" claims and **"Not Entered"** claims may only have a **"Canceled"** or **"Not Entered"** status identifier after the claim number. The text must not be supplied.

New or added claims must have "**New**" as a status identifier.

Other than amendments in reissue applications, do not underline the text of the new claims.

Grouping of Claims – consecutive "**Canceled**" claims or "**Not Entered**" claims may be aggregated into one line. For example:

Claims 1-5 (canceled)

Claims 6-10 (not entered)

13.2.6 MARKINGS IN CLAIMS TO SHOW CHANGES

Replacement text, paragraphs, or sections in abstracts, currently amended claims, and specifications must include markings to show all changes relative to the immediate prior version.

- Added text must be shown by underlining.
- Deleted text must be shown by strikethrough (e.g., ~~strikethrough~~) with two exceptions.
- For deletion of five or fewer consecutive characters, double brackets [[ ]] may be used (e.g., [[eroor]]).
- If strikethrough cannot be easily perceived, deleted text must be shown by double brackets [[ ]] around the deleted text characters. For example:

Changing "4 corners" to "three corners" should be indicated by "three[[4]] corners".

- For changes of punctuation marks or difficult to perceive characters, Applicant may delete text before and after with strikethrough, and then insert such text along with the change by underlining, e.g., ~~number 4 as~~number 14 as.

13.2.7 AMENDMENTS TO THE DRAWINGS

Drawing changes must be made by presenting replacement figures which incorporate the desired changes. An explanation of the changes made must be presented either in the drawing amendments or remarks sections of the amendment, and may be accompanied by a marked-up copy of one or more of the figures being amended, with annotations. Any replacement drawing sheet must be identified in the top margin as "Replacement Sheet" and include all of the figures appearing on the immediate prior version of the sheet, even though only one figure may be amended. Any marked-up (annotated) copy showing changes must be labeled "Annotated Sheet" and accompany the replacement sheet in the amendment (e.g., as an appendix).

The figure or figure number of the amended drawings must not be labeled as "amended." If the changes to the drawing figures are not accepted by the Examiner, Applicant will be notified of any required corrective action in the next Office Action. No further drawing submission will be required, unless Applicant is notified.

Amendments to drawings must include:

1. Replacement drawing sheets showing amended figures which include the desired changes, without markings; and
2. Explanation of the changes in the remarks, or preferably, in the drawing amendments section, of the amendment paper.

An "Annotated" drawing sheet is a marked-up copy of the amended figure(s) with annotations showing the changes to be submitted, or required by the Examiner. In order to avoid confusion between a replacement sheet and an annotated sheet, replacement drawings must be identified in the top margin as "Replacement Sheet" and annotated drawing sheets must be identified in the top margin as "Annotated Sheet".

Annotated drawing sheets will not be entered as part of the official drawings for the application.

The replacement drawing sheets and annotated drawing sheets, if any, should follow the last page of the amendment paper, as attachments.

If the drawings are not acceptable, the Applicant will be notified of any objections or additional requirements.

Drawings in reissue applications may be amended in a similar manner as described above.

Deletion of a figure requires the following:

* An instruction to delete the figure;
* A replacement sheet which does not include the canceled figure, unless no other figure is on the same sheet as the canceled figure;
* An amendment to the specification to make corresponding changes to the description of the drawings (e.g., deletion of the description of the canceled figure); and
* If other figures need to be renumbered, those figures also need to be amended with revised figure numbers via replacement drawing sheets.

13.3 Preliminary Amendment

Before the Examiner examines the application, the Applicant may file a Preliminary Amendment to make changes to the specification, claims, abstract, and drawings, if necessary. A Preliminary Amendment can be filed at any time before a first Office Action from the Examiner is received.

13.3.1 Preliminary Amendment Shell Template

The Paralegal may be asked by his/her Practitioner to prepare the following Preliminary Amendment shell before the examination of the application.

Consult with the Practitioner on the style on which he/she prefers in preparing the Preliminary Amendment Shell.

If any of these sections are not needed (specification, claims and/or drawings), remove these sections from the shell.

IN THE UNITED STATES PATENT AND TRADEMARK OFFICE

In re Patent Application of:
First Named Inventor: Art Unit:
Appln. No.:   Examiner:

Filed: Confirmation No.:
For:

● ● ●

PRELIMINARY AMENDMENT

Commissioner for Patents
P.O. Box 1450
Alexandria, VA 22313-1450

Commissioner:

Prior to examination, please amend the above-identified patent application as indicated below.

Amendments to the Specification begin on page 2 of this paper.

Amendments to the Claims are reflected in the listing of claims which begins on page __ of this paper.

Amendments to the Drawings begin on page __ of this paper and include both an attached replacement sheet and an annotated sheet showing changes.

Remarks begin on page __ of this paper.

(NEXT PAGE)
Amendments to the Specification:

<u>In the title</u>:

Please change the title to read as follows:

Please replace paragraph [0001] with the following amended paragraph:
[0001]

Please add the following <u>new</u> paragraph after paragraph [0001]:
[0001.1]

<u>IN THE ABSTRACT</u>:

Please replace the original Abstract with the accompanying Abstract on a separate sheet.

(NEXT PAGE)
Amendments to the Claims:

This listing of claims will replace all prior versions, and listings, of claims in the application:

Listing of Claims:

1. (include status identifier in each claim)

(NEXT PAGE)
Amendments to the Drawings:

The attached sheet of drawings includes changes to __.

Attachment: Replacement Sheet
          Annotated Sheet Showing Changes

(NEXT PAGE)

REMARKS

INSERT

The Commissioner is hereby authorized to charge to Deposit Account No. _____ (Attorney Docket No. _____) any fees under 37 C.F.R. §§ 1.16 and 1.17 that may be required by this paper and to credit any overpayment to that Account. If any extension of time is required in connection with the filing of this paper and has not been separately requested, such extension is hereby requested.

Respectfully submitted,

Date: _____   By: _____
                                  Attorney Name
                                  Reg. No. _____

Firm Name
Firm Address
Firm Phone No.
Firm Email

13.3.2 eFILING A PRELIMINARY AMENDMENT VIA EFS-WEB

The basic steps to efile a Preliminary Amendment via EFS-Web are as follows:

1. After EFS-Web certification, under "*Main Functions", click "Existing application/patent/proceeding".
2. Select Type of Submission: Click "Document/Fees for an existing application/proceeding".
3. Type in the Application Number and Confirmation Number of the existing patent application. Click "Continue" for the next screen.
4. Files to be Submitted: Browse for the file (in PDF format) and upload it to this filing.
5. Underneath the uploaded document, it states: "Does your PDF file contain multiple documents?" Click "Yes".
6. The following basic document descriptions are used for filing a Preliminary Amendment:

Category	Document Description
Amendment	Preliminary Amendment (Transmittal)
Amendment	Specification (Amendments to the Specification)

Amendment	Claims (Amendments to the Claims)
Amendment	Applicant Arguments/Remarks Made in an Amendment (Amendments to the Drawings)
Amendment	Applicant Arguments/Remarks Made in an Amendment (Remarks)
Amendment	Abstract
Amendment	Drawings – only black and white line drawings

7. Click "Upload & Validate" to make sure that there are no validation errors. If there is a validation error, there will be a prompt on the screen of an error or a warning! If there is an error, the error must be corrected at this point. If there is a warning, click "Continue" to go to the next screen.

For the remainder of the steps, see **Section 6.2.2** to complete the efiling of the Preliminary Amendment via EFS-Web.

TIP: The Preliminary Amendment does not have to be separated into the document descriptions listed above. The USPTO will also accept one document description, i.e., Preliminary Amendment via EFS-Web.

13.4 NON-FINAL AMENDMENT

After an examination "on the merits," an Office Action will be mailed concerning patentability issues.

If all the pending claims are considered allowable then a first action allowance will be sent.

If the Examiner rejects one or more claims and/or objects to the specification, he/she will send a written Office Action explaining the rejections and/or objections.

If, after receiving an Office Action, the Applicant chooses to continue to pursue the application, Applicant must file a written response on or before the due date, which is normally three (3) months from the mailing date of the Office Action. This written response is commonly referred to as a "Non-Final Amendment". In the response, the Applicant will request that the Examiner reconsider the application, and can amend the specification, claims, and/or drawings to conform to the Examiner's requirements.

13.4.1 Non-Final Amendment Shell Template

The Paralegal may be asked by his/her Practitioner to prepare the following Non-Final Amendment shell.

Consult with the Practitioner on the style on which he/she prefers in preparing the Non-Final Amendment Shell.

If any of these sections are not needed (specification, claims and/or drawings), remove these sections from the shell.

37 CFR 1.111: Reply by Applicant or Patent Owner to Office Action after the first examination.

IN THE UNITED STATES PATENT AND TRADEMARK OFFICE

In re Patent Application of:
First Named Inventor: Art Unit:
Appln. No.:   Examiner:

Filed: Confirmation No.:
For:

● ● ●

AMENDMENT UNDER 37 C.F.R. §1.111

Mail Stop <u>Amendment</u>
Commissioner for Patents
P.O. Box 1450
Alexandria, VA 22313-1450

Commissioner:

In response to the Office Action of _____, please amend the above-identified application as follows:

    Amendments to the Specification begin on page 2 of this paper.
    Amendments to the Claims are reflected in the listing of claims which begins on page __ of this paper.

Amendments to the Drawings begin on page __ of this paper and include both an attached replacement sheet and an annotated sheet showing changes.

Remarks begin on page __ of this paper.

(NEXT PAGE)
Amendments to the Specification:

<u>In the title</u>:

Please change the title to read as follows:

Please replace paragraph [0001] with the following amended paragraph:
[0001]

Please add the following <u>new</u> paragraph after paragraph [0001]:
[0001.1]

<u>IN THE ABSTRACT</u>:

Please replace the original Abstract with the accompanying Abstract on a separate sheet.

(NEXT PAGE)
<u>Amendments to the Claims:</u>

This listing of claims will replace all prior versions, and listings, of claims in the application:

<u>Listing of Claims</u>:

1. **(include status identifier in each claim)**

(NEXT PAGE)
<u>Amendments to the Drawings:</u>

The attached sheet of drawings includes changes to __.

Attachment: Replacement Sheet
              Annotated Sheet Showing Changes

(NEXT PAGE)

REMARKS

INSERT

The Commissioner is hereby authorized to charge to Deposit Account No. _____ (Attorney Docket No. _____) any fees under 37 C.F.R. §§ 1.16 and 1.17 that may be required by this paper and to credit any overpayment to that Account. If any extension of time is required in connection with the filing of this paper and has not been separately requested, such extension is hereby requested.

Respectfully submitted,

Date: _____   By: _____

Attorney Name

Reg. No. _____

Firm Name
Firm Address
Firm Phone No.
Firm Email

13.4.2 eFILING A NON-FINAL AMENDMENT VIA EFS-WEB

The basic steps to efile a Non-Final Amendment via EFS-Web are as follows:

1. After EFS-Web certification, under "*Main Functions", click "Existing application/patent/proceeding".
2. Select Type of Submission: Click "Document/Fees for an existing application/proceeding".
3. Type in the Application Number and Confirmation Number of the existing patent application. Click "Continue" for the next screen.
4. Files to be Submitted: Browse for the file (in PDF format) and upload it to this filing.
5. Underneath the uploaded document, it states: "Does your PDF file contain multiple documents?" Click "Yes".
6. The following basic document descriptions are used for filing a response to the Non-Final Office Action:

Category	Document Description
Amendment	Amendment/Req. Reconsideration After Non-Final Reject
Amendment	Specification (Amendments to the Specification)
Amendment	Claims (Amendments to the Claims)

Amendment	Applicant Arguments/Remarks Made in an Amendment (Amendments to the Drawings)
Amendment	Applicant Arguments/Remarks Made in an Amendment (Remarks)
Amendment	Abstract
Amendment	Drawings – only black and white line drawings

7. Click "Upload & Validate" to make sure that there are no validation errors. If there is a validation error, there will be a prompt on the screen of an error or a warning! If there is an error, the error must be corrected at this point. If there is a warning, click "Continue" to go to the next screen.

For the remainder of the steps, see ***Section 6.2.2*** to complete the efiling of the Non-Final Amendment via EFS-Web.

13.5 AFTER FINAL REJECTION

A second or subsequent Office Action can be "made final" by the Examiner. When an Office Action is made final, the Examiner will insert a standard paragraph at the end of the text of the Office Action, stating in CAPITALS that the action is final. This is also indicated by the Examiner checking a box on the cover sheet of the Office Action. If the action is not indicated as FINAL, yet the box is checked (or vice versa), request clarification from the Examiner.

A response to an After-Final Rejection ("AFR") must be filed within six (6) months from the date of the AFR in order to avoid abandonment of the application. Therefore, the Paralegal must notify the Practitioner immediately so that he/she can prepare a letter to the Applicant giving options available to the Applicant for responding to the AFR in a timely manner.

13.5.1 ADVISORY ACTION

If the Practitioner files a response to the AFR and the response does not place the application in condition for allowance, the Examiner will issue an Advisory Action briefly explaining why the final rejection is not overcome by the response. After receiving an Advisory Action, if Practitioner does not subsequently authorize filing a Notice of Appeal, an RCE, or a Divisional, Continuation, or Continuation-In-Part Application before the end of the six (6)-month statutory period for response, the application will become abandoned.

There is an advantage to filing a response within two (2) months after the date of the AFR. For example, assume that an AFR is mailed on September 1, 2008, a response to the AFR is filed on November 1, 2008, and an Advisory Action is mailed December 19, 2008. If the Applicant desires to appeal the AFR, the

Notice of Appeal can be filed on or before January 19, 2009, without having to pay an extension of time fee. On the other hand, if the Advisory Action is mailed on November 29, 2008, the Notice of Appeal must be filed by December 1, 2008, in order to avoid payment of an extension of time fee.

13.5.2 AFTER FINAL AMENDMENT

When an amendment or a request for reconsideration is filed in response to an Office Action under Final Rejection, type the following in the upper right-hand corner of the first page of the paper (e.g., under docket numbers).

RESPONSE UNDER 37 CFR 1.116
EXPEDITED PROCEDURE – EXAMINING GROUP ____

This information will assist the USPTO in acting promptly after a final rejection. Otherwise, the Examiner may not get the response for a month or so after it was filed which may result in filing an extension of time fee to file a Notice of Appeal.

Any After Final Amendment or Amendment filed with a Request for Continued Examination ("RCE"), must include markings showing the changes relative to the last entered amendment.

Do not include markings to show changes relative to any unentered amendment.

If an Advisory Action or Notice of Allowability has not been received at least two (2) weeks before the end of the six (6)-month statutory period to respond to an Office Action, check PAIR, or call the Examiner, to determine whether the After Final Amendment has been entered before and advise the Practitioner as to the status of the After Final Amendment.

If Practitioner wishes to file an RCE after filing more than one After Final Amendment that has not been entered, consult with the Practitioner as to whether claims will be amended.

A claim listing which includes any unentered claims must be presented using the status identifier "not entered" (e.g., claims 20-25 (not entered)). Any new claims must be numbered consecutively beginning with the number next following the highest numbered claim previously presented (whether entered or not).

13.5.3 AFTER FINAL AMENDMENT SHELL TEMPLATE

The Paralegal may be asked by his/her Practitioner to prepare the following After Final Amendment.

Consult with the Practitioner on the style on which he/she prefers in preparing the After Final Amendment Shell.

If any of these sections are not needed (specification, claims and/or drawings), remove these sections from the shell.

37 CFR 1.116: Amendments and affidavits or other evidence after final action and prior to appeal.

RESPONSE UNDER 37 CFR 1.116
EXPEDITED PROCEDURE – EXAMINING GROUP _____

IN THE UNITED STATES PATENT AND TRADEMARK OFFICE

In re Patent Application of: Art Unit:
First Named Inventor:
Appln. No.:   Examiner:

Filed: Confirmation No.:
For:

● ● ●

AMENDMENT AFTER FINAL REJECTION

Mail Stop AF
Commissioner for Patents
P.O. Box 1450
Alexandria, VA 22313-1450

Commissioner:

In response to the Office Action of _____, please amend the above-identified application as follows:

    Amendments to the Specification begin on page 2 of this paper.
    Amendments to the Claims are reflected in the listing of claims which begins on page __ of this paper.

Amendments to the Drawings begin on page __ of this paper and include both an attached replacement sheet and an annotated sheet showing changes.

Remarks begin on page __ of this paper.

(NEXT PAGE)

Amendments to the Specification:

In the title:

    Please change the title to read as follows:

    Please replace paragraph [0001] with the following amended paragraph:
    [0001]

    Please add the following <u>new</u> paragraph after paragraph [0001]:

    [0001.1]

IN THE ABSTRACT:

    Please replace the original Abstract with the accompanying Abstract on a separate sheet.

(NEXT PAGE)

Amendments to the Claims:

    This listing of claims will replace all prior versions, and listings, of claims in the application:

Listing of Claims:

    1. (include status identifier in each claim)

(NEXT PAGE)

Amendments to the Drawings:

    The attached sheet of drawings includes changes to __.

Attachment: Replacement Sheet
                    Annotated Sheet Showing Changes

(NEXT PAGE)

REMARKS

INSERT

The Commissioner is hereby authorized to charge to Deposit Account No. _____ (Attorney Docket No. _____) any fees under 37 C.F.R. §§ 1.16 and 1.17 that may be required by this paper and to credit any overpayment to that Account. If any extension of time is required in connection with the filing of this paper and has not been separately requested, such extension is hereby requested.

Respectfully submitted,

Date: _____   By: _____

Attorney Name

Reg. No. _____

Firm Name
Firm Address
Firm Phone
Firm Email

13.5.4 AFTER FINAL CONSIDERATION PILOT PROGRAM 2.0

The USPTO implemented the After Final Consideration Pilot Program 2.0 ("AFCP 2.0") on May 19, 2013, which is part of the USPTO's ongoing efforts towards compact prosecution and increased collaboration between Examiners and the IP community.

AFCP 2.0 authorized additional time for Examiners to search and/or consider responses after final rejection. Under AFCP 2.0, Examiners will also use the additional time to schedule and conduct an interview to discuss the results of their search and/or consideration with the Practitioner.

AFCP 2.0 has been extended through **September 30, 2017**; therefore, any request to consider a response after-final rejection under AFCP 2.0 must be filed **on or before September 30, 2017**.

Form PTO/SB/434 is to be used to request consideration under AFCP 2.0 at *www.uspto.gov/forms/sb0434.pdf.*

Guidelines for Consideration of Responses After-Final Rejection under 37 CFR 1.116(b) under the AFCP 2.0 can be found at *www.uspto.gov/patents/init_events/afcp_guidelines.pdf.*

The following basic document description is used when filing the Pilot:

<u>Category</u>   <u>Document Description</u>

Pilot Programs	After Final Consideration Program Request
	(Form PTO/SB/434)

13.5.5 POST-PROSECUTION PILOT PROGRAM

The Post-Prosecution Pilot ("P3") Program was developed to test its impact on enhancing patent practice during the period subsequent to final rejection and prior to the filing of a notice of appeal. Effective features of two programs currently aimed at improving this area of prosecution are (1) the After Final Consideration Pilot 2.0 program and (2) the Pre-Appeal Brief Conference Pilot program, which have been incorporated into a single program that adds new, requested features, such as providing Applicants an opportunity to present arguments to a panel at a conference.

The P3 Program began on July 11, 2016, and will continue to **January 11, 2017**, or when 1,600 requests have been accepted into the P3 Program, whichever comes first. Each individual technology center will accept no more than 200 compliant requests, which means that the P3 Program may close with respect to an individual technology center that has accepted 200 compliant requests, even as it continues to run in other technology centers that have yet to accept 200 compliant requests.

The P3 Program is open to nonprovisional and international, utility applications filed under 35 USC 111(a) or 35 USC 371 that are under final rejection. Reissue, design, and plant applications, as well as reexamination proceedings, are not eligible to participate in the P3 Program.

The following documents are required for entry into the P3 Program:

- A **Certification and Request for Consideration Under the Post-Prosecution Pilot Program (P3) (PTO/SB/444)** form at *www.uspto.gov/sites/default/files/documents/sb0444.pdf* filed via EFS-Web within two (2) months of the mailing date of the final rejection and prior to filing a notice of appeal.
- A statement (contained with the Request Form) that the Applicant is willing and available to participate in a P3 conference with the panel of examiners.
- A response comprising no more than five (5) pages of arguments under 37 CFR 1.116 to the outstanding final rejection, exclusive of any amendments.
- Optionally, proposed non-broadening amendments to one or more claim(s).

P3 Program Requirements

The P3 Program has the following requirements:

- There are no fees to participate in the P3 Program.
- Applicant cannot have previously filed a proper request to participate in the Pre-Appeal or the AFCP 2.0 programs in response to the same outstanding final rejection.
- Once a P3 Program request has been accepted, no additional response(s) under 37 CFR 1.116 will be entered, unless requested by the Examiner.
- It is also not possible to request to participate in the Pre-Appeal program or request consideration under AFCP 2.0 once a P3 Program request has been accepted.

P3 Program Process

Once the P3 Program has been accepted, the USPTO will contact the Applicant to schedule the P3 conference. Such contact should result in a P3 conference within ten (10) calendar days of the initial contact with the Applicant or the P3 Program request could be considered improper at that time.

The Applicant will make an oral presentation to the panel of examiners, with such participation being limited to twenty (20) minutes:

After Applicant's presentation, the Applicant will be excused from the conference.

The Applicant will be informed of the panel's decision, in writing, following complete consideration of the P3 Program request.

The P3 Program process will be terminated if Applicant files any of the following after the filing of the P3 Program request but prior to the notice of decision from the panel:

- A notice of appeal
- A Request for Continued Examination
- An express abandonment under 37 CFR 1.138
- A request for the declaration of interference
- A petition requesting the institution of a derivation proceeding

The following basic document description is used when filing the Pilot:

Category	Document Description
Pilot Programs	Prosecution Conference Pilot Request

13.5.6 eFILING AN AFTER FINAL AMENDMENT VIA EFS-WEB

The basic steps to efile an After Final Amendment via EFS-Web are as follows:

1. After EFS-Web certification, under "*Main Functions", click "Existing application/patent/proceeding".
2. Select Type of Submission: Click "Document/Fees for an existing application/proceeding".
3. Type in the Application Number and Confirmation Number of the existing patent application. Click "Continue" for the next screen.
4. Files to be Submitted: Browse for the file (in PDF format) and upload it to this filing.
5. Underneath the uploaded document, it states: "Does your PDF file contain multiple documents?" Click "Yes".
6. The following basic document descriptions are used for filing an After Final Amendment:

Category	Document Description
Pilot Programs	After Final Consideration Program Request (if needed) (Form PTO/SB/434)
Amendment	Response After Final Action
Amendment	Specification (Amendments to the Specification)
Amendment	Claims (Amendments to the Claims)
Amendment	Applicant Arguments/Remarks Made in an Amendment (Amendments to the Drawings)
Amendment	Applicant Arguments/Remarks Made in an Amendment (Remarks)
Amendment	Abstract
Amendment	Drawings – only black and white line drawings

7. Click "Upload & Validate" to make sure that there are no validation errors. If there is a validation error, there will be a prompt on the screen of an error or a warning! If there is an error, the error must be corrected at this point. If there is a warning, click "Continue" to go to the next screen.

For the remainder of the steps, see **Section 6.2.2** to complete the efiling of the After Final Amendment via EFS-Web.

13.6 REQUEST FOR RECONSIDERATION

If there is no need to file any amendments to the specification, claims, abstract, and drawings, the Practitioner may submit a "Request for Reconsideration" in response to any Office Action.

13.6.1 eFILING A REQUEST FOR RECONSIDERATION VIA EFS-WEB

The basic steps to efile a Request for Reconsideration via EFS-Web are as follows:

1. After EFS-Web certification, under "*Main Functions", click "Existing application/patent/proceeding".
2. Select Type of Submission: Click "Document/Fees for an existing application/proceeding".
3. Type in the Application Number and Confirmation Number of the existing patent application. Click "Continue" for the next screen.
4. Files to be Submitted: Browse for the file (in PDF format) and upload it to this filing.
5. Underneath the uploaded document, it states: "Does your PDF file contain multiple documents?" Click "Yes".
6. The following basic document descriptions are used for filing a Request for Reconsideration:

Category	Document Description
Amendment	Amendment/Req. Reconsideration After Non-Final Reject or Response After Final Action
Amendment	Applicant Arguments/Remarks Made in an Amendment (Remarks)

7. Click "Upload & Validate" to make sure that there are no validation errors. If there is a validation error, there will be a prompt on the screen of an error or a warning! If there is an error, the error must be corrected at this point. If there is a warning, click "Continue" to go to the next screen.

For the remainder of the steps, see **Section 6.2.2** to complete the efiling the Request for Reconsideration via EFS-Web.

13.7 EX PARTE QUAYLE ACTION

When an application is in condition for allowance, prosecution on the merits is closed. Where there are "formal matters" to be corrected, such as minor administrative matters and/or obvious mistakes, the USPTO issues an *Ex parte* Quayle Action to request the Applicant to correct these "formal matters" which preclude fully closing the prosecution.

An *Ex parte* Quayle Action has a two (2)-month shortened statutory period, which can be extended up to four (4) additional months for a total of six (6) months with proper extensions of times and fees. The Practitioner will prepare a response to the *Ex parte* Quayle Action.

13.7.1 eFiling a Response to *Ex Parte* Quayle Action via EFS-Web

The basic steps to efile a Response to *Ex parte* Quayle Action via EFS-Web are as follows:

1. After EFS-Web certification, under "*Main Functions", click "Existing application/patent/proceeding".
2. Select Type of Submission: Click "Document/Fees for an existing application/proceeding".
3. Type in the Application Number and Confirmation Number of the existing patent application. Click "Continue" for the next screen.
4. Files to be Submitted: Browse for the file (in PDF format) and upload it to this filing.
5. Underneath the uploaded document, it states: "Does your PDF file contain multiple documents?" Click "No".
6. The following basic document description is used for filing a Response:

Category	Document Description
Amendment	Response After *Ex parte* Quayle Action

7. Click "Upload & Validate" to make sure that there are no validation errors. If there is a validation error, there will be a prompt on the screen of an error or a warning! If there is an error, the error must be corrected at this point. If there is a warning, click "Continue" to go to the next screen.

For the remainder of the steps, see **Section 6.2.2** to complete the efiling of the response to Quayle Action via EFS-Web.

13.8 Non-Compliant Amendments

If an amendment submitted fails to comply with the requirements of 37 CFR 1.121, the USPTO will notify Applicant by a Notice of Non-Compliant Amendment, Form **PTOL-324**, and identify: (i) which section of the amendment is non-compliant (e.g., the amendments to the claims section); (ii) items that are required for compliance (e.g., a claim listing in compliance with 37 CFR 1.121); and (iii) the reasons why the section of the amendment fails to comply with 37 CFR 1.121 (e.g., the status identifiers are missing).

If the non-compliant amendment would otherwise place the application in condition for allowance, the Examiner may enter the non-compliant amendment and provide an Examiner's Amendment to correct the non-compliance (e.g., an incorrect status identifier).

The Notice of Non-Compliant Amendment usually sets a two (2)-month time period to correct the deficiency unless it accompanies a Non-Final Office Action. Failure to reply to this notice will result in abandonment of the application. Applicant's reply is required to include the corrected section of the amendment.

If the Applicant files an amendment in response to a Final Rejection (or after allowance) and the amendment is found noncompliant, the Applicant is given no new time period. If Applicant wishes to resubmit the non-compliant after final amendment with corrections, the entire corrected amendment must be resubmitted.

13.9 TIMES TO RESPOND TO OFFICE ACTIONS

USPTO Paper	Time to Reply	Max Extension of Time Permitted
Non-Final Office Action	3 months	3 months
After-Final Rejection	3 months	3 months
Restriction Requirement/ Election of Species	2 months	4 months
Ex parte Quayle Action	2 months	4 months
Notice of Non-Compliant Amendment (before Final Rejection)	2 months	None

13.10 Petition for Extension of Time

The Practitioner has a maximum of six (6) months from the mailing date of an Office Action within which to respond. However, the usual practice of the USPTO is to give the Practitioner a SSP of three (3) months in which to respond to the Office Action, without the need for a Petition for Extension of Time. If the response is submitted after the three (3)-month SSP period, the Practitioner must request a Petition for Extension of Time and pay the required fee. Due dates can be extended in one (1)-month increments. As a safety net, if the Practitioner has a Deposit Account, the Response to the Office Action should include the following paragraph authorizing the USPTO to charge all required fees to the Practitioner's USPTO Deposit Account:

> The Commissioner is hereby authorized to charge to Deposit Account No. _____ any fees that may be required by this paper and to credit any overpayment to that Account. If any extension of time is required in connection with the filing of this paper and has not been separately requested, such extension is hereby requested.

13.11 Reporting Amendment

The following template can be used to report an Amendment to the client:

> RE: U.S. Patent Application No. _____
>   Title:
>   Your Ref.:
>   Our Ref.:
>
> Dear _____:
>
> Enclosed is a copy of an Amendment which was filed in the U.S. Patent and Trademark Office on _____.
>
> As soon as we receive word from the U.S. Patent and Trademark Office, we will let you know.

CHAPTER 14
Restriction Requirements

● ● ●

14.1 WHAT IS A RESTRICTION REQUIREMENT?

THE FIRST SUBSTANTIAL STEP THE Examiner takes is to look at the claims and determine if there are one or more "separate and distinct" inventions claimed. If the Examiner determines that more than one separate and distinct invention is claimed, he/she will issue a Restriction Requirement.

The Restriction Requirement requires an Applicant to elect claims to prosecute. The non-elected claims are "withdrawn" from consideration in the present application and are not examined. However, the claims may be pursued later in a DIV application. The requirement may be traversed. Traverse means that the Practitioner submits arguments as to why the Restriction Requirement is improper.

Effective December 18, 2013, a response to Restriction Requirement is due within two (2) months of mailing date of the Restriction Requirement. A petition requesting up to four (4) months extensions of time from the due date of the Restriction Requirement can be filed. If no response is timely filed, with or without an extension of time, the application will become abandoned.

When the response to the Restriction Requirement has been finalized, it must be checked thoroughly for accuracy including application number, filing date, docket number, inventor information, etc.

NOTE: Restriction Requirements that have been made final can be petitioned to the Tech Center Director. The petition may be deferred until after-final rejection or allowance of claims to the invention elected, but must be filed no later than the filing date of the notice of appeal. A Restriction Requirement cannot be appealed.

14.1.1 EFILING A RESPONSE TO RESTRICTION REQUIREMENT VIA EFS-WEB

The basic steps to efile a Response to Restriction Requirement via EFS-Web are as follows:

1. After EFS-Web certification, under "*Main Functions", click "Existing application/patent/proceeding".
2. Select Type of Submission: Click "Document/Fees for an existing application/proceeding".
3. Type in the Application Number and Confirmation Number of the existing patent application. Click "Continue" for the next screen.
4. Files to be Submitted: Browse for the file (in PDF format) and upload it to this filing.
5. Underneath the uploaded document, it states: "Does your PDF file contain multiple documents?" Click "No".
6. The following basic document description is used for filing a Response to Restriction Requirement:

Category	Document Description
Amendment	Response to Election / Restriction Filed

7. Click "Upload & Validate" to make sure that there are no validation errors. If there is a validation error, there will be a prompt on the screen of an error or a warning! If there is an error, the error must be corrected at this point. If there is a warning, click "Continue" to go to the next screen.

For the remainder of the steps, see **Section 6.2.2** to complete the efiling of the Response to Restriction Requirement via EFS-Web.

14.2 WHAT IS AN ELECTION OF SPECIES?

An election of species is similar to a Restriction Requirement, in that the Practitioner will have to choose one claim or group of claims to be examined. The difference is that in an election of species, the Examiner believes that it is possible that the claims in the application would cover more than one variation ("species") of a single invention. If a "generic" claim (one which covers more than one species) is allowed as a result of the examination process, then other non-elected species which would be covered by that generic claim would also be allowed.

If there are no claims which are "generic", it will be necessary to file a DIV application covering the non-elected species, just as in the restriction requirement.

14.2.1 EFILING A RESPONSE TO ELECTION OF SPECIES VIA EFS-WEB
The basic steps to efile a Response to Election of Species via EFS-Web are as follows:

1. After EFS-Web certification, under "*Main Functions", click "Existing application/patent/proceeding".
2. Select Type of Submission: Click "Document/Fees for an existing application/proceeding".
3. Type in the Application Number and Confirmation Number of the existing patent application. Click "Continue" for the next screen.
4. Files to be Submitted: Browse for the file (in PDF format) and upload it to this filing.
5. Underneath the uploaded document, it states: "Does your PDF file contain multiple documents?" Click "No".
6. The following basic document descriptions are used for filing a Response to Election of Species:

Category	Document Description
Amendment	Response to Election / Restriction Filed

7. Click "Upload & Validate" to make sure that there are no validation errors. If there is a validation error, there will be a prompt on the screen of an error or a warning! If there is an error, the error must be corrected at this point. If there is a warning, click "Continue" to go to the next screen.

For the remainder of the steps, see **Section 6.2.2** to complete the efiling of the Response to the Election of Species via EFS-Web.

14.3 Petition for Extension of Time

The Practitioner has a maximum of six (6) months from the mailing date of an Office Action (Election of Species) within which to respond. However, the usual practice is to give the Practitioner a SSP of two (2) months in which to respond to the Election of Species, without the need for a Petition for Extension of Time. If the response is submitted after the two (2)-month SSP period, then the Practitioner must request a Petition for Extension of Time and pay the required fee. Due dates can be extended in one (1)-month increments. As a safety net, if the Practitioner has a Deposit Account, the response to the Election of Species should include the following paragraph authorizing the USPTO to charge all required fees to the Practitioner's USPTO Deposit Account:

The Commissioner is hereby authorized to charge to Deposit Account No. _____ any fees that may be required by this paper and to credit any overpayment to that Account. If any extension of time is required in connection with the filing of this paper and has not been separately requested, such extension is hereby requested.

14.4 Reporting Response to Restriction Requirement and/or Election of Species

The following template can be used to report a response to Restriction Requirement and/or Election of Species to the client:

RE: U.S. Patent Application No. _____
         Title:
         Your Ref.:
         Our Ref.:

Dear _____:

Enclosed is a copy of a Response to Restriction Requirement (or Election of Species) which was filed in the U.S. Patent and Trademark Office on _____.

As soon as we receive word from the U.S. Patent and Trademark Office, we will let you know.

CHAPTER 15

Examiner Interviews

● ● ●

15.1 WHAT ARE EXAMINER INTERVIEWS?

AN EXAMINER INTERVIEW IS A discussion between the Examiner and the Practitioner to enable the Practitioner and the Examiner to discuss and resolve issues in the prosecution of a patent application. The interview is often initiated by the Practitioner, but it can be initiated by the Examiner. Interviews can be by telephone, video conference, email, or in-person at the UPSTO. Interviews are an effective tool to advance the prosecution of an application. The USPTO encourages Examiners to take a proactive approach to examination by reaching out in order to shorten prosecution.

Properly conducted, an interview can bridge the gap between an Examiner and an Applicant with regard to the substantive matters at issue in an application. Interviews often help to advance prosecution and identify patentable subject matter. Positions presented during an interview should be advanced with decorum and courtesy.

All discussions between the Applicant and the Examiner regarding the merits of a pending application should be made of record and in writing. This includes any and all records or communications received in connection with the interview, whether the interview was conducted in-person or through a telephone conversation, video conference, and email, or other electronic message system. Where an electronic record is created as part of the interview, e.g., a series of electronic messages, a copy of the electronic record is to be made of record in the application. Where an electronic record is not created, a summary of the interview must be made of record and in writing.

15.2 USPTO AIR

The USPTO Automated Interview Request ("AIR") Form is a new web-based tool that allows Applicants to schedule an interview with an Examiner for his/her pending patent application. The form is located at *www.uspto.gov/patent/uspto-automated-interview-request-air-form.html*. After the form is submitted, an Examiner will email the requestor to confirm the request within two (2) business days. Go to *www.uspto.gov/interviewpractice* to watch the USPTO's Interview Practice short video for a brief introduction to AIR and other available USPTO interview resources. AIR is a convenient online form for submitting requests for interviews.

15.3 Video Conferencing

Video conferencing with an Examiner gives the Applicant the ability to have face-to-face meetings, no matter the location of the Examiner or Applicant. See Video Conferencing and Collaboration at *www.uspto.gov/about-us/contact-us/video-conferencing-and-collaboration*, for instructions on how to join a USPTO-hosted video conference, and information and links on how to use WebEx collaboration tools, including audio/video conferencing and file sharing.

15.4 Technology Center Interview Specialist

Each Technology Center ("TC") has an Interview Specialist. This person is an expert on interview practice and policy and is available to assist in interviews, including facilitating and assisting with technical issues that may arise (e.g., WebEx problems, public interview room setup).

15.5 Scheduling and Conducting an Interview

An interview should normally be arranged in advance, either by letter, facsimile, electronic mail, or telephone call, in order to insure that the Primary Examiner and/or the Examiner in charge of the application will be available. When Applicant is initiating a request for an interview, an **Applicant Initiated Interview Request Form (PTOL-413A)** at *www.uspto.gov/sites/default/files/documents/PTOL413A.pdf* should be submitted to the Examiner prior to the interview in order to permit the Examiner to prepare in advance for the interview and to focus on the issues to be discussed. This form should identify the participants of the interview, the proposed date of the interview, whether the interview will be personal, telephonic, instant message system or video conference, and a brief description of the issues to be discussed.

With the Practitioner's guidance and/or instructions, the Paralegal can contact the Examiner on how he/she wants to receive the agenda when setting up the interview. The interview agenda can be e-mailed to the Examiner, faxed to the Examiner's direct number, or uploaded to PAIR.

> **Note:** An **Authorization for Internet Communications in a Patent Application or Request to Withdraw Authorization for Internet Communications (PTO/SB/43)** form at *www.uspto.gov/sites/default/files/documents/sb0439.pdf* must be submitted at the USPTO in order to use video conferencing, instant messaging, or e-mail with the Examiner.

15.6 Examiner Preparation for Interviews

Before the interview, for efficiency and where appropriate, the Examiner should complete a form **PTOL-413B**, including identifying the rejections, claims and prior art documents to be discussed and optionally the interview participants, date, and type of interview, and bring a copy of this form to the interview.

CHAPTER 16
Request for Continued Examinations

● ● ●

16.1 WHAT IS A REQUEST FOR CONTINUED EXAMINATION?

ONCE PROSECUTION IN AN APPLICATION is closed, an Applicant may request continued examination of the application by filing a Request for Continued Examination, commonly known as an RCE.

An RCE is used commonly in the following situations:

- Continue prosecution after-final rejection.
- Entry of an IDS after prosecution is closed.

For purposes of filing an RCE, prosecution is closed when:

- Application is under appeal.
- Last Office Action is a Final Rejection.
- Notice of Allowance has been issued.
- Action that otherwise closes prosecution in the application.

An RCE must be accompanied by a submission and a fee.

The submission can include:

- Information Disclosure Statement.
- An Amendment to an outstanding Final Rejection that the Examiner has not considered previously.
- Arguments in the Appeal Brief or Reply Brief previously filed.
- An Affidavit(s) or Declaration(s).

There is no limit to the number of RCEs that can be filed for the same application, but the fee (regular undiscounted or small entity) for a second or subsequent RCE significantly increases.

An RCE is not a new application. It keeps the same application number and filing date, and uses the same declaration.

Fees (regular undiscounted or small entity) for a Petition for Extension of Time need to be paid if three (3) months from the mailing date of the Office Action has past the initial deadline. After the initial deadline, a Petition for Extension of Time can be filed for up to three (3) months in response to the Office Action, i.e., RCE.

An RCE cannot be requested in the following types of applications:

* Provisional applications
* Utility or plant applications filed before June 8, 1995
* International applications filed before June 8, 1995
* Design patent applications
* Patent under Reexaminations

The USPTO has made it available to use a fillable RCE form via EFS-Web. This form can only be submitted electronically. The form is found at *www.uspto.gov/ebc/portal/efs/sb0030e_fill.pdf* with instructions at *www.uspto.gov/ebc/portal/efs/sb0030e_fill.doc* to use this form. If this form is used, make sure that the document is saved as a PDF file for filing via EFS-Web.

16.1.1 eFiling an RCE via EFS Web

The basic steps to efile an RCE via EFS-Web are as follows:

1. After EFS-Web certification, under "*Main Functions", click "Existing application/ patent/proceeding".
2. Click "Documents/Fees for an existing application/proceeding".
3. Type in the Application Number and Confirmation Number of the existing patent application. Click "Continue" for the next screen.
4. Files to be Submitted: Browse for the file (in PDF format) and upload it to this filing.
5. Underneath the uploaded document, it states: "Does your PDF file contain multiple documents?" Click "Yes".
6. The following basic document descriptions are used for filing the RCE, Amendment and IDS:

Category	Document Description
Continued Prosecution	Request for Continued Examination (RCE) (Form PTO/SB/30EFS)

Continued Prosecution	Amendment Submitted/Entered with Filing of CPA/RCE
Amendment	Specification (Amendments to the Specification)
Amendment	Claims (Amendments to the Claims)
Amendment	Applicant Arguments/Remarks Made in an Amendment (Amendments to the Drawings)
Amendment	Applicant Arguments/Remarks Made in an Amendment (Remarks)
Amendment	Abstract
Amendment	Drawings – only black and white line drawings

If efiling an Information Disclosure Statement, use the following document descriptions:

Category	Document Description
IDS/References	Transmittal Letter
IDS/References	Information Disclosure Statement (IDS) Form (SB08)
IDS/References	Foreign Reference
IDS/References	Non-Patent Literature

7. Click "Upload & Validate" to make sure that there are no validation errors. If there is a validation error, there will be a prompt on the screen of an error or a warning! If there is an error, the error must be corrected at this point. If there is a warning, click "Continue" to go to the next screen.

For the remainder of the steps, see **Section 6.2.2** to complete the efiling of the RCE, Amendment and IDS via EFS-Web.

16.2 PETITION FOR EXTENSION OF TIME
The Practitioner has a maximum of six (6) months from the mailing date of an Office Action within which to respond. However, the usual practice of the USPTO is to give the Practitioner a SSP of three (3) months in which to respond to the Office Action, without the need for a Petition for Extension of Time.

If the response is submitted after the three (3)-month SSP period, then the Practitioner must request a Petition for Extension of Time and pay the required fee. Due dates can be extended in one (1)-month increments. As a safety net, if the Practitioner has a Deposit Account, Practitioner should insert the following paragraph in the Amendment Accompanying RCE authorizing that the USPTO to charge all required fees to the Practitioner's Deposit Account:

> The Commissioner is hereby authorized to charge to Deposit Account No._____ any fees that may be required by this paper and to credit any overpayment to that Account. If any extension of time is required in connection with the filing of this paper and has not been separately requested, such extension is hereby requested.

16.3 REPORTING RCE, AMENDMENT AND IDS

The following template can be used to report an RCE, Amendment and IDS to the client:

RE: U.S. Patent Application No. _____
        Title:
        Your Ref.:
        Our Ref.:

Dear _____:

Enclosed are copies of a Request for Continued Examination, an Amendment Accompanying Request for Continued Examination and an Information Disclosure Statement which were filed in the U.S. Patent and Trademark Office on _____.

As soon as we receive word from the U.S. Patent and Trademark Office, we will let you know.

CHAPTER 17
Allowance of Patent Applications

• • •

17.1 WHAT IS A NOTICE OF ALLOWANCE?

ONCE ALL THE FORMALITIES HAVE been met and there are no objections or rejections to the patent application, the Examiner will issue a Notice of Allowance and Fee(s) Due ("NOA"), Form **PTOL-85**.

The patent application file must be checked thoroughly to ensure that no information is incorrect or missing. If there is incorrect or missing information, notify the USPTO immediately to complete the file. The NOA checklist can be found in **Appendix A.15**. Also, it is very important to check that all references (or prior art) have been cited and acknowledged by the Examiner before paying the issue fee. If some of the references have not been acknowledged by the Examiner, send a Request for Acknowledgement for Information Disclosure Statement to the Examiner immediately.

Check with the Practitioner to determine if a Divisional, Continuation, or Continuation-In-Part Application must be filed. This is very important if the Divisional, Continuation, or Continuation-in-Part is not filed by the issued date of the patent, a priority date will be lost. If so, prepare the application as instructed by the Practitioner. This application must be filed before the parent patent issues so that the parent patent can be co-pending.

The issue fee must be paid within three (3) months from the mailing date of the NOA. There are no extensions and no exceptions. If the fee is not paid on time, the application is abandoned.

17.2 ISSUE FEE PAYMENT

After checking the NOA to make sure that all requirements have been met and the client has authorized payment of the issue fee, complete fillable form of the **Part B - Fee(s) Transmittal Form (PTOL-85B)** at *www.uspto.gov/forms/ptol85b.pdf* or complete the form received from the USPTO. Double check to make sure that the information on the form is correct, especially the Assignee information. The USPTO prints information from the Transmittal Form in the issued patent. After checking and verifying the data on the Transmittal Form, forward the Transmittal Form to the

Practitioner for review and signature. If, for some reason, the Assignee information was not submitted at the time the issue fee was paid, the Practitioner must wait until after the patent issues and file a Request for Certificate of Correction Under 37 CFR 3.81(b) and **Certificate of Correction (PTO/SB/44)** form at *www.uspto.gov/forms/sb0044.pdf*, provided that the assignment was previously recorded at the UPSTO before payment of the issue fee.

17.2.1 eFILING AN ISSUE FEE TRANSMITTAL VIA EFS-WEB
The basic steps to efile an Issue Fee Transmittal via EFS-Web are as follows:

1. After EFS-Web certification, under "*Main Functions", click "Existing application/patent/proceeding".
2. Select Type of Submission: Click "Document/Fees for an existing application/proceeding".
3. Type in the Application Number and Confirmation Number of the existing patent application. Click "Continue".
4. On the next screen, browse for the signed Issue Fee Transmittal (in PDF format) and upload it to this filing.
5. Underneath the uploaded document, it states: "Does your PDF file contain multiple documents?" Click "Yes" or "No" (depending if multiple documents are submitted).
6. The following basic document descriptions are used for filing an Issue Fee Payment, along with the Fee Address Indication Form (if needed):

Category	Document Description
General Transmittal	Issue Fee Payment (PTO-85B)
Change Requests	Maintenance Fee Address Change

7. Click "Upload & Validate" to make sure that there are no validation errors. If there is a validation error, there will be a prompt on the screen of an error or a warning! If there is an error, the error must be corrected at this point. If there is a warning, click "Continue" to go to the next screen.
8. If there are no validation errors, click "Continue".
9. The next page is "Calculate Fees". Check the box "Post Allowance & Post Issuance Fees", and select the appropriate fee to pay the issue fee and click "Calculate", then click "Continue".
10. On the next screen, check to make sure that all of the information is correct before clicking "Submit". Also, at this point, the submission can be saved by clicking "Save for Later Submission". The submission can be saved for up to 7 calendar days.
11. After clicking "Submit", there will be a prompt to either pay fees due by USPTO Deposit Account, Charge Credit Card, or Electronic Funds Transfer. Follow the screen instructions to pay the fees.

If, for some reason, EFS-Web is down, there are two options available for submission of the completed and signed Transmittal Form. Sign and date the Certificate of Mailing or Transmission (on the Form) and mail to:

Mail Stop ISSUE FEE
Commissioner for Patents
P.O. Box 1450
Alexandria, VA 22313-1450

or fax the Form to:

(571) 273-2885

17.3 DOCKETING AFTER PAYMENT OF ISSUE FEE

Once the issue fee has been paid, docket a four (4)-month status check to ensure that the issued patent has been received in your office. If the issued patent has not been received within four (4) months, call the publishing division of the USPTO to check on the status of the patent.

17.4 AMENDMENTS AFTER NOTICE OF ALLOWANCE

Any Amendment filed before the payment of the issue fee may be entered at the discretion of the Examiner, without withdrawing the application from issue. However, it is no longer possible to file any amendments after payment of the issue fee. If the Practitioner must file an Amendment and/or IDS after payment of the issue fee, a Petition to Withdraw the Application from Issue must be submitted, and an RCE must be filed.

17.5 ISSUE NOTIFICATION

After the issue fee has been paid and the application goes through the publication process, just prior to publication, an Issue Notification from the USPTO will be sent to the correspondence address providing the patent number and issue date.

NOTE: It is important to file any Divisional, Continuation, or Continuation-In-Part Applications before the issued date of the patent, so that the new application will be copending with the parent patent and a priority date is not lost.

CHAPTER 18

Appeal of Examiner's Rejection

● ● ●

18.1 NOTICE OF APPEAL

IF AN APPLICANT FOR A patent is dissatisfied with the Primary Examiner's decision in the second rejection of the claims, he/she may appeal to the Patent Trial and Appeal Board ("PTAB") for review of the Examiner's rejection by filing a Notice of Appeal and submitting the required fee. The Applicant now becomes the Appellant.

An extension of time petition may also be required also to be filed with the Notice of Appeal on or before the end of the six (6)-month statutory period for response set forth in the Office Action from which an appeal is taken.

The use of a separate letter containing the Notice of Appeal is strongly recommended. Use **Notice of Appeal from the Examiner to the Patent Trial and Appeal Board (PTO/AIA/31)** form at *www.uspto. gov/forms/aia0031.pdf* for filing a Notice of Appeal. The Appeal Brief must be filed and accompanied by the fees within two (2) months from the date of filing the Notice of Appeal, and has up to five (5) months extensions of time available.

18.1.1 DEFECTIVE NOTICE OF APPEAL

If a Notice of Appeal is defective, the USPTO will notify the Practitioner with a Notice of Defective Notice of Appeal. A Notice of Appeal is not a proper reply to the last Office Action if none of the claims in the application has been twice rejected. A Notice of Appeal can be defective if it was not timely filed within the time period set forth in the last Office Action, or the Notice of Appeal fee was not timely filed. The Practitioner must be notified immediately of the Notice of Defective Notice of Appeal.

18.1.2 eFILING A NOTICE OF APPEAL VIA EFS-WEB

The basic steps to efile a Notice of Appeal via EFS-Web are as follows:

1. After EFS-Web certification, under "*Main Functions", click "Existing application/patent/ proceeding".
2. Select Type of Submission: Click "Document/Fees for an existing application/proceeding".
3. Type in the Application Number and Confirmation Number of the existing patent application. Click "Continue" for the next screen.
4. Files to be Submitted: Browse for the file (in PDF format) and upload it to this filing.
5. Underneath the uploaded document, it states: "Does your PDF file contain multiple documents?" Click "No".
6. The following basic document description is used for filing a Notice of Appeal:

<u>Category</u>   <u>Document Description</u>

BPAI   Notice of Appeal Filed

7. Click "Upload & Validate" to make sure that there are no validation errors. If there is a validation error, there will be a prompt on the screen of an error or a warning! If there is an error, the error must be corrected at this point. If there is a warning, click "Continue" to go to the next screen.

For the remainder of the steps, see **Section 6.2.2** to complete the efiling of the Notice of Appeal via EFS-Web.

18.2 Appeal Brief

An Appeal Brief must be filed within two (2) months of the filing date of the Notice of Appeal, but five (5)-month extensions of time are available for a fee. Note that once the Notice of Appeal is filed, the time period for reply given in the last Office Action is tolled and is no longer relevant for the time period for filing an Appeal.

If an Appeal Brief is not filed within the allowed period, an Appeal stands dismissed, and the application will become abandoned unless the application contains allowed claims.

There is no PTO form for the Appeal Brief. It must be prepared by the Practitioner and have the following headings:

1. Real party in interest;
2. Related appeals and interferences;
3. Status of Claims;
4. Status of Amendments;

5. Summary of claimed subject matter;
6. Grounds of rejection to be reviewed on appeal;
7. Argument;
8. Claims appendix;
9. Evidence appendix; and
10. Related proceedings appendix.

The Appeal Brief must be signed by the Practitioner and accompanied by the appropriate fee, including any extension of time fees. If filed by first class mail, facsimile, or hand-delivery/courier, the Appeal Brief must be filed in triplicate. If filing the Appeal Brief electronically, triplicate copies are not required.

When the Appeal Brief reaches the USPTO, it will initially go to the Examiner. Upon considering the Brief, the Examiner will have the opportunity to change his/her mind, and reopen prosecution. If this is done, the Practitioner will get another opportunity to answer the last Office Action and submit amendments as a matter of right.

If the Examiner does not reopen prosecution, then he/she will determine if the Appeal Brief complies with all the required formalities. If the Appeal Brief does not comply with all of the formalities, the Examiner will issue a Notice of Non-Compliant Appeal Brief, and the Practitioner will be given thirty (30) days from the mailing date of the Notice to supply an amended Appeal Brief that complies with all the required rules and fees. The Notice of Non-Compliant Appeal Brief must be given to the Practitioner immediately after receipt. If the Practitioner does not file an Amended Brief correcting all the defects within the time period set in the Notice, the Appeal will stand dismissed.

If the Appeal Brief is complete, then the Examiner will do one of the following:

* File an Examiner's Answer to the Appeal Brief; or
* Forward the application to the PTAB.

18.2.1 eFiling an Appeal Brief via EFS-Web
The basic steps to efile an Appeal Brief via EFS-Web are as follows:

1. After EFS-Web certification, under "*Main Functions", click "Existing application/patent/proceeding".
2. Select Type of Submission: Click "Document/Fees for an existing application/proceeding".
3. Type in the Application Number and Confirmation Number of the existing patent application. Click "Continue" for the next screen.

4. Files to be Submitted: Browse for the file (in PDF format) and upload it to this filing.
5. Underneath the uploaded document, it states: "Does your PDF file contain multiple documents?" Click "No".
6. The following basic document description is used for filing an Appeal Brief:

Category	Document Description
BPAI	Appeal Brief Filed

7. Click "Upload & Validate" to make sure that there are no validation errors. If there is a validation error, there will be a prompt on the screen of an error or a warning! If there is an error, the error must be corrected at this point. If there is a warning, click "Continue" to go to the next screen.

For the remainder of the steps, see **Section 6.2.2** to complete the efiling of the Appeal Brief via EFS-Web.

18.3 EXAMINER'S ANSWER

An Examiner's Answer is a statement by the Examiner responding to the arguments in the Appeal Brief. It may be sent to the Practitioner within two (2) months after receipt of the Appeal Brief. Docket two (2) months from the date of mailing of the Examiner's Answer to file a Reply Brief.

18.4 REPLY BRIEF

A Reply Brief is a response to the Examiner's Answer. The Practitioner is given two (2) months from the date of the Examiner's Answer in which to file the Reply Brief. It is optional for the Practitioner to file a Reply Brief. The Reply Brief is not required to be filed. The time period for filing the Reply Brief is extendible, but only "for cause". The petition to extend the time period must be filed before the due date.

The Reply Brief must be signed by the Practitioner and accompanied by the appropriate fee, including any extension of time fees. If filed by first class mail, facsimile, or hand-delivery (courier), the Reply Brief must be filed in triplicate. If the Reply Brief is filed electronically, triplicate copies are not required.

18.4.1 eFILING A REPLY BRIEF VIA EFS-WEB

The basic steps to efile a Reply Brief via EFS-Web are as follows:

1. After EFS-Web certification, under "*Main Functions", click "Existing application/patent/proceeding".
2. Select Type of Submission: Click "Document/Fees for an existing application/proceeding".
3. Type in the Application Number and Confirmation Number of the existing patent application. Click "Continue" for the next screen.
4. Files to be Submitted: Browse for the file (in PDF format) and upload it to this filing.
5. Underneath the uploaded document, it states: "Does your PDF file contain multiple documents?" Click "No".
6. The following basic document description is used for filing a Reply Brief:

Category	Document Description
BPAI	Reply Brief Filed

7. Click "Upload & Validate" to make sure that there are no validation errors. If there is a validation error, there will be a prompt on the screen of an error or a warning! If there is an error, the error must be corrected at this point. If there is a warning, click "Continue" to go to the next screen.

For the remainder of the steps, see **Section 6.2.2** to complete the efiling of the Reply Brief via EFS-Web.

18.5 Request for Oral Hearing

The Practitioner may request an Oral Hearing. The request must be made within two (2) months from the date of the Examiner's Answer, no extensions of time are available.

To request an Oral Hearing, the Practitioner must file a separate paper entitled "Request for Oral Hearing" specifically requesting for such a hearing. The request must be accompanied by the appropriate fee. Use **Form PTO/AIA/32** at *www.uspto.gov/forms/aia0032.pdf* for filing a Request for Oral Hearing.

A date for the oral hearing will be set by the PTAB, and a notice for the hearing will be given to the Practitioner. At the Oral Hearing, arguments are presented by the Practitioner on behalf of the Applicant. The Primary Examiner can also request to attend and present arguments. Arguments are usually limited to about twenty (20) minutes for the Practitioner and fifteen (15) minutes for the Primary Examiner. The Practitioner speaks first and may reserve time for rebuttal. Generally, the Practitioner can only present arguments previously presented in the written record and that have been previously entered and considered by the Primary Examiner. Likewise, the Primary Examiner may only rely on argument and evidence already presented and relied upon.

Any Request for Oral Hearing may be rejected by the PTAB if the PTAB decides that a hearing is not necessary.

The Request for Oral Hearing can be filed by hand-delivery/courier, Priority Mail Express, first class mail, facsimile or electronically.

If no Request for Oral Hearing is requested, the appeal will be decided by the PTAB on the written record in the file.

18.5.1 eFILING A REQUEST FOR ORAL HEARING VIA EFS-WEB
The basic steps to efile a Request for Oral Hearing via EFS-Web are as follows:

1. After EFS-Web certification, under "*Main Functions", click "Existing application/patent/proceeding".
2. Select Type of Submission: Click "Document/Fees for an existing application/proceeding".
3. Type in the Application Number and Confirmation Number of the existing patent application. Click "Continue" for the next screen.
4. Files to be Submitted: Browse for the file (in PDF format) and upload it to this filing.
5. Underneath the uploaded document, it states: "Does your PDF file contain multiple documents?" Click "No".
6. The following basic document description is used for filing a Request for Oral Hearing:

Category	Document Description
BPAI	Request for Oral Hearing

7. Click "Upload & Validate" to make sure that there are no validation errors. If there is a validation error, there will be a prompt on the screen of an error or a warning! If there is an error, the error must be corrected at this point. If there is a warning, click "Continue" to go to the next screen.

For the remainder of the steps, see *Section 6.2.2* to complete the efiling of the Request for Oral Hearing via EFS-Web.

18.6 SUPPLEMENTAL EXAMINER'S ANSWER

The Examiner does respond to the Practitioner's Reply Brief, unless specifically directed by the PTAB to submit a Supplemental Answer. The Supplemental Examiner's Answer is mailed to the Practitioner. When received, the Supplemental Examiner's Answer must be brought to the attention of the Practitioner, who can respond by filing a Supplemental Reply Brief.

18.7 BOARD OF PATENT TRIAL AND APPEAL

The PTAB may affirm or reverse any decision of the Examiner, in whole or in part, or may remand the application to the Examiner for further consideration with its suggestions. Upon remand, the Examiner may file a Supplemental Examiner's Answer, and the Practitioner may file a Reply Brief or reopen prosecution. The PTAB may also include new grounds for rejection. The PTAB's decision may include an explicit statement that claims will be allowable if certain amendments are made. In this event, the Practitioner is given the opportunity to amend the claims as directed by the PTAB. If so available, the Examiner is required to allow those claims.

If the PTAB presents new grounds for rejection, its decision must be given to the Practitioner immediately. The Practitioner has two (2) months from the date of the PTAB's decision to respond in order to avoid dismissal of the Appeals proceeding and abandonment of the patent application.

18.8 REQUEST FOR PRE-APPEAL BRIEF CONFERENCE

Under certain circumstances, the Practitioner may request a pre-appeal conference. If the request is filed, a panel of examiners (including the Examiner of Record) will consider the merits of the appeal and will issue a written decision as to the status of the application. The Request for a Pre-Appeal Brief Conference must be filed with the Notice of Appeal. **Use Pre-Pre-Appeal Brief Request for Review (PTO/AIA/33)** at *www.uspto.gov/forms/aia0033.pdf* for filing the Pre-Appeal Brief Request for Review form. The request is limited to five (5) pages.

18.9 TIMES TO RESPOND AFTER FILING A NOTICE OF APPEAL

Paper	Response Paper	Time to Reply	Max Extension of Time Period
Office Action – claims rejected twice	Notice of Appeal	3 months	3 months
Notice of Appeal	Appeal Brief	2 months from Notice of Appeal filed	5 months
Examiner's Answer	Reply Brief	2 months	None
Examiner's Answer	Request for Oral Hearing	2 months	None
Supplemental Examiner's Answer	Supplemental Reply Brief	2 months	None

CHAPTER 19

Issued Patents

• • •

19.1 UTILITY LETTERS PATENT

AFTER AN APPLICATION HAS BEEN issued as a patent, an original Utility Letters Patent will be sent to the Practitioner of record. Once it is received, thoroughly check the accuracy of the data on the first page of the patent and check the claims to make sure that there are no typographical printing errors. If typographical or printing errors are found, a Certificate of Correction should be prepared immediately for the Practitioner's signature (see **Section 19.3**).

Once a Utility Letters Patent issues, maintenance fees are required to be paid at 3 ½, 7 ½, and 11 ½ years from the date of issuance in order to keep the patent in force.

19.2 DESIGN LETTERS PATENT

After a design application has been issued as a patent, the original Design Letters Patent will be sent to the Practitioner of record. Once the original Design Letters Patent has been received, check the accuracy of the data on the inside first page of the patent and the claims to make sure that there are no typographical errors. If typographical errors are found, prepare a Certificate of Correction immediately to be signed by the Practitioner and filed in the USPTO (see *Section 19.3*).

The term of the design patent is fourteen (14) years for applications filed prior to May 13, 2015. For applications filed on or after May 13, 2015, in accordance with the Hague Agreement, the design patent term is fifteen (15) years. Design patents cannot be renewed. Also, there is no maintenance fees associated with design patents.

19.3 CERTIFICATE OF CORRECTION

Once the patent is granted, the USPTO no longer has jurisdiction over the patent. However, if there is an error in the patent due to an error by the USPTO, a Certificate of Correction may be filed and the USPTO may issue, without a fee, a certificate correcting the error. The errors subject to correction are mostly printing errors. Some minor errors of a typographical nature made by the Practitioner may also be corrected by a Certificate of Correction, but a fee is required. Consult with the Practitioner to determine if Certificate of Correction is permitted or appropriate in these circumstances.

In order to file a Certificate of Correction, use the fillable **Form (PTO/SB/44)** at *www.uspto.gov/forms/sb0044.pdf*, also referred to as Form **PTO-1050**.

19.4 REISSUE
When the patent is defective with respect to non-USPTO error(s) made during prosecution, the Patentee may apply for a reissue patent to bring the patent within the jurisdiction of the USPTO.

> NOTE: In order to broaden claims in a patent, the reissue application must be filed within two (2) years after the issued date of the patent.

19.5 REEXAMINATION
Any person may file a request for reexamination of a patent. There is a required fee to institute reexamination proceeding. However, this proceeding is limited to determine patentability of claims based on patents and printed publications only. At the conclusion of the reexamination proceedings, a certificate setting forth the results of the reexamination proceeding is issued.

19.6 MAINTENANCE FEES
All utility patents that issue from applications filed on and after December 12, 1980, are subject to the payment of maintenance fees, which must be paid to maintain the patent in force. The fees are due at 3 ½, 7 ½, and 11 ½ years from the date the patent is granted and can be paid without a surcharge during the "window-period" which is the six (6)-month period preceding each due date (see Maintenance Fee Schedule below).

MAINTENANCE FEE SCHEDULE

Maintenance Fee	First Window (beginning due date)	Due Date (from the issued date of patent)	Last Window (final due date with surcharge fee)
1st	3 years	3 ½ years	4 years
2nd	7 years	7 ½ years	8 years
3rd	11 years	11 ½ years	12 years

When submitting maintenance fee and any necessary surcharge, the patent number, and the application number of the U.S. application for the patent must be included with the submission. If the payment includes identification only of the patent number, the USPTO may not accept the payment and return the payment to the sender.

Failure to timely pay the current maintenance fee will result in expiration of the patent. A six (6)-month grace period is provided when the maintenance fee may be paid with a surcharge. The grace period is the six (6)-month period immediately following the due date. The USPTO does not mail notices to patent owners that maintenance fees are due.

19.6.1 Fee Payment Options
Patent maintenance fees can be paid by using one of the following four options:

1. **Pay online**: Visit the Patent Maintenance Fees Storefront at *https://fees.uspto.gov/MaintenanceFees* and pay immediately with a credit/debit card, USPTO Deposit Account, or EFT. Do not submit payment via EFS-Web.
2. **Pay by wire**: See the instructions for sending a wire payment (*www.uspto.gov/learning-and-resources/fees-and-payment/fees-payments-faqs#type-wire-payments*) to the UPSTO.
3. **Pay by fax**: Complete the **Maintenance Fee Transmittal Form (PTO/SB/45)** at *www.uspto.gov/sites/default/files/forms/sb0045.pdf* and **Credit Card Payment Form (PTO-2038)** at *www.uspto.gov/sites/default/files/documents/PTO-2038.pdf* (if paying with a credit/debit card), and fax to (571) 273-6500.
4. **Pay by mail:** Complete the **Maintenance Fee Transmittal Form (PTO/SB/45)** at *www.uspto.gov/sites/default/files/forms/sb0045.pdf* and **Credit Card Payment Form (PTO-2038)** at *www.uspto.gov/sites/default/files/documents/PTO-2038.pdf* (if paying with a credit card/debit card). If using a check or money order, it should be made payable to the "Director of the USPTO", and mail to:

> Director of the U.S. Patent and Trademark Office
> Attn: Maintenance Fees
> 2051 Jamieson Avenue, Suite 300
> Alexandria, VA 22314

19.6.2 Update the Entity Status or Fee Address
Private PAIR users may submit entity status or address change requests online. Such submissions are processed immediately. The application must be associated to the Practitioner's Customer Number, or the attorney or agent of record must have been given Power of Attorney.

Go to **Change Entity Status Quick Start Guide** at *www.uspto.gov/sites/default/files/documents/QSG-Entity%20Status-Final.pdf* for more information.

Once the entity status change has been made via Private PAIR, allow five-seven (5-7) business days for the request to be processed before attempting to pay the maintenance fee. If paying by mail, the change requests should be included with the maintenance fee payments. All change requests must be signed by a recognized party.

The correspondence address for the application that issued as the patent will be regarded as the maintenance fee address. The maintenance fee address can be changed by submitting the **Fee Address" Indication Form (PTO/SB/47)** at *www.uspto.gov/forms/sb0047.pdf*. Submission of this form is necessary to have correspondence related solely to maintenance fees mailed to a different address other than the correspondence address for the application. If there is no Customer Number, a **Request for Customer Number (PTO/SB/125)** form at *www.uspto.gov/sites/default/files/web/forms/sb0125.pdf* must be completed first and a Customer Number obtained before filing the "Fee Address Indication Form". To change only the correspondence address after a patent is issued, submit **a Change of Correspondence Address (Patent) (PTO/SB/123)** form at *www.uspto.gov/sites/default/files/forms/aia0123.pdf*. The maintenance fee address will automatically be updated with the change in the correspondence address.

19.6.3 CHECK THE CURRENT STATUS OF A PATENT
Bibliographic data, payment dates, and the fee amounts due for a specific patent are available through the Financial Manager at *https://fees.uspto.gov/FinancialManager*.

19.6.4 REINSTATE AN EXPIRED PATENT
If a maintenance fee has not been paid in a timely manner and the owner of the patent wants to reinstate the patent, a petition and proper fees are required. Any petition to accept an unintentionally delayed payment of a maintenance fee must include: (1) the required maintenance fee set forth in 37 CFR 1.20 (e) through (g); (2) the petition fee as set forth in 37 CFR 1.17(m); (3) a statement that the delay in payment of the maintenance fee was unintentional; and (4) be signed in compliance with 37 CFR 1.33(b).

If the date of expiration of the patent is less than twenty-four (24) months after the maintenance fee is due, file a petition using the Web-based ePetition in EFS-Web. By filing electronically, the petition is automatically processed and granted immediately upon submission if the petition meets all of the above-mentioned requirements.

If the date of expiration of the patent is more than twenty-four (24) months after the maintenance fee is due, file a petition by submitting completed **Petition to Accept Unintentionally Delayed Payment of Maintenance Fee in an Expired Patent (37 CFR 1.378(b)) (PTO/SB/66)** form at *www.uspto.gov/sites/default/files/sb0066.pdf* and pay the proper fees.

> NOTE: There may be significant processing delays and the filing does not guarantee that the petition will be granted.

19.6.5 MAINTENANCE FEE CORRESPONDENCE OTHER THAN PAYING FEES ONLINE

Any correspondence related to maintenance fees that does NOT accompany a maintenance fee payment (e.g., entity status changes, fee address changes) should be sent to:

Mail Stop M Correspondence
Commissioner for Patents
P.O. Box 1450
Alexandria, VA 22313-1450

or

Facsimile: (571) 273-6500

19.6.6 PATENT TERM CALCULATOR

The USPTO does not calculate the expiration dates for patents, but has a resource to help the public estimate the expiration date of a patent. See the "Patent Term Calculator" at *www.uspto.gov/patent/laws-and-regulations/patent-term-calculator* page for more information.

19.6.7 INQUIRIES TO THE USPTO REGARDING MAINTENANCE FEES

Questions concerning payment of maintenance fees should be directed to the Maintenance Fee Branch by calling **(571) 272-6500**.

CHAPTER 20
Accelerated Examination of Applications

● ● ●

20.1 PETITION FOR ACCELERATED EXAMINATION APPLICATIONS

THE USPTO HAS ESTABLISHED PROCEDURES under which the examination of a patent application may be accelerated. Under these procedures, the USPTO will advance an application out of turn for examination if the Practitioner files a Petition to Make Special Under the Accelerated Examination Program ("AE"), which is subsequently granted by the USPTO. The goal for the AE is to achieve a final decision by the Examiner within twelve (12) months from the filing date of the application.

On or after August 25, 2006, any petition for AE, and any other petition to make an application special (except petitions based on Applicant's health or age or the PPH pilot program), must be filed electronically via EFS-Web.

In order to meet the twelve (12)-month goal, the Practitioner will be required to provide additional information with the AE program, and comply with the procedures throughout the examination process, to assist the Examiner in expeditiously arriving at a final disposition.

The application must be filed with the **Petition to Make Special Under Accelerated Examination Program (PTO/SB/28)** form at *www.uspto.gov/web/forms/sb0028_fill.pdf*, and the fee under 37 CFR 1.17(h), or a statement that the claimed subject matter is directed to environmental quality, energy, or countering terrorism (no fee required). This form also includes an Instruction Sheet for the AE program.

20.2 CONDITIONS FOR PROPER REQUEST FOR ACCELERATED EXAMINATION

AE applications must meet the following conditions:

1. Be filed via EFS-Web.
   a. All follow-on documents must also be filed via EFS-Web.
   b. The Practitioner must be a registered user to file follow-on papers via EFS-Web.

2. Use **Petition to Make Special Under Accelerated Examination Program (PTO/SB/28)** form at *www.uspto.gov/web/forms/sb0028_fill.pdf* for filing the petition.
3. Must be a non-reissue utility or design application.
4. All fees must be paid at time of electronic filing.
5. No preliminary amendments present on the filing date of the application.
6. No petition for a non-signing inventor.
7. Be complete and correct.

20.3 CONTENTS FOR COMPLETE APPLICATION

To be complete, the AE application must contain the following:

1. **Petition to Make Special Under Accelerated Examination Program (PTO/SB/28)** form at *www.uspto.gov/web/forms/sb0028_fill.pdf.*
2. Statement of Pre-examination Search – A statement that a pre-examination search was conducted, including an identification of the field of search by United States class and subclass and the date of the search, where applicable, and for database searches, the search logic or chemical structure sequence used as a query, the name of the file or files search and the database service, and the date of the search. The search must involve U.S. patents and patent application publications, foreign patent documents, and non-patent literature.
3. Examination Support Document – A document that includes an information disclosure statement citing each reference deemed most closely related to the subject matter of each of the claims, identification of all the limitations in the claims that are disclosed by the reference specifying where the limitation is disclosed for each reference cited, a detailed explanation of how each of the claims are patentable over the references cited, a concise statement of the utility of the invention as defined in each of the independent claims, a showing of where each limitation of the claims finds support in the written description of the specification, and identification of any cited references that may be disqualified as prior art.
4. The application must include the following parts:
   * Specification and at least one claim must be in English.
   * Three (3) or fewer independent claims.
   * Twenty (20) or fewer total claims.
   * The claims must be directed to a single invention.
   * The application must not contain any multiple dependent claims.An Abstract.
   * If necessary: Application size fee, Drawings, Non-English Specification, translation of Foreign Priority Documents, and/or Application Data Sheet.
   * Basic filing, search, and examination fees and petition fee under 37 CFR 1.17(h).

- Executed Oath or DeclarationInformation Disclosure Statement in Support of Petition to Make Special.
- Transmittal letter: the Transmittal letter must include suggested classification, by class and subclass. Class and subclass could also be submitted using the USPTO form fillable ADS.
- A statement that the Practitioner will agree to make an election without traverse in a telephonic interview.
- A statement that Practitioner will agree to have an interview when requested by the Examiner.
- A statement that Practitioner will agree not to separately argue the patentability of any dependent claim during any appeal.
- A statement that a pre-examination search was conducted.
- An accelerated examination support document (ESD).

The Practitioner should contact the USPTO if a decision on the Petition to Make Special is not received by the Practitioner after three (3) months from the filing of the petition.

20.4 eFiling an Accelerated Exam Application via EFS-Web

The basic steps to efile an Accelerated Exam Application via EFS-Web are as follows:

1. After EFS-Web certification, under "*Main Functions", click "New application/proceeding".
2. Click "Utility" under "Select Type of New Application/Proceeding".
3. Click "Accelerated Exam".
4. Click "Continue" for the next screen.
5. Enter the following information:
   - Title of Invention
   - Attorney Docket Number
   - First Named Inventor
   - Correspondence Address (select the Practitioner's Customer Number with the drop down arrow)
6. After all this information has been entered, click "Continue". This saves the filing up to this point.
7. Browse for the file (in PDF format) and upload it to this filing.
8. Underneath the uploaded document, it states: "Does your PDF file contain multiple documents?" Click "Yes".
9. The following basic document descriptions are used for filing an Accelerated Examination application:

Category	Document Description
General Transmittal or Petition	Petition for 12-month Accelerated Exam (Use the fillable form PTO/SB/28 – Petition to Make Special Under Accelerated Examination Program)
General Transmittal or Petition	Statement of pre-examination search
General Transmittal or Petition	Examination support document
Application Part	Oath or Declaration Filed
Application Part	Application Data Sheet
Change Requests	Power of Attorney
IDS/References	Transmittal Letter
IDS/References	Information Disclosure Statement (IDS) Form (SB08)
IDS/References	Foreign Reference
IDS/References	NPL Documents
Application Part	Specification
Application Part	Claims
Application Part	Abstract
Application Part	Drawings-only black and white line drawings

10. Click "Upload & Validate" to make sure that there are no validation errors. If there is a validation error, there will be a prompt on the screen of an error or a warning! If there is an error, the error must be corrected at this point. If there is a warning, click "Continue" to go to the next screen.

For the remainder of the steps, see **Section 6.2.2** to complete the efiling of the Accelerated Examination Application via EFS-Web. All fees must be paid at time of electronic filing.

CHAPTER 21

Claim For Foreign Priority

● ● ●

21.1 WHAT IS A CLAIM FOR FOREIGN PRIORITY?

AN APPLICANT FILING A U.S. Nonprovisional Application, who wishes to secure the right of priority to a foreign filed patent application for the same invention, must comply with certain formal requirements under 35 USC 119. If these requirements are not satisfied, the right of priority to the filing date of the first filed foreign application is lost and cannot thereafter be asserted.

For U.S. applications filed prior to November 29, 2000, a claim must be made and a certified copy of the original foreign application must be submitted to the USPTO before the U.S. application issues as a patent. For Nonprovisional Applications filed (other than a design application) on or after November 29, 2000, in addition to the above, the foreign application must be identified by its application number, the intellectual property authority or country in which the foreign application was filed, and the date of filing of the foreign application. Further, the claim for priority must be made within four (4) months after the filing of the U.S. application or sixteen (16) months from the filing date of the foreign application. This time period is not extendable, but a petition to accept an unintentionally delayed claim for priority can be filed. For an application that entered the national stage from a Patent Cooperative Treaty ("PCT") international application, the claim for priority must be made during the pendency of the application and within the time limit set forth in the PCT regulations. The claim for priority can be made by completing the appropriate blocks on the oath or declaration or in a separate document. If in a separate document, the Practitioner should be consulted.

If a claim for foreign priority is made in a document to be signed by the Practitioner, the Paralegal must perform the following:

- Verify that the document states that Applicant claims priority to a foreign application.
- Identify the foreign application in the document by its application number, the intellectual property authority or country in which the foreign application was filed, and the date of filing of the foreign application.

* Obtain and include a certified copy of the foreign application from the Applicant and attach it to the document.
* If the document to be submitted is not being filed within the time periods set forth above, consult with the Practitioner.

21.2 Certified Copy of Foreign Priority Document

Certified copies of foreign priority documents should be submitted by hand-delivery/courier or by first class mail. When a document that is required by statute to be certified must be filed, a copy (including a photocopy, facsimile transmission or via EFS-Web) of the certification is not acceptable. Note that it may be possible for the USPTO to retrieve an electronic copy of a priority document through the priority document exchange program.

21.3 Manner of Filing a Claim for Priority

Documents for claiming priority can be filed directly with the USPTO or by using certificate of mailing.

21.3.1 Hand-Delivery/Courier

A Certified Copy of Foreign Priority Document that is hand-delivered to the USPTO must be filed at the Customer Window at the following address:

Customer Service Window
U.S. Patent and Trademark Office
Randolph Building
401 Dulany Street
Alexandria, VA 22131-1450

Best practice is to prepare a filing receipt identifying the patent application and documents to be filed so that the receipt can be date-stamped by the clerk at the Customer Service Window.

21.3.2 Certificate of Mailing

A Certificate of Mailing by First Class Mail is a statement signed by the person doing the mailing certifying that the document was deposited with the USPS, with sufficient first class postage, addressed to the USPTO, on a certain date.

This is an example text to be placed on the Certified Copy of Foreign Priority Document transmittal if the document is to be mailed to the USPTO:

CERTIFICATE OF MAILING

I hereby certify that this correspondence is being deposited with the United States Postal Service with sufficient postage as First Class Mail in an envelope addressed to Commissioner for Patents, P.O. Box 1450, Alexandria, VA 22313-1450, on the date shown below.

Date:_____   (Signature of person mailing the correspondence)

21.4 RETRIEVING DOCUMENTS FROM THE EPO, JPO, OR KIPO

The USPTO can electronically exchange priority documents directly with the European Patent Office (EPO), the Japanese Patent Office (JPO), and the Korean Intellectual Property Office (KIPO).

Use the form **Request to Retrieve Electronic Priority Application(s) (PTO/SB/38)** form at *www. uspto.gov/forms/sb0038.pdf* if the Practitioner wants to retrieve priority documents from the EPO, JPO, or KIPO.

Also, for more information, go to this document which explains the procedures to follow to Retrieve Documents from the EPO, JPO, or KIPO at *www.uspto.gov/patents/process/file/pdx_index.jsp*.

CHAPTER 22

ePetitions

● ● ●

22.1 What are ePetitions?

Filing ePetitions online via EFS-Web is a fast and convenient process providing Petitioners with instant feedback to ensure that all requirements are met for immediate petition grant. The USPTO offers eleven (11) web-based ePetitions and two (2) existing PDF-based ePetitions that are available to be filed via EFS-Web.

22.2 PDF-based ePetitions

The PDF-based ePetitions require the download and completion of the respective EFS-Web fillable PDF form:

- Petition to Make Special Based on Age (37 CFR 1.102)
- Petition to Accept Unintentional Delayed Payment of the Maintenance Fee (37 CFR 1.378(b))

22.3 Web-based ePetitions

Unlike the two (2) existing legacy ePetitions, which require the petition fillable PDF form to be completed and attached in EFS-Web, the Web-based ePetitions can be completed online through Web-based screens. The ePetitions are auto-processed and granted immediately upon submission if the petition meets all of the requirements.

By using ePetition, Petitioners will have more control as to when their petitions are filed and answered. This is especially advantageous for critical petitions, such as petitions to withdraw from issue. Deciding petitions electronically decreases the need for renewed petitions, since petitioners know instantly whether all requirements have been met and there are no EFS-Web fillable forms required. To process any of the auto-granted ePetitions, fees must be paid immediately which then provide users more financial flexibility. A paper-filed petition includes a fee but does not guarantee a granted petition.

The following Web-based ePetitions are available to users:

- Petition to Make Special Based on Age (37 CFR 1.102)
- Request for Withdrawal as Attorney or Agent of Record (37 CFR 1.36)
- Petitions to Withdraw from Issue After Payment of the Issue Fee
  - Petition to Withdraw from Issue After Payment of the Issue Fee (37 CFR 1.313(c)(1) or (2))
  - Petition to Withdraw from Issue After Payment of the Issue Fee (37 CFR 1.313(c)(3))
  - Petition to Withdraw from Issue After Payment of the Issue Fee (37 CFR 1.313(c)(1) or (2) with Assigned Patent Number)
  - Petition to Withdraw from Issue After Payment of the Issue Fee (37 CFR 1.313(c)(3) with Assigned Patent Number)
- Petitions for Revival
  - Petition to Accept Late Payment of Issue Fee – Unintentional Late Payment (37 CFR 1.137(a))
  - Petition for Revival of an Application based on Failure to Notify the Office of a Foreign or International Filing (37 CFR 1.137(f))
  - Petition for Revival of an Application for Continuity Purposes Only (37 CFR1.137(a))
  - Petition for Revival of an Abandoned Patent Application Abandoned Unintentionally (37 CFR 1.137(a)) (For Cases Abandoned After 1st Action and Prior to Notice of Allowance)
- Petition to Correct Assignee After Payment of Issue Fee (37 CFR 3.81(b))
- Petition to Accept Unintentional Delayed Payment of the Maintenance Fee (37 CFR 1.378(b))

22.4 BASIC GUIDELINES FOR eFILING ePETITIONS

- The Petitioner must be a registered eFiler.
- The Petitioner must be able to access the EFS-Web.
- Registered eFilers are strongly advised to transmit electronic filings early in the day to allow time for an alternative paper filing when transmission cannot be initiated or correctly completed. Note that paper filed petitions require a fee.
- The ability to submit an ePetition under EFS-Web Contingency is not permitted.

WARNING: For eFiler protection, an EFS-Web session will time-out after one (1) hour of in-activity. An ePetition request that has not been submitted after one (1) hour of inactivity will be lost unless it is saved. In the event the session times out, logon to EFS-Web again and re-enter the required ePetition information.

22.5 ePetition Process

Once signed into EFS-Web, the eFiler will need to certify that he or she is a certificate holder or working under the authority of the certificate holder.

To submit an ePetition, select the radio button located next to Existing application/patent. The Web screen will expand to display additional options. Select the radio button next to ePetition (for automatic processing and immediate grant, if all petitions requirements are met).

When the ePetition option is selected, the screen will display all available ePetition types – the two (2) legacy PDF-based ePetitions and the eleven (11) Web-based ePetitions.

Filing instructions for the two PDF-based ePetitions and the Quick Start Guide for the EFS-Web ePetitions can be located on the ePetition Resource Page at:

www.uspto.gov/patents/process/file/efs/guidance/epetition-info.jsp

CHAPTER 23
Patent Term Adjustment

● ● ●

23.1 WHAT IS PATENT TERM ADJUSTMENT?

PATENT TERM ADJUSTMENT ("PTA") EXTENDS the patent term if the USPTO fails to issue the patent within three (3) years from the Applicant requested examination.

23.2 PATENT TERM

Patent applications filed on or after June 8, 1995, if are granted have a term of enforceability that starts on the day of issue and ends twenty (20) years from the date the application was originally filed. If the application claims priority to an earlier-filed application, then the expiration date will be twenty (20) years from the date of filing of the earlier-filed application.

If a patent application was filed before June 8, 1995, the patent term is seventeen (17) years from the date of the patent issue or twenty (20) years from earliest-filing date of an earlier-filed application, whichever is longer.

23.3 CALCULATION OF PATENT TERM

The PTA provides day-for-day adjustment of the patent term for each day's delay in prosecution. If delay is the fault of the USPTO, then the Patentee gets extra days added to the patent term. If the Patentee causes the delay, then these days are subtracted from the adjusted total. However, the patent term will never be less than the unadjusted term. There are three (3) reasons for which the term may be extended:

- If the USPTO fails to take certain actions within specified time frames ("A" delay).
- If the USPTO fails to issue a patent within three (3) years of the actual filing date (assuming the application is fully patentable and should be issued) ("B" delay).
- If there are delays due to interference, secrecy order or successful appeal to the Patent Trial and Appeal Board ("C" delay).

The PTA is automatically calculated by the USPTO "PALM" system. If there is an extension granted, it is printed on the Issue Notification, which is mailed approximately three (3) weeks prior to the issuance of the patent. The PTA will be printed on the face of the issued patent.

23.4 ADJUSTMENT DUE TO USPTO DELAYS

There are three types of USPTO delays: "A" delay, "B" delay and "C" delay.

23.4.1 "A" DELAY

"A" delay accrues in four types of USPTO delays (the 14+4+4+4 Rule).

* First Office Action, including a Restriction Requirement, must issue within fourteen (14) months of the filing date.
* An Examiner must respond to Applicant's Reply within four (4) months.
* An Examiner must respond to a Board decision within four (4) months.
* USPTO must issue a patent within four (4) months of payment of the issue fee.

23.4.2 "B" DELAY

"B" delay accrues for each day issues after three (3) years of prosecution until the patent issues. Three (3) years is measured from the U.S. filing date of the application or the commencement of the national stage examination. A foreign priority date or a U.S. provisional filing date is not considered in determining a "B" delay.

Exceptions to a "B" delay:

* Time consumed by an RCE begins on the date the RCE is filed and ends on the date a Notice of Allowance is mailed. (37 CFR 1.703(b)(1) amended January 9, 2015).
* If an RCE is filed after Allowance, there is an Applicant delay unless the RCE is filed with an IDS having a statement.
* Other "B" delay exceptions are from review by the Board of a Federal court and Applicant requested delay.

23.4.3 "C" DELAY

"C" delay fills the gaps of the "B" delay exceptions due to delays for interference or derivation proceeding, secrecy order, successful civil action, and successful PTAB appeal.

23.5 PTA Limitations

PTA shall not exceed the actual number of days of delay (no double count overlapping delays). There is no adjustment beyond any date specified in a terminal disclaimer and Applicant delay.

23.6 Applicant Delay Not Considered in Determining PTA

The following types of delay by Applicant will not be considered in determining PTA:

- The PTA is reduced by the number of days Applicant "failed to engage in reasonable efforts to conclude prosecution".
- Applicant's failure to respond to any Notice or Office Action within three (3) months of mailing date.
- For any PTO Notice or Office Action setting a two (2)-month due date, the first-month extension does not reduce PTA; e.g., response to restriction, filing appeal brief or RCE following notice of appeal, response to missing parts, or corrected application papers, etc.

Other Types of Applicant Delay that will not be considered:

- Applicant-granted petition to suspend action.
- Applicant's request to defer of issuance of a patent.
- Abandonment or late issue fee payment.
- Failure to petition to withdraw abandonment or petition to revive.
- Conversion from Provisional to Nonprovisional Application.
- Submission of a preliminary amendment less than one (1) month before an Office Action.
- Submission of a reply having an omission.
- Submission of a supplemental reply.
- Submission of an Amendment after a Board decision less than one (1) month before issuance of an Office Action or Notice of Allowance.
- Submission of Amendment under 37 CFR 1.312 after a Notice of Allowance.
- Failure to file an Appeal Brief within three (3) months.
- Submission of an RCE after a Notice of Allowance.
- Failure to provide an application in condition for examination within eight (8) months of filing.

The following documents filed after Notice of Allowance will not be considered in calculating the PTO:

- Issue Fee Transmittal (PTOL-85B).
- Power to Inspect.
- Change of Address.

- Change of entity status (micro/small/undiscounted regular).
- Response to the Examiner's reasons for allowance or a request to correct an error or omission in the Notice of Allowance.
- Letter related to government interests.
- Request for acknowledgement of IDS provided that Applicant requested consideration of the IDS prior to issuance of a Notice of Allowance.
- Comments on the substance of an interview where an Applicant-initiated interview resulted in a Notice of Allowance.
- Status Letters.
- Request for Refund.
- Inventor's Oath or Declaration.

23.7 EXAMPLES OF CALCULATING PTA
Example 1 (Facts)

- Application filed under 111(a) on 5/1/2009
- RCE filed on 3/5/2013
- Notice of Allowance mailed on 7/1/2013
- Patent issued on 10/1/2013
- There were no "A" delays or "C" delays
- No Applicant delays under 37 CFR 1.704(b) and (c)

Example 1 (Calculation)

- Days from filing to issue is (5/1/2009 – 10/1/2013) = 1615
- Days RCE to NOA is (3/5/2013 – 7/1/2013) = 119
- Days considered as "B" days = 1615 – 119 = 1496
- Overall "B" delay = 1496 – 1097 = 399
- Overall PTA = A + B + C - overlap – Applicant delay
- PTA = 0 + 399 + 0 – 0 + 0 = 399 days

Example 2 (Facts)

Application filed on 5/1/2009
RCE filed on 6/1/2011
Notice of Allowance mailed on 10/12/2012
Patent issued on 3/10/2013
There were no "A" delays or "C" delays

No Applicant delays under 37 CFR 1.704(b) and (c)

Example 2 (Calculation)

* Days from filing to issue is (5/1/2009 – 3/10/2013 = 1410
* Days from RCE to NOA is (6/1/2011 – 10/12/2012 = 500
* Days considered as "B" days = 1410 – 500 = 910
* Overall "B" delay is 910 – 1097 = 0
* PTA = A + B + C – overlap – Applicant delay
* PTA = 0 + 0 + 0 – 0 = 0 days

Example 3 (Facts)

* Application filed 5/1/2008
* RCE filed 8/1/2011
* Notice of Allowance 10/5/2012
* Issue fee paid 1/5/2013
* Patent issues 9/5/2013

Example 3 (Calculation)

* Filing to issue date (5/1/2008 – 9/5/2013) = 1954
* Days from RCE to NOA (8/1/2011 – 10/5/2012) = 432
* Days considered as "B" days is 1954 – 432 = 1522
* "B" delay is 1522 – 1096 = 426
* "A" delay (issue more than 4 months after (IFEE) is 5/6/2013 to 9/5/2013) = 123
* Overlap is 5/6/2013 to 9/5/2013 = 123
* "No "C" delays or Applicant delays
* PTA = A + B + C – Overlap – Applicant delay
* PTA = 123 + 426 + 0 – 123 – 0 = 426

23.8 REQUEST FOR RECONSIDERATION OF USPTO PTA CALCULATION

Pursuant to the AIA Technical Corrections Act of January 14, 2013, requests for reconsideration of the PTA calculation determination may now be filed no later than two (2) months from the date the patent was granted. However, extensions up to five (5) months can be requested for a fee. A separate $400 processing fee will also be required. This will bring the total time period in which to challenge the USPTO's PTA calculation determination to seven (7) months from the patent grant date.

CHAPTER 24
Supplemental Examinations

• • •

THE PATENT OWNER MAY REQUEST a supplemental examination for a patent so that the USPTO can consider, reconsider, or correct information believed to be relevant to the patent. The information is not limited to patents or printed publications, but instead may include information concerning any ground or patentability, i.e., patent eligible subject matter, anticipation, obviousness, written description, enablement, best mode, and indefiniteness.

The supplemental examination provision in the AIA became effective on September 16, 2012.

The **Request for Supplemental Examination Transmittal (PTO/SB/59)** form at *www.uspto.gov/forms/ sb0059.pdf* must contain the following items:

- A list of each item of information that is requested to be considered, reconsidered, or corrected.
- An identification of each claim of the patent for which supplemental examination is requested.
- A separate explanation of the relevance and manner of applying each item of information to each claim of the patent for which it was identified.
- A summary of the relevant portions of any submitted document, other than the request, that is over fifty (50) pages in length.
- Supplemental Examination fees.

As of January 1, 2014, a request for supplemental examination must be accompanied by a total fee of $16,500 for a regular undiscounted ($8,250 for small entity or $4,125 for micro entity). Broken down, these fees comprise as (i) a fee of $4,400 for a regular undiscounted ($2,200 for small entity or $1,100 for micro entity) for processing and treating a request for supplemental examination, and (ii) a fee of $12,100 for a regular undiscounted ($6,050 for small entity or $3,025 for micro entity) for *ex parte* reexamination ordered as a result of a supplemental examination proceeding, and any applicable document size fees.

The document size fees apply only to non-patent documents that have more than twenty (20) pages. Non-patent documents having twenty (20) pages or less are not subject to the document size fees. Non-patent documents include, for example, non-patent literature, transcripts of audio or video recordings, and court documents.

CHAPTER 25
Terminal Disclaimers

• • •

25.1 WHAT IS A TERMINAL DISCLAIMER?

TERMINAL DISCLAIMERS ARE SEPARATE AND independent from PTA. A Terminal Disclaimer is filed in response to an obviousness double patenting rejection of claims by the Examiner in an Office Action.

To have a Terminal Disclaimer filed and recorded in the USPTO, it must:

* Be signed by the Applicant, Assignee, or the Practitioner.
* Specify the portion of the term of the patent being disclaimed.
* State the present extent of the Applicant's or the Assignee's ownership interest in the patent to be granted.
* Be accompanied by a fee.

25.1.1 TERMINAL DISCLAIMER FORMS

The USPTO has two forms that can be used for Terminal Disclaimers:

* **Terminal Disclaimer to Obviate a Provisional Double Patenting Rejection Over a Pending Application (PTO/SB/25)** form at *www.uspto.gov/web/forms/sb0025.pdf.*
* **Terminal Disclaimer to Obviate a Double Patenting Rejection Over a Prior Patent (PTO/SB/26)** form at *www.uspto.gov/web/forms/sb0026.pdf.*

25.1.2 eFILING A TERMINAL DISCLAIMER VIA EFS-WEB

The basic steps to efile a Terminal Disclaimer via EFS-Web are as follows:

1. After EFS-Web certification, under "*Main Functions", click "Existing application/patent/ proceeding".
2. Select Type of Submission: Click "Document/Fees for an existing application/ proceeding".

3. Type in the Application Number and Confirmation Number of the existing patent application. Click "Continue" for the next screen.
4. Files to be Submitted: Browse for the file (in PDF format) and upload it to this filing.
5. Underneath the uploaded document, it states: "Does your PDF file contain multiple documents?" Click "No".
6. The following basic document description is used for filing a Terminal Disclaimer:

Category	Document Description
Application Part	Terminal Disclaimer Filed

7. Click "Upload & Validate" to make sure that there are no validation errors. If there is a validation error, there will be a prompt on the screen of an error or a warning! If there is an error, the error must be corrected at this point. If there is a warning, click "Continue" to go to the next screen.

For the remainder of the steps, see **Section 6.2.2** to complete the efiling of the Terminal Disclaimer via EFS-Web.

25.2 WHAT IS AN eTERMINAL DISCLAIMER?
The basic guidelines for efiling eTerminal Disclaimers via EFS-Web are as follows:

* Registered eFiler must be able to access EFS-Web.
* Registered eFiler is strongly advised to transmit his/her electronic filings sufficiently early in the day to allow for alternative paper filing when transmission cannot be initiated or correctly completed.
* Submitting an eTerminal Disclaimer under EFS-Web Contingency is not permitted.
* The fee (Terminal disclaimer = Statutory disclaimer) to be paid upon filing a request for eTerminal Disclaimer is required.
* eTerminal Disclaimers via EFS-Web are accepted only for Nonprovisional Applications, national stage applications, reissue, reexam and design applications.
* Terminal Disclaimers for plant applications, reexaminations and terminal disclaimers based on a joint research agreement must be filed by paper.
* Registered Practitioner acting in a representative capacity may not file eTerminal Disclaimers.
* Registered Practitioner must have Power of Attorney over the entered application number. The entered registration number must be valid.
* No documents need to be attached for this submission.

25.2.1 eFiling an eTerminal Disclaimer via EFS-Web

The basic steps to efile an eTerminal Disclaimer via EFS-Web are as follows:

1. After EFS-Web certification, select the radio button located next to "Existing application/patent". The Web screen will expand to display additional options.
2. Select the radio button next to "eProcessing (Electronic Terminal Disclaimer and other requests for automatic processing)"
3. Select eTerminal Disclaimer (for automatic processing and immediate approval, if all requirements are met).
4. A valid application and confirmation number must be entered followed by the certification statement.
5. Under the *Application Data* tab, complete all of the necessary fields in order to save the submission for later.
6. At the bottom of the screen, the option to click "Save for Later Submission" or "Save & Continue" is available.
7. On the Application Data screen, both certification statements must be selected in order to proceed. If unable to select any of the statements, the eTerminal Disclaimer cannot be submitted via EFS-Web.
8. In the Owner field, up to 240 characters may be entered into the text box. A counter will reveal how many characters you have left.
9. In the Ownership Percentage field, enter the percentage number.
10. Click "Add owner" button. If this button is not clicked, the entry will not be stored.
11. If an entry needs to be deleted, click the "Remove" button.
12. Additional owners can be added. At least one owner must be added in this section.
13. In the eTerminal Disclaimer request over "reference" application section, the application number needs to have a matching filing date. Similar to the owner section, click the "Add Application" to add the entry. Multiple applications can be added in this section.
14. In the eTerminal Disclaimer request over "prior" patent section, enter the patent number and click the "Add Patent" button to add the entry. A valid patent number must be entered. Multiple patents may be added in this section.
15. Indicate if the fees have been previously filed or will accompany the eTerminal Disclaimer. Also, indicate the current entity status. If the terminal disclaimer fee has already been paid, the entity status section will not appear.
16. At the bottom of the screen, enter the name of the Practitioner, except for the S-signature.
17. The Practitioner provides a S-signature, submit the eTerminal Disclaimer, and can follow the next screens accordingly.
18. Click "Save & Continue" to proceed to the next screen.

19. On the calculate fees screen, the required fee is automatically displayed as "Statutory" or "Terminal" disclaimer. Click "Continue" to proceed.

20. On the next screen, check to make sure that the choices selected are correct.

21. Once the selections have been confirmed, click the "File & Pay" button to file the eTerminal Disclaimer. The fee payment must be successfully processed in order for the eTerminal Disclaimer Approval Letter to be generated.

22. When paying fees, the options available for paying are: Charge USPTO Deposit Account, Charge Credit Card, or Electronic Funds Transfer. Select the radio button for the method of payment.

23. The review fees section of the Pay Fees screen will display the fees being collected for the application. The Total Payment is listed on the bottom right of the screen. To make a payment, click the "Start online payment process" button located at the bottom of the screen.

24. Once the necessary payment information has been paid and received by the USPTO, print/save an Acknowledgement Receipt of the filing. This is proof of the actual filing.

25. The eTerminal Disclaimer filed will appear in Private PAIR within minutes.

Track One Prioritized Examinations

● ● ●

26.1 TRACK ONE PRIORITIZED EXAMINATIONS

TRACK ONE PRIORITIZED EXAMINATION is an accelerated examination that allows Applicants to have their application accorded special status during prosecution before the Patent Examiner. Prioritized Examination for newly filed applications (Track One) and continued examination (PE-RCE) provide Applicants with greater control over the order in which applications are examined.

The resource page for Prioritized Examination can be located at *www.uspto.gov/aia_implementation/track-1-quickstart-guide.pdf.*

Prioritized Examination requests via EFS-Web are accepted only for Nonprovisonal Applications. Requests for prioritized examination for plant applications must be filed by paper.

If a Prioritized Examination request has been submitted, but a necessary component has been omitted, the omitted component must be submitted as a follow-on paper on the same day as the original submission.

A Prioritized Examination request that is complete on the day the request is submitted will be accepted.

26.1.1 REQUIREMENTS FOR FILING A REQUEST FOR PRIORITIZED EXAMINATION

The following are the basic requirements for filing a Request for Prioritized Examination:

* The user must be able to access EFS-Web.
* Filer must be a registered eFiler, except that an unregistered eFiler may file a new application which includes a request for Track One prioritized application.
* It is strongly advised to transmit the electronic filing sufficiently early in the day to allow time for alternative filing such as EFS-Web Contingency when transmission cannot be initiated or correctly completed.
* It is strongly recommended to use the USPTO's certification and request form (**PTO/AIA/424** or equivalent) to request prioritized examination, but the form is not required.

26.1.2 REQUIRED FEES
The fees required for Track One Prioritized Examination must be paid upon filing a request for prioritized examination.

Consult the current Fee Schedule for these fees at:

www.uspto.gov/learning-and-resources/fees-and-payment/uspto-fee-schedule

The following fees must be paid:

* Basic filing fee
* Search fee
* Examination fee
* Prioritized examination processing fee
* Prioritized examination fee
* If applicable, any application size fee, due because the specification and drawings exceed 100 sheets of paper
* If applicable, any excess independent claim fee, due because the number of independent claims exceeds three (3) but no more than four (4) total independent claims
* If applicable, any excess claim fee, due because the number of claims exceeds twenty (20) but no more than thirty (30) total claims
* If requesting prioritized examination for an RCE, RCE fee

26.1.3 eFILING A REQUEST FOR PRIORITIZED EXAMINATION VIA EFS-WEB
The basic steps to efile a Request for Prioritized Examination via EFS-Web are as follows:

1. After EFS-Web certification, under "*Main Functions", click "New application/proceeding".
2. Click "Utility" under "Select Type of New Application/Proceeding".
3. Click on "Track I Prioritized Examination - Nonprovisional Application under 35 USC 111(a)".
4. Click "Continue" for the next screen.
5. Enter the following information:
   * Title of Invention
   * Attorney Docket Number
   * First Named Inventor
   * Correspondence Address (select the Practitioner's Customer Number with the drop down arrow)

6. After all this information has been entered, click "Continue". This saves the filing up to this point.

7. Browse for the file (in PDF format) and upload it to this filing.

8. Underneath the uploaded document, it states: "Does your PDF file contain multiple documents?" Click "Yes".

9. The following basic document descriptions are used for filing a Track 1 Prioritized Examination Application:

Category	Document Description
Track I - Prioritized Examination	TrackOne Request
Application Part	Application Data Sheet
Application Part	Specification
Application Part	Abstract
Application Part	Drawings-only black and white line drawings
Application Part	Oath or Declaration Filed
Amendment	Preliminary Amendment (if any)
Application Part	Claims
Application Part	Abstract
Application Part	Drawings-only black and white line drawings
Application Part	Oath or Declaration Filed

10. Click "Upload & Validate" to make sure that there are no validation errors. If there is a validation error, there will be a prompt on the screen of an error or a warning! If there is an error, the error must be corrected at this point. If there is a warning, click "Continue" to go to the next screen.

For the remainder of the steps, see ***Section 6.2.2*** to complete the efiling of the Track 1 Prioritized Examination Application via EFS-Web.

26.2 SPECIAL STATUS

An application accorded special status will continue to be special throughout its entire course of prosecution until one of the following occurs:

* Filing a petition for extension of time to extend the time period for filing a reply.
* Filing an amendment to amend the application to contain more than four (4) independent claims, more than thirty (30) total claims, or a multiple dependent claim.
* Filing a Request for Continued Examination.
* Filing a Notice of Appeal.
* Filing a Request for Suspension of Action.
* Mailing a Notice of Allowance.
* Mailing of a Final Rejection.
* Abandonment of the application.

CHAPTER 27

Patent Cooperation Treaty

● ● ●

27.1 WHAT IS THE PATENT COOPERATION TREATY?

THE PATENT COOPERATION TREATY ("PCT") is a multilateral treaty that was concluded in Washington, D.C., in 1970 and implemented in the U.S. in 1978. It is administered by the International Bureau of the World Intellectual Property Organization ("WIPO"), located in Geneva, Switzerland.

The PCT is an international treaty with more than 145 Contracting States. The PCT makes it possible to seek patent protection for an invention simultaneously in a large number of countries by filing a single "international" patent application instead of initially filing separate national or regional patent applications in countries where patent protection is sought. The granting of patents remains under the control of the national or regional patent Offices in what is called the "national phase".

A PCT application (also called "international patent application") has two (2) phases. The first phase is the international phase in which patent protection is pending under a single patent application filed with the patent office of a contracting state of the PCT. The second phase is the national and regional phase, which follows the international phase in which rights are continued by filing necessary documents with the patent offices of separate contracting states of the PCT. A PCT application, as such, is not an actual request that a patent be granted, and it is not converted into one unless and until it enters the "national phase".

27.2 PCT PROCEDURE

The main advantages of the PCT procedure are the possibility to maximally delay:

* The national or regional procedures;
* The respective fees and translation costs; and
* The unified filing procedure.

The PCT procedure includes:

- **Filing**: file the PCT international application in a receiving office or WIPO, complying with the PCT formality requirements, in one (1) language, and pay one (1) set of fees.
- **International Search**: an "International Searching Authority" ("ISA") (one of the world's major patent Offices) identifies the published patent documents and technical literature ("prior art") which may have an influence on whether the invention is patentable, and establishes a written opinion on the invention's potential patentability at sixteen (16) months from the priority date.
- **International Publication**: as soon as possible, after the expiration of expiration of eighteen (18) months from the earliest filing date, the content of the international application is published to the world.
- **Supplementary International Search (optional)**: a second ISA identifies, by request, published documents which may not have been found by the first ISA which carried out the main search because of the diversity of prior art in different languages and different technical fields.
- **International Preliminary Examination (optional)**: one of the ISAs, by request, carries out an additional patentability analysis, usually on an amended version of the application.
- **National Phase**: after the end of the PCT procedure, usually at thirty (30) months from the earliest filing date of the initial application, from the claim priority, start to pursue the grant of the patents directly before the national (or regional) patent Offices of the countries in which you want to obtain them.

For any countries remaining whose national laws are not compatible with the thirty (30)-month period, the filing of a demand for an international preliminary examination electing such countries within nineteen (19) months from the priority date will result in an extension of the period for entering the national stage to thirty (30) months from the priority date.

The PCT facilitates the obtaining of protection for inventions where such protection is sought in any or all of the PCT Contracting States (see Appendix B).

27.3 RECEIVING OFFICE

The PCT International Application must be filed in the Receiving Office prescribed by the PCT Treaty. The USPTO will act as a Receiving Office for United States residents and nationals. Also, the International Bureau of the World Intellectual Property Organization ("WIPO") will act as a Receiving Office for U.S. residents and nationals. The Receiving Office functions as the filing and formalities review organization for international applications.

Where a priority claim is made, the date of the earliest-filed application that priority is claimed is used as the date for determining the timing of international processing, including the various transmittals, payment of certain international and national fees, and publication of the application. Where no priority claim is made, the international filing date will be considered to be the "priority date" for timing purposes.

The International Application is subject to the payment of certain fees within one (1) month from the date of receipt. The Receiving Office will grant an international filing date to the application, collect fees, handle informalities by direct communication with the Applicant, and monitor all corrections. At thirteen (13) months from the priority date, the Receiving Office should prepare and transmit to the International Searching Authority, a copy of the international application (called the search copy), and forward the original application (called the record copy) to the International Searching Authority to the International Bureau. Once the Receiving Office has transmitted copies of the application, the International Searching Authority becomes the focus of international processing.

27.4 INTERNATIONAL SEARCHING AUTHORITY

The basic functions of the International Searching Authority are to conduct a prior art search of inventions claimed in international applications and to issue a written opinion which will normally be considered to be the first written opinion of the International Preliminary Examining Authority where international preliminary examination is required.

For most applications filed with the United States Receiving Office, the Applicant may choose (in the Request form) the USPTO, the European Patent Office, the Korean Intellectual Property Office, the Australian Patent Office, the Federal Service for Intellectual Property (Rospatent) (Russian Federation), the Israel Patent Office, or the Japan Patent Office to act as the International Searching Authority.

An international search report and written opinion are issued by the International Searching Authority within three (3) months from the receipt of the search copy, usually about sixteen (16) months after the priority date. The international search report will contain a listing of prior art documents found to be relevant to the claimed invention and will identify the claims in the application to which the prior art is pertinent. The written opinion indicates whether each claim appears to satisfy the criteria of "novelty", "inventive step", and "industrial applicability".

27.5 INTERNATIONAL BUREAU

The basic functions of the International Bureau are to maintain the master file of all international applications and to act as the publisher and central coordinating body under the Treaty. WIPO in Geneva, Switzerland, performs the duties of the International Bureau.

The Applicant has two (2) months from the date of transmittal of the international search report within which to amend the claims by filing an amendment (PCT Article 19) and may file a brief statement directly with the International Bureau explaining the amendment. The International Bureau will publish the international application, along with the search report and any amended claims at the eighteen (18) months from the priority date.

27.6 DESIGNATED OFFICE AND ELECTED OFFICE

The designated Office is the national Office, i.e., USPTO, acting for the state or region designated under Chapter I. Similarly, the elected Office is the national Office acting for the state or region elected under Chapter II.

If the Applicant desires to obtain the benefit of delaying the entry into the national stage until thirty (30) months from the priority date in one or more countries, a Demand for international preliminary examination must be filed with an appropriate International Preliminary Examining Authority within nineteen (19) months of the priority date.

PCT Rule 54*bis* requires the Demand to be made prior to the expiration of whichever of the following periods expires later:

* Three (3) months from the date of transmittal to the Applicant of the international search report or of the declaration referred to in PCT Article 17(2)(a), and of the written opinion under PCT Rule 43*bis*.1.
* Twenty-two (22) months from the priority date.

However, Applicant may desire to file the Demand by nineteen (19) months from the priority date to extend the national stage entry deadline in the following countries: Luxembourg, the United Republic of Tanzania, and Uganda.

27.7 INTERNATIONAL PRELIMINARY EXAMINING AUTHORITY

The International Preliminary Examining Authority ("IPEA") starts the examination process when it is in possession of:

* The Demand.
* The prescribed filing and search fees.
* A translation, if the Applicant is required to furnish a translation under PCT Rule 55.2.
* Either the international search report or a notice of the declaration by the International Searching Authority that no international search report will be established.
* The written opinion established under PCT Rule 43*bis*.1.

However, the IPEA will not start the international preliminary examination before expiration of the later of three (3) months from the transmittal of the international search report (or declaration that no international search report will be established) and written opinion; or the expiration of twenty-two (22) months from the priority date unless the Applicant expressly requests an earlier start. However, see the exception of the situations provided for in PCT Rule 69.1(b).

An Examiner in the IPEA prepares the international preliminary examination report entitled "International Preliminary Report on Patentability". The report designates each claim is "novel", involves "inventive step", and is "industrially applicable". The report is issued normally by twenty-eight (28) months from the priority date.

The PCT Applicant must complete the requirements for entering the national stage by the expiation of thirty (30) months from the priority date in order to avoid any question of withdrawal of the application. However, some elected Offices provide for a longer period to complete the requirements. A listing of all national and regional offices, and the corresponding time limits for entering the national stage after PCT Chapter I and PCT Chapter II, is in Appendix C.

27.8 Required Documents for a PCT International Application to be Accorded a PCT Filing Date

* **PCT Request (Form PCT/RO/101)**

A standard form generally used to meet some of the requirements set forth in PCT Article 11. When filing the standard form via EFS-Web, the request may be filed in one of two different forms: (1) conventional format and (2) PCT Safe Easy format. The request may be filed via EFS-Web in conventional format by uploading the pdf format of the Request (Form PCT/RO/101, which includes the last sheet – EFS-Web).

Category	Document Description
PCT Form and PCT Application Part	RO/101 Request for new IA conventional

Alternatively, the request may be filed via EFS-Web in PCT-Safe Easy format by uploading a zip file containing the request which is created using the PCT-Safe Easy mode software.

Category	Document Description
PCT Form and PCT Application Part	RO/101 Request for new IA PCT-Easy format

NOTE: The request does not need to be signed in order to obtain an international filing date. The receiving Office will invite the Applicant to correct any defect by sending any invitation to correct.

* Description, Claim or Claims, Abstract, and Drawings

Category	Document Description
PCT Application Part	Specification
PCT Application Part	Claims
PCT Application Part	Abstract
PCT Application Part	Drawings – other than black and white line drawings

* Sequence listing part of the description (when required)

Category	Document Description
PCT Application Part	Sequence listing

27.9 DOCUMENTS WHICH OFTEN ACCOMPANY A NEW INTERNATIONAL APPLICATION FILED UNDER THE PCT

* **Transmittal Letter (Form PTO-1382)**

Category	Document Description
PCT General Transmittal or PCT Application Part	PCT transmittal letter

* **Fee Calculation Sheet Annex**

Category	Document Description
PCT General Transmittal or PCT Application Part	RO/101 Annex (fee calculation sheet)

* **Sequence Listing Cover Letter**

Category   Document Description

PCT General Transmittal or
PCT Application Part   Seq Listing Cover Sheet/Stmt under PCT
                                                     Rule 13ter

* **Sequence Listing Statement**

Category   Document Description

PCT General Transmittal or
PCT Application Part   PCT transmittal letter

* **Power of Attorney**

Category   Document Description

PCT General Transmittal or
PCT Application Part   Power of Attorney

* **General Power of Attorney**

Category   Document Description

PCT General Transmittal or
PCT Application Part   Power of Attorney

* **PCT-Easy Validation Log**

Category   Document Description

PCT General Transmittal or
PCT Application Part   PCT Easy validation log

* **Reference to Deposited Microorganisms or Biological Material**

Category   Document Description

PCT General Transmittal or
PCT Application Part   RO/134 Deposited microorganisms/Bio material

* **Request for Restoration of Right of Priority Under PCT Rule 26bis.3**

Category   Document Description

PCT Change Request and
PCT Petition   Evidence for restore of priority claims

27.10 NOT REQUIRED FOR A PCT INTERNATIONAL APPLICATION FILING DATE

Payment of fees, Applicant's signature, title of the invention, abstract, and formal drawings are not required at the time of initial filing of this PCT application. If any of these items are missing at the time of initial filing, an Invitation to Correct Defects will be mailed to the correspondence address with a prescribed time limit to correct these items without losing the international filing date.

27.11 PCT REQUEST FORM

Where the international application is filed on paper, the request must be made on printed Form PCT/RO/101 and filled in with the required information. A filled-in sample and a blank copy of the Form PCT/RO/101 can be downloaded at *www.wipo.int/pct/en/forms*. The request, and instructions on how to complete the editable version, are also available from that site.

An Applicant's or Agent's File Reference may be indicated, if desired. It should not exceed twelve (12) characters. Characters in excess of twelve (12) will be disregarded by the Receiving Office or any International Authority.

Details for filing the Request form are given below in respect of each Box of that form.

Box No. I: Title of Invention

The title of the invention must be short (preferably two (2) to seven (7) words, when in English, or translated into English) and precise. It must be identical with the title heading of the description.

Box Nos. II and III: Applicants, Inventors

At least one of the Applicants named must be a resident or national of a PCT Contracting State for which the Receiving Office acts.

The Applicant must be identified by providing his/her name and address and by marking next to that indication, the check-box "This person is also inventor" in Box No. II, or "Applicant and inventor" in Box No. III.

Where the Applicant is a corporation or other entity, the check-box "Applicant only" must be marked. Where the Applicant is registered with the Receiving Office, the number or other indication under which the Applicant is so registered may also be indicated in Box Nos. II or III. The Applicant's nationality and residence must also be indicated.

The names of persons must be indicated by the family name followed by the given name(s). The family name should preferably be written in capital letters.

The name of a corporation or other entity must be indicated by its full official designation (preferably in capital letters).

Addresses must be indicated in such a way as to satisfy the requirements for prompt postal delivery at the address indicated and must consist of all the relevant administrative units up to and including the house number (if any). The address must also include the country and postal code.

It is recommended that the telephone number, facsimile number or email address of the Applicant, named first in the request, be given, if no agent or common representative is indicated in Box No. IV.

Box No. IV: Agent or Common Representative

Any person who can act as an agent before the Office, which acts as Receiving Office, may be appointed as an agent for any international application filed with that Office. Where the international application is filed with the International Bureau as Receiving Office, any person who has the right to practice before the national (or regional) Office of, or acting for, a Contracting State of which the Applicant(s) is a resident or national may be appointed as agent. An appointed agent who has the right to represent the Applicant before the Receiving Office is automatically also entitled to act before the International Bureau, the International Searching Authority and the International Preliminary Examining Authority.

Where the agent is registered with the national or regional Office that is acting as Receiving Office, the request may indicate the number or other indication under which the agent is registered.

Box No. V: Designation of States

The designation of States is the indication of Contracting States that are bound by the Treaty on the international filing date.

Box No. VI: Priority Claim and Restoration of the Right of Priority

Any international application may contain a declaration claiming the priority of one (1) or more previous applications filed in or for any country party to the Paris Convention for the Protection of Industrial Property or in or for a member of the World Trade Organization that is not party to that Convention. Any priority claim must be made in the request and contain the necessary indications which allow the earlier application to be uniquely identified.

In order for the request to restore the right of priority to be successful, the following requirements must be met:

* The international application must contain a priority claim to an earlier application and within two (2) months from the date of the expiration of the priority period.
* The request to restore should state the reasons for the failure to file the international application within the priority period. The statement of reasons should be submitted as a separate document and accompany the request for restoration in the request form.
* A fee for requesting restoration before the expiration of the time limit.
* If required by the receiving Office, a declaration or other evidence in support of the statement of reasons should preferably be furnished together with the request to restore but may also be furnished upon invitation by the receiving Office.

Box No. VII: International Searching Authority

The Applicant must indicate which Authority is to be chosen to carry out the international search. Competent International Searching Authorities include:

ISA/US	U.S. Patent and Trademark Office
ISA/EP	European Patent Office
ISA/KR	Korean Intellectual Property Office
ISA/AU	Australian Patent Office
ISA/RU	Russian Federation
ISA/IL	Israel Patent Office
ISA/JP	Japan Patent Office

Box No. VIII: Declarations

The Applicant may, for the purposes of the national law applicable in one (1) or designated States, include any of these declarations.

If the Applicant chooses not to make any declaration at the time of filing, the international application or if the declarations are not yet available at the time of filing, the request should not include the optional sheets for declarations and nothing should be marked in the check-boxes in Box No. VIII.

Box No. IX: Check List
This box should be completed by the Applicant to allow the Receiving Office to verify the completeness of the documents constituting and/or accompanying the international application and, in particular, to check whether the international application as filed actually contains the number of sheets in paper form indicated in items (a) to (f).

The Applicant must further indicate in Box No. IX, the figure number of the drawings (if any), which is suggested to accompany the abstract for publication and language of filing of the international application.

Box No. X: Signature of Applicant, Agent or Common Representative
Next to each signature, indicate the name of the person signing and the capacity in which the person signs (if such capacity is not obvious from reading the request). Also, include the agent's PTO registration number (if any) next to his/her name.

PCT Fee Calculation Sheet (Annex to the Request)
The fee calculation sheet is intended to help the Applicant to calculate the total amount of fees payable to the receiving Office. The sheet is usually annexed to the request form which the Applicant obtains from the receiving Office. It is not part of the form and is not counted as a sheet of the request; however, its use is not mandatory.

27.12 eFiling PCT International Application via EFS-Web
PCT International Applications can be filed via EFS-Web using the PDF format or using PCT-SAFE (free software which is available on the internet).

Electronic filing requirements:

- The required page size for a PCT international application filed via EFS-Web in PDF format is A4.
- All PDF documents submitted via EFS-Web must have a minimum resolution of 300 dpi.

27.12.1 PDF Format (Without Using PCT-SAFE Software)

The basic steps to efile in PDF format (without using PCT-SAFE software) via EFS-Web are as follows:

1. After EFS-Web certification, under "*Main Functions", click "New application/proceeding".
2. Click "Utility" under "Select Type of New Application/Proceeding".
3. Click "International Application (PCT) for filing in the US receiving office".
4. Click "Continue" for the next screen.
5. Enter the following information:

    *   Title of Invention
    *   Attorney Docket Number
    *   First Named Inventor
    *   Correspondence Address (select the Practitioner's Customer Number with the drop down arrow)

6. After all this information has been entered, click "Continue". This saves the filing up to this point.
7. Are you attaching a PCT-EASY zip file? "No".
8. Browse for the file (in PDF format) and upload it to this filing.
9. Underneath the uploaded document, it states: "Does your PDF file contain multiple documents?" Click "Yes".
10. The following basic document descriptions are used for filing a PCT International Application:

Category	Document Description
PCT Application Part	PCT-Transmittal
PCT Form	RO/101 – Request form for new IA–Conventional
PCT Application Part	Specification
PCT Application Part	Claims
PCT Application Part	Abstract
PCT Application Part	Drawings-only black and white line drawings

11. Click "Upload & Validate" to make sure that there are no validation errors. If there is a validation error, there will be a prompt on the screen of an error or a warning! If there is an error, the error must be corrected at this point. If there is a warning, click "Continue" to go to the next screen.

For the remainder of the steps, see **Section 6.2.2** to complete the efiling of the PCT International Application via EFS-Web.

27.12.2 PCT-SAFE SOFTWARE

WIPO's electronic filing software, PCT-SAFE (SAFE = Secure Applications Filed Electronically) offers PCT users the means to prepare international applications in electronic form and to file them via secure online transmission or using physical media such as CD-R.

PCT-SAFE software is available at *www.wipo.int/pct-safe/en/* for free to download. The software creates the Request in a validated electronic form and creates a. ZIP file for filing via EFS-Web. The Request contains the same information as the PCT/RO/101, yet in a different character coded format.

The basic steps to efile a PCT-SAFE.ZIP file via EFS-Web are as follows:

1. After EFS-Web certification, under "*Main Functions", click "New application/proceeding".
2. Click "Utility" under "Select Type of New Application/Proceeding".
3. Click "International Application (PCT) for filing in the US receiving office", which is located in the "Application Data" section. In this section, a correspondence address is mandatory; however, but if the firm has a Customer Number, enter it in the "Application Data" section.
4. Click "Continue" for the next screen and enter the following information:

   * Title of Invention
   * Attorney Docket Number
   * First Named Inventor
   * Correspondence Address (select the Practitioner's Customer Number with the drop down arrow)

5. Click "Continue". This saves the filing up to this point.
6. The next screen is the "Attached file" section. EFS-Web will ask "Are you attaching a PCT Zip file?", select YES if the RO/101 has been prepared with PCT-SAFE software. Browse for the .ZIP file and upload it. Click "Upload and Validate". Only attach the PCT-SAFE .ZIP file, upload and validate. After the successful upload of the PCT-SAFE .ZIP file, continue uploading the application parts (Specification, Claims, Abstract, and Drawings as PDF files. These files cannot be added to the .ZIP file, as EFS-Web will not extract them for processing. The RO/101 and Fee sheet, in the .ZIP file, are all that EFS-Web extracts for processing.
7. The following basic document descriptions are used for filing a PCT International Application:

Category	Document Description
PCT Application Part	PCT-Transmittal
PCT Form	RO/101 – Request form for new IA – PCT EASY Format
PCT Form	RO/101 – Annex (fee calculation sheet)
PCT Application Part	Specification
PCT Application Part	Claims
PCT Application Part	Abstract
PCT Application Part	Drawings-only black and white line drawings

8. Click "Continue" and proceed to the "Calculated Fees" section.

9. "Calculated Fee" section provides the PCT filing fees. After selecting the appropriate fees, review the selections by clicking "Calculate". If the calculation is correct, click "Continue", proceed to the next screen: "Confirm and Submit" section.

10. "Confirm and Submit" section allows one to review the application with the uploaded files.

11. Click "Submit". Once submitted, the application is officially received by the USPTO. An International Application Number is automatically assigned to the application.

12. Once the PCT application has been successfully submitted, the following option is presented: "Do you want to pay fees at this time?" If click "Yes! I want to pay fees", three (3) different payment methods will be provided. Select one of these methods. If click "No, I want to pay later", the "Receipt" section will appear acknowledging receipt as confirmation of the PCT application submission.

27.13 CORRECTION OF FORMALITY DEFECTS

The Receiving Office ("RO") reviews the International Application ("IA") with Rule 11 only to the extent necessary for "reasonably uniform publication".

The RO will Invite Correction of a listing of defects and set a prescribed time for correction of the following:

* crudely executed drawings
* missing or incomplete payment of fees
* improper signature, e.g., improper S-signature
* incorrect margins
* use of incorrect size paper, etc.

NOTE: The correction of these defects does not affect the international filing date. Also, as a reminder, do not stamp "Substitute" or "Replacement" sheets on the drawings.

CHAPTER 28

Entry Into The U.S. National Phase

● ● ●

28.1 Entry into the U.S. National Phase

The time limits applicable for entry into the U.S. national phase in the USPTO Receiving Office are:

Under PCT Article 22(1):	thirty (30) months from the priority date
Under PCT Article 39(1)(a):	thirty (30) months from the priority date

The requirements for entry into the U.S. national phase are the following:

* The U.S. National Phase application must be in English.
* Under PCT Article 22: Request, description, claims (if amended, both as originally filed and as amended, together with any statement under PCT Article 19), any text matter in the drawings, abstract.
* Under PCT Article PCT Article 39(1): Request, description, claims, any text matter in the drawings, abstract (if any of those parts has been amended, both as originally filed and as amended by the annexes to the international preliminary report on patentability (Chapter II)).

The Applicant is only required to send a copy of the international application if the national application is filed prior to the publication of the international application. This is necessary when the Applicant expressly requests an earlier start of the national phase under PCT Article 23(2).

No copy of the PCT international application is required if the international application was filed in the USPTO Receiving Office. A copy of the amendments of the claims filed under PCT Article 19 with the International Bureau is required under the conditions indicated in the previous paragraph.

28.2 The Procedure for Filing the U.S. National Phase Application

Applicant(s)

For applications having a filing date prior to September 16, 2012, the Applicant must be the inventor (or, when an invention has been made by two (2) or more persons, the inventors).

For U.S. patent applications filed on or after September 16, 2012, the AIA expanded the potential Applicants for a U.S. patent application. For such applications, the Applicant may be (a) the inventor; (b) the legal representative of a deceased or legally incapacitated inventor; (c) the assignee; (d) an obligated assignee (i.e., a person to whom the inventor is under an obligation to assign the invention); or (e) a person who otherwise shows sufficient proprietary interest the application.

Inventor(s)

The inventorship of a U.S. national phase application having an international filing date before September 16, 2012, is that inventorship set forth in the international application, which includes any changes effected under PCT Rule 92*bis*. The inventorship of a U.S. national phase application having an international filing date on or after September 16, 2012, is the inventor or joint inventors set forth in an ADS accompanying the initial national phase filing. If the ADS is not submitted at the time of initial national phase filing, the inventorship will be effected under PCT Rule 92*bis*.

Form for Entering the National Phase

The USPTO has a special form for the transmittal of the fees and documents required for entering the national phase (**Form PTO-1390**). Use of the Form **PTO-1390** is strongly recommended but not required) because the form clearly identifies the submission as a national phase entry filed under 35 USC 371, as required for proper processing. In addition, **Form PTO-1390** provides Applicants with a checklist of items generally required or potentially applicable to a national phase filing, as well as a mechanism to make specific requests that may be appropriate in a particular national phase application. For example, **Form PTO-1390** contains checkboxes to expressly request that national phase procedures begin immediately, instruct the USPTO not to enter amendments made in the international phase, and to assert small entity status.

Application Data Sheet

In an application with an international filing date before September 16, 2012, an ADS is strongly recommended but not required.

In an application with an international filing date on or after September 16, 2012, an ADS is required to postpone submission of the required oath or declaration of the inventors. See *Chapter 8 - Application Data Sheet*.

Correspondence

It is preferable to file the required national phase items online via EFS-Web.

National phase documents may also be submitted by mail addressed to:

Mail Stop PCT
Commissioner for Patents

P.O. Box 1450
Alexandria, VA 22313-1450

If the Applicant has received a "Notification of Acceptance of Application Under 35 USC 371 and 37 CFR 1.495, the reference to "Mail Stop PCT" must be deleted. If a U.S. application number (e.g., 99/999,999) has been assigned, it must be indicated on the documents.

NOTE: A copy of the international application used to enter the national phase and/or payment of the required basic national fee may not be submitted by facsimile.

Late Furnishing of Translation

If the Applicant pays the basic national fee and a copy of the international application is received within the applicable time limit for national phase entry, but the application is not in English, a notice will be sent to the Applicant which sets a time period for furnishing an English translation. The Applicant can then furnish the translation provided that a processing fee is paid. The time period set in the notice will be two (2) months from the date of the notice or thirty (32) months from the priority date, whichever is later.

U.S. National Filing Fee

The basic national fee must be paid within the time limit for entry into the national phase, which is thirty (30) months after the priority date. This time limit may not be extended. If the basic national fee is not paid with the applicable time period, the National Stage application becomes abandoned.

NOTE: Authorization to charge the national fee to the Deposit Account or a credit card may not be submitted by facsimile.

Search and Examination Fees

If the Applicant pays the basic national fee and a copy of the international application has been received within the time limit for national phase entry, but the search and examination fees have not been paid, a notice is sent to the Applicant which sets a time period for payment of the search and examination fees. The Applicant can then pay the search and examination fees, along with a surcharge fee, in response to the notice.

NOTE: The time period set in the notice is extendable.

Application Size Fee

For any U.S. national phase application or national application, where the specification and drawings exceed one hundred (100) sheets, for each additional fifty (50) sheets, or fraction thereof, an application size fee will apply. For a U.S. national phase application, the application size fee is calculated on the basis of the number of sheets of description, claims, drawings, and abstract in the published international application, without regard to the language of the publication.

Additional Claims Fee

The number of additional claims for the purposes must be computed on the basis of the claims valid at the beginning of the national phase, which includes any amendments filed, claims as amended under PCT Article 19, or the claims as amended in a preliminary amendment. Where the Applicant fails to pay the correct amount of the additional claims fee, the USPTO will invite him/her to pay the missing amount at the current fee amount.

Fee Reduction for "Small Entity" or "Micro Entity" Status

Applicants having a "small entity" or "micro entity" status are entitled to a reduction of 50% or 75%, respectively, in certain fees.

Fees

> NOTE: Fees are subject to change so check the current Fee Schedule at *www.uspto.gov/learning-and-resources/fees-and-payment/uspto-fee*-schedule for the national stage fees. The fee may be paid by the following methods:

- Cash payment
- U.S. Postal Service money order
- Check
- UPSTO Deposit Account
- Credit Card (MasterCard, VISA, American Express, and Discover)

Money orders and checks must be payable in United States dollars to the "Director of the USPTO." Remittance from foreign countries must be payable and immediately negotiable in the United States of America for the full amount of the fee required. Cash sent by mail will be at the risk of the sender; letters containing cash should be registered. All payments must indicate the complete application number, the name of Applicant and the type of fee being paid.

Inventor's Oath or Declaration

For applications with an international filing date before September 16, 2012, if the Applicant pays the basic national fee and a copy of the international application is received within the time limit for entry into the national phase, but an oath or declaration of the inventor is not furnished, a notice shall be sent to the Applicant which sets a time period for furnishing the oath or declaration. The Applicant can then furnish the oath or declaration provided that a surcharge is paid. The time period set in the notice will be two (2) months from the date of the notice or thirty-two (32) months from priority date, whichever is later.

> NOTE: The time period set in the notice is extendable.

For applications with an international filing date on or after September 16, 2012, the submission of an ADS identifying each inventor and providing each inventor's residence and mailing address will permit the Applicant to postpone submission of the oath or declaration of the inventor (or substitute statement, if applicable) until the application is otherwise in condition for allowance. In such cases, the USPTO will issue a Notification of Acceptance (Form PCT/DO/EO/903) and refer the application for publication and examination; however, the Notification of Acceptance (Form PCT/DO/EO/903) will indicate that the oath or declaration has not yet been satisfied.

Power of Attorney
No representation of the Applicant by an attorney or agent is required, but where an attorney or agent is to represent an Applicant, a Power of Attorney signed by the Applicant/Inventor to an attorney or agent registered to practice before the USPTO is required. It is highly advisable to be represented by an attorney or agent.

Information Disclosure Statement
An Information Disclosure Statement ("IDS") must be filed in the UPSTO no later than three (3) months from the date of entry of the national phase. The IDS must disclose all information of which the Applicant, or any other person substantively involved with the preparation of the application or its prosecution, is aware which is material to the patentability of the invention.

The IDS must include:

* A listing (preferably on Form PTO/SB/08) of patents, applications, publications or other information;
* A copy of each listed item except for U.S. patents and U.S. patent application publications; and
* For each item listed which is not in the English language, a concise explanation of its relevance.

Amendments of the U.S. National Phase Application
The Applicant may make the following amendments, provided no new matter is introduced in the disclosure of the invention:

* Before the final decision of the USPTO to grant or to reject the patent, the Applicant may file amendments to the description, claims and drawing(s) of his own/her own volition or when specifically required by the Examiner.
* After the final decision, amendments may be made only by (canceling) claims or complying with any requirement of form which has been made by the Examiner, or by presenting rejected claims in better form for reconsideration on appeal.

Fee for Grant of Patent

A patent issue fee and any required publication fee must be paid within a nonexpendable period of three (3) months after the mailing of a written notice of allowance.

Maintenance Fees

After a patent has been issued, a fee must be paid for maintaining the patent in force beyond four (4) years after grant. The first such fee is due by three (3) years and six (6) months after issue of the patent. Where the Applicant fails to pay within that time limit, the fee payer may receive a Maintenance Fee Reminder from the USPTO. Payment can then still be made together with a surcharge within six (6) months following the due date. If payment is not made by the surcharge date, then the USPTO will mail a Notice of Patent Expiration to the fee payer for non-payment of maintenance fees.

Early Start of U.S. National Phase before the USPTO

If the Applicant desires the examination by the USPTO of his/her application to start earlier than the expiration of the time limit for entry into the national phase, he/she must file in writing an express request and submit the basic national fee, a copy of the international application, a translation of the international application (if required), and an oath or declaration of the inventor. The express request may be accomplished by checking the appropriate box on the Form-1390 for entry into the national phase.

> NOTE: The mechanism for deferring submission of the oath or declaration of the inventor by filing an ADS is not applicable where the Applicant requests early examination by the USPTO. Such early examination of the application requires submission of the oath or declaration (or the substitute statement, if applicable).

Continuation, Continuation-In-Part or Divisional of the PCT International Application

The Applicant may, instead of entering the national phase, file a continuation, continuation-in-part, or divisional of the PCT international application ("the continuing application"), provided the international application designates the U.S. and has not been withdrawn or abandoned at the time of filing the continuation application. An international application is considered abandoned after the expiration of the time limit for entry into the national phase, which is thirty (30) months from the priority date, if a copy of the international application and the basic national fee have not been received in the USPTO.

When the basic national fee has been paid and a copy of the PCT international application has been communicated by the International Bureau within the time limit for entry into the national phase, but the application is not in English, or the oath or declaration has not been received, a notice will be sent to the Applicant to furnish an English translation and/or an oath or declaration of the inventor. If the Applicant does not timely respond to the notice within the time period set by the USPTO, the international application will become abandoned.

The normal procedure for filing continuing applications applies. The Applicant must submit an ADS claiming the benefit of the international filing date of the international application designating the United States.

Recording Assignment Documents
The USPTO will record assignments relating to international patent applications which designate the United States. The assignment must identify the application by the international application number.

Publication of Applications
Each international application in compliance with 35 USC 371 and continuing application from an international application will be published promptly after the expiration of eighteen (18) months from the earliest filing date for which a benefit is sought, unless the application is:

- No longer pending
- Subject to national security provisions
- Issued as a patent
- Filed with a nonpublication request

28.3 eFILING A U.S. NATIONAL PHASE APPLICATION VIA EFS-WEB
The basic steps to file a U.S. National Phase Application via EFS-Web are as follows:

1. Go to *www.uspto.gov*.
2. Under "Patents" tab, click "Filing Online" under "Application Process" section.
3. On the "File Online" page, click "EFS-Web".
4. On the "About EFS-Web" page, click "Launch EFS-Web Registered eFiler".
5. Security Warning: "Allow access to the following application from this website?" Click "Allow".
6. When the User Authentication screen appears, browse for the Practitioner's .epf file. (Hint: Save the Practitioner's .epf file on the desktop for easier access.)
7. Enter the Practitioner's password.
8. Check box at left side of screen in order to proceed to the next screen.
9. Under "*Main Functions", click "New application/proceeding".
10. Click "Utility" under "Select Type of New Application/Proceeding".
11. Click "U.S. National Stage under 35 USC 371".

12. Type in the International Application Number and International Filing Date. Click "Continue" for the next screen.
13. Enter the following information:
    * Title of Invention
    * Attorney Docket Number
    * First Named Inventor
    * Correspondence Address (select the Practitioner's Customer Number using the drop down arrow).
14. After all the foregoing information has been entered, click "Continue". This saves the filing up to this point.
15. Browse for the file (in PDF format) and upload it to this filing.

NOTE: When naming the PDF file, make sure that there are no spaces or the PDF file attachment will be rejected.

16. Underneath the uploaded document, it states: "Does your PDF file contain multiple documents?" Click "Yes".
17. The following basic document descriptions are used for filing a National Phase Application:

Category	Document Description
Application Part	Application Data Sheet
Application Part	Specification
Application Part	Claims
Application Part	Abstract
Application Part	Drawings-only black and white line drawings
Application Part	Oath or Declaration Filed
Amendment	Preliminary Amendment (if any)

NOTE: The Preliminary Amendment does not have to be broken down into document descriptions. The USPTO will accept both ways via EFS-Web.

Category	Document Description
Amendment	Preliminary Amendment
Amendment	Specification (Amendments to the Specification)

Amendment	Claims
	(Amendments to the Claims)
Amendment	Applicant Arguments/Remarks Made in an Amendment
	(Amendments to the Drawings)
Amendment	Applicant Arguments/Remarks Made in an Amendment
	(Remarks)
Amendment	Abstract
Amendment	Drawings – only black and white line drawings

If filing an Information Disclosure Statement, use the following document descriptions:

Category	Document Description
IDS/References	Transmittal Letter
IDS/References	Information Disclosure Statement (IDS) Form (SB08)
IDS/References	Foreign Reference
IDS/References	Non-Patent Literature

18. Click "Upload & Validate" to make sure that there are no validation errors. If there is a validation error, there will be a prompt on the screen of an error or a warning! If there is an error, the error must be corrected at this point. If there is a warning, click "Continue" to go to the next screen. For the remainder of the steps, see *Section 6.2.2* to complete the efiling of the National Phase Application via EFS-Web.

CHAPTER 29

Resources and Blogs

● ● ●

29.1 PATENT ELECTRONIC RESOURCES

THE FOLLOWING PATENT ELECTRONIC WEBSITES are excellent resources concerning general patent information, procedures, and petitions:

* General Information Concerning Patents (*www.uspto.gov/patents/resources/general_info_concerning_patents.pdf*) - Provides information in nontechnical language concerning the application for and granting of patents.
* Manual of Patent Examining Procedure (MPEP) (*www.uspto.gov/web/offices/pac/mpep/index.html*) - USPTO Patent Examiners' guide to examination practice.
* Petitions (*www.uspto.gov/patents-application-process/petitions*) – provides information on petitions and reference materials.

29.2 USPTO SERVICES

The following USPTO services are excellent resources for information on all aspects of the patent process:

* USPTO Web Patent Database (*patft.uspto.gov/*) - Full text of all U.S. patents issued since January 1, 1976 and images and PDFs of every patent issued since 1790.
* Search patent assignments (*assignments.uspto.gov/assignments/q?db=pat*) – This searchable database contains all recorded patent assignment information back to August 1980.
* Order copies (*ebiz1.uspto.gov/oems25p/index.html*) – Order copies of U.S. patent application documents.
* USPTO Subscription Center (*enews.uspto.gov*) - This is the place to sign up to receive the latest news, updates, alerts via email.
* First Office Action Estimator (*www.uspto.gov/learning-and-resources/ statistics/first-office-action-estimator*) - Check current estimates on how long it will take for a first Office Action on a patent application by entering an Art Unit or Class and Subclass associated with a current or potential application.

- e-Office Action Quick Start Guide (*www.uspto.gov/sites/default/files/documents/e-oa_quick_start_guide_Mar2015.pdf*) - Learn more about the e-Office Action program and receiving e-notifications of USPTO communications.

- Patent Term Calculator (*www.uspto.gov/patent/laws-and-regulations/patent-term-calculator*) – USPTO is providing a downloadable patent term calculator as a resource to help the public estimate the expiration date of a patent.

- Entity Status Quick Start Guide (*www.uspto.gov/sites/default/files/documents/QSG-Entity%20Status-Final.pdf*) – Learn how to update the Entity Status for an application.

- USPTO Webinars, Public Training Portal and IP E-Learning Modules (*www.uspto.gov/learning-and-resources/global-intellectual-property-academy-gipa/uspto-webinars-and-ip-e-learning*) – USPTO intellectual property webinar series.

- Corrections to Patents (*www.uspto.gov/patents-maintaining-patent/data-management-services*) - Data Management Services provides information in correcting patent publications and granted patents.

- Electronic Data Products (*www.uspto.gov/learning-and-resources/electronic-bulk-data-products*) - The USPTO makes patent public data available in bulk form, which can be used to load into databases or other analytical tools for research and analysis. Bulk data is generally provided in the form of ZIP or TAR files containing TIFF or PDF images, concatenated XML or structured ASCII files.

- Expired Patent Number Search (*www.uspto.gov/patents/process/expform.jsp*) – Search expired patents for failure to pay maintenance fees.

- Products and Services (*www.uspto.gov/learning-and-resources/public-information-products-services*) - One stop resource for assignment recordation, ordering copies, electronic bulk data products, general information, libraries, and patent statistical reports.

- Patent Application Initiatives Timeline (*www.uspto.gov/patent/initiatives/uspto-patent-application-initiatives-timeline*) - Displays various programs and initiatives that are available to Applicants during each phase of the application process.

- Patent Terms Extended (*www.uspto.gov/patent/laws-and-regulations/patent-terms-extended*) – patent terms extended under 35 USC 155 and 35 USC 156.

- Issue Years and Patent Numbers Since 1836 (*www.uspto.gov/web/offices/ ac/ido/oeip/taf/issuyear.htm*) – Table of issue years and patent numbers for selected document types issued since 1836.

- Patent Statistics by Calendar Year (*www.uspto.gov/web/offices/ac/ido/oeip/ taf/reports.htm*) – Calendar year patent statistics (January 1 to December 31) and general patent statistics reports are available for viewing.

- USPTO Systems Status and Availability (*www.uspto.gov/blog/ebiz*) - Check this page for the latest information on operating status and availability of the USPTO online business systems.

- How to Conduct a Preliminary U.S. Patent Search: A Step by Step Strategy (*www.uspto.gov/video/cbt/ptrcsearching*) – Video web based tutorial (36 minutes).

- The Seven-Step Strategy (*www.uspto.gov/learning-and-resources/support-centers/patent-and-trademark-resource-centers-ptrc/resources/seven*) - Outlines a suggested procedure for patent searching.

29.3 PUBLICATIONS

The following publication websites are excellent resources to search for patent-related notices and gazettes:

* Official Gazette for Patents (*www.uspto.gov/learning-and-resources/official-gazette/official-gazette-patents*) - Published each Tuesday in electronic form only, and contains bibliographic text and a representative drawing from each patent issued that week.
* Daily Official Gazette for Certificates (*www.uspto.gov/learning-and-resources/official-gazette/patents/daily-official-gazette-certificates-current-week*) - Each Tuesday's Official Gazette for Patents will report the daily certificates that issued during the preceding workweek (Monday-Friday).
* Notices: Recent Patent-Related (*www.uspto.gov/patent/laws-and-regulations/patent-related-notices/patent-related-notices-2015*) – Most recent pre-Official Gazette, Official Gazette and Federal Register notices.

29.4 INTERNATIONAL PROTECTION

The following International websites are excellent resources relating to PCTs and International Patent Offices:

* Patent Cooperation Treaty (PCT) Legal Administration (*www.uspto.gov/patents-getting-started/international-protection/international-patent-legal-administration-formerly*) – Excellent resource relating to all PCT matters.
* PCT Help Desk (*www.uspto.gov/patents/init_events/pct/index.jsp#helpdesk*) – **Telephone assistance and information** on the PCT process, **(571) 272-4300, is available** from **9:00 am** to **4:30 pm** (ET), **Monday through Friday.**
* GPSN (*gpsn.uspto.gov/*) - Search tool for Chinese patent documentation.
* Search International Patent Offices (*www.uspto.gov/patents/process/search/ index.jsp#heading-9*) – Search tool for free online access to patent documents is provided by many countries including EPO, JPO, WIPO, KIPRIS and SIPO.
* PCT Search Quick Start Guide (*www.uspto.gov/sites/default/files/patents/process/status/ private_pair/pctsearch-v2_09_07_07.pdf*) – Search tool for International application numbers via PAIR.

29.5 GENERAL

The following websites are excellent resources in locating Patent Practitioners, Patent Agents and USPTO Employees.

- Attorneys and Agents Registered to Practice Before the U.S. Patent and Trademark Office (*https://oedci.uspto.gov/OEDCI*) – Search tool for locating registered Practitioners authorized to practice before the USPTO.
- Employee Locator Search (*portal.uspto.gov/EmployeeSearch*) - Search tool for locating USPTO employees.

29.6 Blogs

The following blogs are excellent resources in receiving updates and information regarding the USPTO and AIA, generally:

- USPTO Blog (www.uspto.gov/blog) – Director's Forum: A Blog from USPTO's Leadership.
- AIA Blog (www.uspto.gov/blog/aia/) – This blog has updates and information about various AIA related issues but consult with the AIA Helpdesk for specific requirements on a particular type of AIA filing or if you have any questions.

APPENDIX A

Helpful Checklists

● ● ●

A.1 Opening New Matters

Item	Yes	Requires Attention
Review client instruction letter: Bar date noted? Provisional priority claimed? Foreign priority claimed? Invention disclosure present?		
Assign reference number for matter: Conflict check performed? Client number assigned? Matter number assigned?		
Client file: Sent acknowledgment letter? Hard file created? Client entity size noted on file? All correspondence in file?		
Docketing: Bar and due dates noted? Attorney assigned? Attorney notified of matter?		

A.2 Daily Checklist

Item	Yes	Requires Attention
Review Today's Docket: Attorney aware and working?		
Incoming correspondence: All docketed and correct? If needed, attorney notified? Reported to client?		
Today's filings: Filings ready for review? Filings ready for PTO submission? Filings submitted to PTO? Filing reported? File for matter updated?		
Review Tomorrow's Docket: Attorney aware and working?		

A.3 MONTHLY CHECKLIST

Item	Yes	Requires Attention
Review Monthly Docket: Bar dates and deadlines noted? Attorney aware and working?		
Old Files (after time limit): Abandoned sent to storage? Issued sent to storage? Expired prov. sent to storage?		
Billing: All Attorney time entered? Invoices prepared? Letters prepared? Bills sent to client?		

A.4 PROVISIONAL APPLICATION CHECKLIST

Date: _____ Client/Matter No. _____

_____Have client/inventor complete an Invention Disclosure Record.

_____Docket deadline for filing (priority or statutory bar).

_____Acknowledge receipt of documents to client, if requested, after checking for completeness of documents.

_____Complete client/intake form, obtain client/matter number.

_____Complete file jacket (print).

Checklist for documents:

_____Complete **Application Data Sheet 37 CFR 1.76 (PTO/AIA/14)** form at *www.uspto.gov/forms/aia0014.pdf* to include names and addresses of all inventors.

_____Specification has all consecutive pages (noting page numbers).

_____Drawings required if necessary to understand invention. Drawings must show every feature of the invention disclosed in specification. Check that all figures/drawings described in specification are not missing.

_____After efiling: Executed/signed Assignment is filed through ePAS (if needed).

NOTE: The Nonprovisional Application must be filed within one year from the Provisional Application filing date. If the date falls on a Saturday, Sunday or a holiday, the due date will fall on the next business day.

A.5 Nonprovisional Application Checklist

Date: _____ Client/Matter No. _____

_____Invention Disclosure Record.

_____Docket deadline for filing (priority or statutory bar).

_____Acknowledge receipt of documents to client, if requested, after checking for completeness of documents.

_____Complete client/intake form, obtain client/matter number.

   * All inventors, citizenship, addresses.

_____Complete file jacket (print).

_____Calculate claims on inside file jacket or on **Multiple Dependent Claim Calculation Sheet (PTO/ SB/07)** form at *www.uspto.gov/forms/sb0007.pdf.*

Checklist for documents:

_____Specification has all consecutive pages (noting page and line numbers).

_____Make list of cited references contained in specification (if any).

_____Claims – make sure there is at least one independent claim that appears to be related to the subject matter of the application, e.g., compare with the application title. If there are multiple dependent claims, follow Practitioner practice for preparing Preliminary Amendment amending claims to avoid the multiple dependent claim fee.

_____Abstract of the Disclosure (separate sheet attached at end).

_____Drawings – make sure all drawings mentioned in specification are present and vice-versa. Compare figure designations with specification. **Note:** If figure designations do not agree, discuss with Practitioner.

_____Prepare **Declaration (37 CFR 1.63) for Utility or Design Application Using an Application Data Sheet (37 CFR 1.76) (PTO/SB/01A)** form at *www.uspto.gov/forms/aia0001.pdf* for execution by inventor or unexecuted to be filed.

_____Prepare **Power of Attorney by Applicant (PTO/AIA/82B)** form at *www.uspto.gov/forms/aia0082.pdf* for execution by Applicant or unexecuted to be filed.

_____If executed Declaration is present for filing with the new application:

Check in body of Declaration:

- Inventor's full name (first, middle initial, last)
- Title of invention (corresponds to title on application)
- Date of execution (optional)
- Have all inventors signed the Declaration?

_____If executed Declaration is **NOT** present with the new application:

Optional: If there is no executed Declaration, prepare a Declaration for submitting with unsigned application. Have Declaration proofread. On unsigned applications, Application Number and filing to be inserted in the Declaration for forwarding to client when this information is available.

_____Check to see if this is a small entity or a regular undiscounted entity. If small entity is being claimed, there is a 50% reduction of government fees to be paid.

_____Assignment for US only: (if application is to be assigned)

Check to make sure all inventors on Declaration have signed and dated the Assignment.

Check title of the application.

Compare execution date of Assignment and make sure it agrees with execution dates indicated on Declaration and Power of Attorney. Must be same date as the Declaration or later.

_____Assignment for Worldwide:

If assignee is U.S. company and application is being first filed in the United States, is worldwide assignment being filed?

_____Priority Document (can be filed at a later date) – be sure the deadline for filing is docketed. Make sure Application Number and filing date on certified copy of priority document agree with data on Declaration and information forwarded by client.

_____Biotech Cases:

Sequence Listing: may not file with application filing, but after Notice received from USPTO. (Notice to file sequence listing may appear in first Office Action.)

* Printed sequence listing
* Electronic Version (diskette) of sequence listing (diskette envelope must have copy of diskette label on front)
* Statement to support filing
* Preliminary Amendment (if after filing application)
* Copy of Notice to Comply (if after filing application)
* File in "Box Sequence" (if after filing application)

Preparation of documents for filing case:

_____**Optional** - Prepare **Utility Patent Application Transmittal (PTO/AIA/15)** form at *www.uspto.gov/forms/aia0015.pdf.*

_____Insert Attorney Docket No. (client/matter number)
_____Insert First Named Inventor
_____Insert title of invention
_____Number of pages totaling the Specification, Claims, and Abstract
_____Number of drawing sheets (if no drawings type "0" or "none")
_____Check box for Inventor's Oath or Declaration if submitting either executed or unexecuted
_____Check box for ADS (best to file at initial filing)
_____Check box for small entity, if applicable
_____Check boxes for any other documents accompanying application papers
_____Insert Customer Number for the Correspondence Address
_____Insert registered Practitioner's name and registration number

_____**Required** - Complete **Application Data Sheet 37 CFR 1.76 (PTO/AIA/14)** form at *www.uspto.gov/forms/aia0014.pdf* to include names and addresses of all inventors.

_____Executed or unexecuted new language Declaration from each inventor.

_____Executed/signed Power of Attorney from each inventor and/or Assignee.

_____Information Disclosure Statement (if any).

_____Preliminary Amendment (if needed).

_____After efiling: Executed/signed Assignment is filed through ePAS (if needed).

A.6 Design Patent Application Checklist

Date: _____   Client/Matter No. _____

_____Docket deadline for filing (priority or statutory bar).

_____Acknowledge receipt of documents to client, if requested, after checking for completeness of documents.

_____Complete client/intake form, obtain client/matter number.

_____Complete file jacket (print).

Checklist for documents:

_____Specification has all consecutive pages.

_____Drawings showing all views necessary to understand invention. Drawings must show every feature of the invention disclosed in specification. Check that all figures/drawings described in specification are accounted for.

_____Make list of cited references in specification (if any).

_____Order certified copy of foreign priority application (if any).

Preparation of documents for filing case:

_____**Optional -** Complete the **Design Patent Application Transmittal Form (PTO/SB/18)** form at *www.uspto.gov/web/forms/sb0018_fill.pdf.*

      _____Insert Attorney Docket No. (client/matter number)
      _____Insert First Named Inventor
      _____Insert title of invention
      _____Number of pages totaling the Specification, Claims, and Abstract
      _____Number of drawing sheets (if no drawings type "0" or "none")
      _____Check box for Inventor's Oath or Declaration if submitting either executed or unexecuted

_____Check box for ADS (best to file at initial filing)
_____Check box for small entity, if applicable
_____Check boxes for any other documents accompanying application papers
_____Insert Customer Number for the Correspondence Address
_____Insert registered Practitioner's name and registration number

_____**Required** - Complete **Application Data Sheet 37 CFR 1.76 (PTO/AIA/14)** form at *www.uspto.gov/forms/aia0014.pdf* to include names and addresses of all inventors.

_____Executed or unexecuted new language Declaration from each inventor.

_____Executed/signed Power of Attorney from each inventor and/or Assignee.

_____Information Disclosure Statement (if any).

_____Preliminary Amendment (if needed).

_____After efiling: Executed/signed Assignment is filed through ePAS (if needed).

A.7 Divisional/Continuation Application Checklist

Date: _____ Client/Matter No. _____

_____Invention Disclosure Record.

_____Docket deadline for filing (priority or statutory bar).

_____Acknowledge receipt of documents to client, if requested, after checking for completeness of documents.

_____Complete client/intake form, obtain client/matter number.

    ＊   All inventors, citizenship, addresses.

_____Complete file jacket (print).

_____Calculate claims on inside file jacket or on **Multiple Dependent Claim Calculation Sheet (PTO/SB/07)** form at *www.uspto.gov/forms/sb0007.pdf*.

Checklist for documents:

_____Specification from parent case has all consecutive pages (noting page and line numbers).

_____Make list of cited references contained in specification (if any).

_____Claims – make sure there is at least one independent claim that appears to be related to the subject matter of the application, e.g., compare with the application title. If there are multiple dependent claims, follow Practitioner practice for preparing Preliminary Amendment amending claims to avoid paying the multiple dependent claim fee.

_____Abstract of the Disclosure (separate sheet attached at end).

_____Drawings – make sure all drawings mentioned in specification are present and vice-versa. Compare figure designations with specification. **Note:** If figure designations do not agree, discuss with Practitioner.

_____Copy of executed Declaration (if application filed after 9/16/12) and Power of Attorney from parent application is present. Otherwise, a "new language" Declaration must be signed by the inventors again.

Preparation of documents for filing case:

_____**Optional** - Prepare Utility Patent Application Transmittal (PTO/AIA/15) form at *www.uspto. gov/forms/aia0015.pdf.*

    _____Insert Attorney Docket No. (client/matter number)
    _____Insert First Named Inventor
    _____Insert title of invention
    _____Number of pages totaling the Specification, Claims, and Abstract
    _____Number of drawing sheets (if no drawings type "0" or "none")
    _____Check box for Inventor's Oath or Declaration if submitting either executed or unexecuted
    _____Check box for ADS (best to file at initial filing)
    _____Check box for small entity, if applicable
    _____Check boxes for any other documents accompanying application papers
    _____Insert Customer Number for the Correspondence Address
    _____Insert registered Practitioner's name and registration number

_____**Required** - Complete Application Data Sheet 37 CFR 1.76 (PTO/AIA/14) form at *www.uspto.gov/forms/aia0014.pdf* to include names and addresses of all inventors.

_____Executed or unexecuted new language Declaration from each inventor.

_____Executed/signed Power of Attorney from each inventor and/or Assignee.

_____Information Disclosure Statement (cited references from parent application), if any.

_____Preliminary Amendment (if needed).

_____After efiling: Copy of executed/signed Assignment (from parent application) is filed through ePAS (if needed).

A.8 Continuation-In-Part Application Checklist

Date: _____ Client/Matter No. _____

_____Invention Disclosure Record.

_____Docket deadline for filing (priority or statutory bar).

_____Acknowledge receipt of documents to client, if requested, after checking for completeness of documents.

_____Complete client/intake form, obtain client/matter number.

* All inventors, citizenship, addresses

_____Complete file jacket (print).

_____Calculate claims on inside file jacket or on **Multiple Dependent Claim Calculation Sheet (PTO/ SB/07)** form at *www.uspto.gov/forms/sb0007.pdf.*

Checklist for documents:

_____Specification has all consecutive pages (noting page and line numbers).

_____Make list of cited references contained in specification, (if any).

_____Claims – make sure there is at least one independent claim that appears to be related to the subject matter of the application, e.g., compare with the application title. If there are multiple dependent claims, follow Practitioner practice for preparing Preliminary Amendment amending claims to avoid paying the multiple dependent claim fee.

_____Abstract of the Disclosure (separate sheet attached at end).

_____Drawings – make sure all drawings mentioned in specification are present and vice-versa. Compare figure designations with specification. **NOTE:** If figure designations do not agree, discuss with Practitioner.

_____Prepare **Declaration (37 CFR 1.63) for Utility or Design Application Using an Application Data Sheet (37 CFR 1.76) (PTO/AIA/01)** form at *www.uspto.gov/forms/aia0001.pdf* for execution by inventor or unexecuted to be filed.

_____Prepare **Transmittal for Power of Attorney to One or More Registered Practitioners (PTO/AIA/82)** form at *www.uspto.gov/forms/aia0082.pdf* for execution by inventor/Applicant/assignee or unexecuted to be filed.

A copy of the Declaration and Power of Attorney from the parent application is not to be used for a CIP Application.

_____If executed Declaration is present for filing with the new application:

Check in body of Declaration:

* Inventor's full name (first, middle initial, last)
* Title of invention (corresponds to title on application)
* Citizenship
* Date of execution

_____If executed Declaration is **NOT** present with the new application:

If there is no executed Declaration, prepare a declaration for submitting with unsigned application. Have Declaration proofread. On unsigned applications, Application Number and filing to be inserted in the Declaration for forwarding to client when this information is available.

Preparation of documents for filing case:

_____**Optional** - Complete **Utility Patent Application Transmittal (PTO/SB/05)** form at *www.uspto.gov/forms/sb0005_fill.pdf*.

_____Insert Attorney Docket No. (client/matter number)
_____Insert First Named Inventor
_____Insert title of invention
_____Number of pages totaling the Specification, Claims, and Abstract
_____Number of drawing sheets (if no drawings type "0" or "none")
_____Check box for Inventor's Oath or Declaration if submitting either executed or unexecuted
_____Check box for ADS (best to file at initial filing)

_____Check box for small entity, if applicable
_____Check boxes for any other documents accompanying application papers
_____Insert Customer Number for the Correspondence Address
_____Insert registered Practitioner's name and registration number

_____**Required –** Complete **Application Data Sheet 37 CFR 1.76 (PTO/AIA/14)** form at *www.uspto.gov/forms/aia0014.pdf* to include names and addresses of all inventors.

_____Executed or unexecuted new language Declaration from each inventor.

_____Executed/signed Power of Attorney from each inventor and/or Assignee.

_____Information Disclosure Statement (cited references from parent application), if any.

_____Preliminary Amendment (if needed).

_____Executed/signed Assignment is filed through ePAS after filing the U.S. patent application electronically (if needed).

A.9 Assignment Recordation Checklist

Date: _____ Client/Matter No. _____

No.	Item	Correct or not?
1	Recordation Date	
2	Application No.	
3	Inventor(s) Name(s)	
4	Date signed by inventor(s)	
5	Assignee Name(s)	
6	Assignee Address(es)	
7	Filing Date	

Reel/Frame: _____

A.10 Published Application Checklist

Date: _____ Client/Matter No. _____

When an application is published, and if requested to do so, check the following:

* Application Number
* Title
* Abstract
* All inventors listed
* Assignee (if any listed)
* Specification page count
* Drawing page count
* Filing date
* Make sure no pages are blank
* Make sure all claims are listed
* Priority/benefit claim

A.11 Patent Official Filing Receipt Checklist

Date: _____ Client/Matter No. _____

No.	Item	Correct or not?
1	Application Number	
2	Filing Date	
3	Atty. Docket No.	
4	Correspondence Address/Customer Number	
5	Inventor(s), City/State	
6	Applicant(s), City/State	
7	Domestic Priority Data	
8	Assignment for Published Patent Application	
9	Foreign Applications	
10	Power of Attorney	
11	Entity Status	
12	Title	

Note: No. 7 does not apply to provisional applications

A.12 Amendment Checklist

Date: _____ Client/Matter No. _____

_____Check to make sure the Office Action deadline is correct on docket. The deadline is three (3) months from the mailing date of Office Action, with up to three (3)-month extensions of time available.

_____Calculate claim amendments on inside file jacket – "STATUS OF CLAIMS"

_____Prepare Petition for Extension of Time if required. (If efiling, the EOT Form is not necessary.)

_____If foreign certified priority document is available, prepare Claim for Convention Priority, and file document(s) with Amendment. (This can only be submitted by hand-delivery or by mail via Certificate of Mailing. It is not available to e-file this at the USPTO at the moment.)

_____If disclosure reference(s) in file are not yet submitted, prepare Information Disclosure Statement transmittal letter and Forms **PTO/SB/08a** and/or **PTO/SB/08b** or the USPTO fillable IDS form.

Additional if FINAL REJECTION:

_____Prepare and file Notice of Appeal if 6-month, non-extendible deadline has been reached to prevent abandonment of application. Be aware that the Notice of Appeal deadline is still running in response to a Final Rejection unless the case is allowed or the Notice of Appeal has been filed.

_____Include fee for Notice of Appeal in fee calculation.

_____Expedited handling block in upper right of amendment.

A.13 Restriction Requirement Checklist

Date: _____ Client/Matter No. _____

_____Check to make sure the Office Action (**Restriction Requirement**) deadline is correct on docket. The deadline is two (2) months from the mailing date of **Restriction Requirement**, with up to 4-month extensions of time available.

_____Prepare a **Response to the Restriction Requirement** electing which group of claims, for the Practitioner's signature.

_____Prepare **Petition for Extension of Time,** if any, for the Practitioner's signature. (**If efiling, this form is not necessary.**)

A.14 Rce Checklist

Date: _____ Client/Matter No. _____

If prosecution in an application is closed, an Applicant may file an RCE.

_____Prepare a Request for Continued Examination (RCE) Transmittal Form at *www.uspto.gov/web/forms/sb0030.pdf* or EFS-Web fillable form at *www.uspto.gov/web/forms/sb0030e_fill.pdf.*

Check to make sure the following information is correct on the transmittal:

* Application No.
* Filing Date
* First Named Inventor
* Art Unit
* Examiner
* Attorney Docket No.

_____Submission required under 37 CFR 1.114:

_____Previously submitted filed unentered amendments
_____Amendment Accompanying Request for Continued Examination
_____Information Disclosure Statement
_____Affidavit/Declaration

A.15 Notice Of Allowance/Issue Fee Payment Checklist

Docket No.:_____ Application No: _____ Date: _____

It is recommended that the Notice of Allowance letter should **NOT** be forwarded to client until the following items have been checked and this form signed by the responsible attorney/assisting attorney. Check each line item and, if necessary notify docketing of any dates to be associated with the payment of the Issue Fee.

Paralegal Review

Item	Yes	No	N/A
Are all the inventor(s) names spelled correctly?			
Is the title of the invention correct?			
Is the entity status listed as micro, small or undiscounted still accurate?			
Has assignment been filed? If yes, Reel ____ / Frame ____ Assignee name:			
Has an Oath been filed?			
Has a Power of Attorney been filed?			
Has the proper priority been filed and acknowledged by the USPTO?			
Has an Election or Restriction Requirement issued?			
Do we have instructions to file a Divisional, Continuation or CIP?			
Have all references cited been acknowledged by the Examiner?			
Is correction of drawings needed?			
Have drawings been sent to draftsman?			
Is a biological deposit necessary?			
Were there any Terminal Disclaimers filed in this case?			

Attorney Review

Item	Yes	No	N/A
Examiner Interview Summary Record?			
Acceptable?			
Examiner's Reasons for Allowance?			
Acceptable?			
Examiner's Amendment?			
Acceptable?			
Has the firm received notification from the client that Maintenance fees will be paid through another channel?			

Reviewed By: Paralegal:_____
                Attorney:_____

Notes:_____

A.16 Utility/Design Letters Patent Checklist

Date: _____ Client/Matter No. _____

No.	Item	Correct or not?
1	Cover page	
2	Claims	

APPENDIX B

PCT Contracting States

• • •

(Updated August 18, 2016)

Name of State followed by the Two-letter code

Date on which State became bound by the PCT[1]

Name of State	Date
Albania AL	4 October 1995
Algeria DZ[2]	8 March 2000
Angola AO	27 December 2007
Antigua and Barbuda AG	17 March 2000
Armenia AM[2]	25 December 1991
Australia AU	31 March 1980
Austria AT	23 April 1979
Azerbaijan AZ	25 December 1995
Bahrain BH[2]	18 March 2007
Barbados BB	12 March 1985
Belarus BY[2]	25 December 1991
Belgium BE	14 December 1981
Belize BZ	17 June 2000
Benin BJ	26 February 1987
Bosnia and Herzegovina BA	7 September 1996
Botswana BW	30 October 2003
Brazil BR	9 April 1978
Brunei Darussalam BN	24 July 2012
Bulgaria BG	21 May 1984
Burkina Faso BF	21 March 1989
Cameroon CM	24 January 1978
Canada CA	2 January 1990
Central African Republic CF	24 January 1978

Chad TD .... 24 January 1978

Chile CL[2] ....2 June 2009

China CN[3,4] ....1 January 1994

Columbia CO ....28 February 2001

Comoros KM ....3 April 2005

Congo CG ....24 January 1978

Costa Rica CR ....3 August 1999

Côte d'Ivoire CI..30 April 1991

Croatia HR ....1 July 1998

Cuba CU[2] ....16 July 1996

Cyprus CY ....1 April 1998

Czech Republic CZ ....1 January 1993

Democratic People's Republic of Korea KP ....8 July 1980

Denmark DK...1 December 1978

Dominica DM ....7 August 1999

Dominican Republic DO ....28 May 2007

Djibouti..(will be bound on 23 Sept. 2016)

Ecuador EC ....7 May 2001

Egypt EG...6 September 2003

El Salvador SV...17 August 2006

Equatorial Guinea GQ ....17 July 2001

Estonia EE...24 August 1994

Finland FI[5] ....1 October 1980

France FR[2,6] ....25 February 1978

Gabon GA ....24 January 1978

Gambia GM ....9 December 1997

Georgia GE[2] ....25 December 1991

Germany DE ....24 January 1978

Ghana GH...26 February 1997

Greece GR...9 October 1990

Grenada GD ....22 September 1998

Guatemala GT ....14 October 2006

Guinea GN..27 May 1991

Guinea-Bissau GW ....12 December 1997

Honduras HN ....20 June 2006

Hungary HU[2] ....27 June 1980

Iceland IS ....23 March 1995

India IN[2] ....7 December 1998

Indonesia ID[2] ....5 September 1997
Iran (Islamic Republic of) IR...4 October 2013
Ireland IE..1 August 1992
Israel IL ....1 June 1996
Italy IT...28 March 1985
Japan JP...1 October 1978
Kazakhstan KZ[2] ....25 December 1991
Kenya KE ....8 June 1994
Kyrgyzstan KG[2] ....25 December 1991
Kuwait...(will be bound on 9 Sept. 2016)
Lao People's Democratic Republic LA...........................14 June 2006
Latvia LV ....7 September 1993
Lesotho LS ....21 October 1995
Liberia LR ....27 August 1994
Libya LY ....15 September 2005
Liechtenstein LI ....19 March 1980
Lithuania LT ....5 July 1994
Luxembourg LU ....30 April 1978
Madagascar MG ....24 January 1978
Malawi MW ....24 January 1978
Malaysia MY[2] ....16 August 2006
Mali ML ....19 October 1984
Malta MT[2] ....1 March 2007
Mauritania MR...13 April 1983
Mexico MX...1 January 1995
Monaco MC..22 June 1979
Mongolia MN ....27 May 1991
Montenegro ME..3 June 2006
Morocco MA ....8 October 1999
Mozambique MZ[2] ....18 May 2000
Namibia NA ....1 January 2004
Netherlands NL[7]..10 July 1979
New Zealand NZ ....1 December 1992
Nicaragua NI ....6 March 2003
Niger NE...21 March 1993
Nigeria NG ....8 May 2005
Norway NO[5]...1 January 1980
Oman OM[2] ....26 October 2001

Panama PA..7 September 2012

Papua New Guinea PG ....14 June 2003

Peru PE..6 June 2009

Philippines PH ....17 August 2001

Poland PL[5] ....25 December 1990

Portugal PT..24 November 1992

Qatar QA[2] ....3 August 2011

Republic of Korea KR ....10 August 1984

Republic of Moldova MD[2]..25 December 1991

Romania RO[2] ....23 July 1979

Russian Federation RU[2] ....29 March 1978[8]

Rwanda RW..31 August 2011

Saint Kitts and Nevis KN..27 October 2005

Saint Lucia LC[2] ....30 August 1996

Saint Vincent and the Grenadines VC[2] ....6 August 2002

San Marino SM ....14 December 2004

Sao Tome and Principe ST ....3 July 2008

Saudi Arabia SA...3 August 2013

Senegal SN ....24 January 1978

Serbia RS[9] ....1 February 1997

Seychelles SC...7 November 2002

Sierra Leone SL..17 June 1997

Singapore SG...23 February 1995

Slovakia SK..1 January 1993

Slovenia SI ....1 March 1994

South Africa ZA[2] ....16 March 1999

Spain ES ....16 November 1989

Sri Lanka LK...26 February 1982

Sudan SD ....16 April 1984

Swaziland SZ ....20 September 1994

Sweden SE ....17 May 1978

Switzerland CH..24 January 1978

Syrian Arab Republic SY...26 June 2003

Tajikistan TJ[2]..25 December 1991

Thailand TH[2]..24 December 2009

The former Yugoslav Republic of Macedonia MK ....10 August 1995

Togo TG..24 January 1978

Trinidad and Tobago TT ....10 March 1994

Tunisia TN[2]	10 December 2001
Turkey TR	1 January 1996
Turkmenistan TM[2]	25 December 1991
Uganda UG	9 February 1995
Ukraine UA[2]	25 December 1991
United Arab Emirates AE	10 March 1999
United Kingdom GB[10]	24 January 1978
United Republic of Tanzania TZ	14 September 1999
United States of America US[11, 12]	24 January 1978
Uzbekistant UZ[2]	25 December 1991
Viet Nam VN	10 March 1993
Zambia ZM	15 November 2001
Zimbabwe ZW	11 June 1997

(Total: 150 States)

---

[1] All PCT Contracting States are bound by Chapter II of the PCT relating to the international preliminary examination.

[2] With the declaration provided for in PCT Article 64(5).

[3] Applies also to Hong Kong, China with effect from 1 July 1997.

[4] Not applicable to Macau, China.

[5] With the declaration provided for in PCT Article 64(2)(a)(ii).

[6] Including all Overseas Departments and Territories.

[7] Ratification for the Kingdom in Europe, the Netherlands Antilles and Aruba. The Netherlands Antilles ceased to exist on 10 October 2010. As from that date, the PCT continues to apply to Curacao and Sint Maarten. The PCT also continues to apply to the islands of Bonaire, Sint Eustatius and Saba, which, with effect from 10 October 2010, have become part of the territory of the Kingdom of the Netherlands in Europe.

[8] Date of ratification of the Soviet Union, continued by the Russian Federation as from 25 December 1991.

[9] Serbia is the continuing State from Serbia and Montenegro as from 3 June 2006.

[10] The United Kingdom extended the application of the PCT to the Isle of Man with effect from 29 October 1983.

[11] With the declarations provided for in PCT Articles 64(3)(a) and 64(4)(a).

[12] Extends to all areas for which the United States of America has international responsibility.

Time Limits

• • •

Entering National/Regional Phase under PCT Chapters I and II
(in months from priority date)
(as of August 18, 2016)

Code	Designated/Elected Office	Chapter I (under PCT Article 22)	Chapter II (under PCT Article 39(1))
AE	United Arab Emirates	30	30
AG	Antigua and Barbuda[1]	30	30
AL	Albania[2]	31	31
AM	Armenia[3]	31	31
AO	Angola[1]	30	30
AP	African Regional Intellectual Property Organization[4]	31	31
AT	Austria[2]	30	30
AU	Australia	31	31
AZ	Azerbaijan[3]	30	31
BA	Bosnia and Herzegovina	34	34
BB	Barbados	30	30
BG	Bulgaria[2]	31	31
BH	Bahrain	30	30
BN	Brunei Darussalam	30	30
BR	Brazil	30	30
BW	Botswania[6]	31	31
BY	Belarus[3]	31	31
BZ	Belize	30	30[7]
CA	Canada	30 (42[8])	30 (42[8])
CH	Switzerland[2, 9]	30	30

CL	Chile	30	30
CN	China	30 (32)[8]	30 (32)[8]
CO	Colombia	31	31
CR	Costa Rica	31	31
CU	Cuba	30	30
CZ	Czech Republic[2]	31	31
DE	Germany[2]	30	30
DK	Denmark[2]	31	31
DM	Dominica[1]	30	30
DO	Dominican Republic	30	30
DZ	Algeria	31	31
EA	Eurasian Patent Organization	31	31
EC	Ecuador	31	31
EE	Estonia[2]	31	31
EG	Egypt	30	30
EP	European Patent Organization[10]	31	31
ES	Spain[2]	30	30
FI	Finland[2]	31	31
GB	United Kingdom[2]	31	31
GD	Grenada[1]	30	30
GE	Georgia	31	31
GH	Ghana[6]	30	30
GM	Gambia[6]	30	31
GT	Guatemala	30	30
HN	Honduras	30	30
HR	Croatia[2]	31	31
HU	Hungary[2]	31	31
ID	Indonesia	31[5]	31[5]
IL	Israel	30	30
IN	India	31	31
IR	Iran (Islamic Republic of)	30	30
IS	Iceland[2]	31	31
JP	Japan	30	30
KE	Kenya[6]	30	30
KG	Krgyzstan[3]	31	31
KN	Saint Kitts and Nevis[1]	30	30
KP	Democratic People's Republic of Korea	30	30

KR	Republic of Korea	31	31
KZ	Kazakhstan[3]	31	31
LA	Lao People's Democratic Republic[1]	30	30
LC	Saint Lucia[1]	30	30
LK	Sri Lanka	30	30
LR	Liberia[6]	30	31
LS	Lesotho[6]	30	31
LU	Luxembourg[2]	20[11]	30
LY	Libya[1]	30	30
MA	Morocco	31	31
MD	Republic of Moldova[3]	31	31
ME	Montenegro[1]	30	30
MG	Madagascar	30	30
MK	The former Yugoslav Republic of Macedonia[2]	31	31
MN	Mongolia	31	31
MW	Malawai[6]	30	30
MX	Mexico	30	30
MY	Malaysia	30	30
MZ	Mozambique[6]	31	31
NA	Namibia[6]	31	31
NG	Nigeria	30	30
NI	Nicaragua	30	30
NO	Norway[2]	31	31
NZ	New Zealand	31	31
OA	African Intellectual Property Org.[13]	30	30
OM	Oman	30	30
PA	Panama[1]	30	30
PE	Peru	30	30
PG	Papua New Guinea	31	31
PH	Philippines	30 (31[8])	30 (31[8])
PL	Poland[2]	30	30
PT	Portugal[2]	30	30
QA	Qatar	30	30
RO	Romania[2]	30	30
RS	Serbia[2]	30[13]	30[13]
RU	Russian Federation[3]	31	31
RW	Rwanda[1]	30	30

SA	Saudi Arabia	30	30
SC	Seychelles	31	31
SD	Sudan[6]	30	30
SE	Sweden[2]	31	31
SG	Singapore	30[14]	30[14]
SK	Slovakia[2]	31	31
SL	Sierra Leone[6]	31	31
SM	San Marino[2]	31	31
ST	Sao Tome and Principe[1]	30	30
SV	El Salvador	30	30
SY	Syrian Arab Republic	31	31
TH	Thailand	30	30
TJ	Tajikistan[3]	30	31
TM	Turkmenistan[3]	30	31
TN	Tunisia[1]	30	30
TR	Turkey[2]	30 (33[8])	30 (33[8])
TT	Trinidad and Tobago	30	31
TZ	United Republic of Tanzania[6]	21[11]	31
UA	Ukraine	31	31
UG	Uganda[6]	21[11]	31
US	United States of America	30	30
UZ	Uzbekistan	31	31
VC	Saint Vincent and the Grenadines	31	31
VN	Viet Nam	31	31
ZA	South Africa	31	31
ZM	Zambia[6]	30	30
ZW	Zimbabwe[6]	30	31

---

[1] In the absence of information from the Office concerned, the time limits shown are those which would normally apply under PCT Articles 22(1) and 39(1)(a). If the Office decides to apply longer time limits, that information will be published in the PCT Newsletter.

[2] If designated/elected for a European patent, see EP as DO/EO for the applicable time limits.

[3] If designated/elected for a Eurasian patent, see EA as designated/elected Office (DO/EO) for the applicable time limits.

[4] The Office acts as DO/EO for the following State which does not act in the capacity of DO/EO: SZ.

5   This time limit may be extended provided that the Applicant pays an additional fee for late entry into the national phase (see national phase for details).

6   If designated/elected for an ARIPO patent, see AP as DO/EO for the applicable time limits.

7   May be extended upon written request of the Applicant.

8   Time limit applicable if Applicant pays an additional fee for late entry into the national phase (see national phase for details: CA, CN, PH, TR).

9   The Office acts as DO/EO for the following State which does not act in the capacity of DO/EO: LI.

10   The Office acts as DO/EO for the following States which do not act in the capacity of DO/EO: BE, CY, FR, GR, IE, IT, LT, LV, MC, MT, NL, SI.

11   The Office has notified the International Bureau of the non-applicability of the 30-month time limit under PCT <u>Article 22(1)</u>, as modified with effect from 1 April 2002 – it does not yet apply the 30-month time limit for entering the national phase.

12   The Office acts as DO/EO for the following States which do not act in the capacity of DO/EO: BF, BJ, CF, CG, CI, CM, GA, GN, GQ, GW, KM, ML, MR, NE, SN, TD, TG.

13   The time limit may be extended by 30 days if the Applicant pays an additional fee for late entry into the national phase.

14   The time limit may be extended by up to eighteen (18) months provided the Applicant pays the prescribed fee (see national phase for details).

GLOSSARY OF PATENT TERMS

Term Definition

Abandonment
A patent application becomes abandoned for failure to file a complete and proper reply as the condition of the application may be required within the time period.

Abstract of the disclosure
A concise statement of the technical disclosure including that which is new in the art to which the invention pertains.

ADS
Application **D**ata **S**heet

Agent (patent)
One who is not a registered attorney or Practitioner but is authorized to act for and in place of the Applicant(s) before the USPTO.

Applicant
Inventor or joint inventors who are applying for a patent on their own invention or the person who is applying for a patent in place of the inventor.

Application
An application for patent that includes all types of patent applications (e.g., utility, design, plant, and reissue) except Provisional Applications. The Nonprovisional Application establishes the filing date and initiates the examination process. A Nonprovisional Patent Application must include a specification, including a claim or claims; drawings, when necessary; an oath or declaration; and the prescribed filing fee.

Application number (patent)
The unique number assigned to a patent application when it is filed. The application number includes a two digital series code and a six digit serial number.

Assignment
A transfer of ownership of a patent application or patent from one entity to another. Record all assignments with the USPTO Assignment Services Division to maintain clear title to pending patent applications and patents.

Attorney	An individual who is a member in good standing of the bar of any United States court or the highest court of any State and who is registered to practice before the USPTO.
AU	**Art Unit**
BPAI	Patent Trial and Appeal Board, now known as the Patent Trial and Appeal Board.
CN	**Customer Number**
Canceled claim	A claim that is canceled or deleted. "Canceled" is the status identifier that should be used when a claim is canceled in an application.
Certificate of Mailing	A certificate for each piece of correspondence mailed, prior to the expiration of the set period of time for response, stating the date of deposit with the U.S. Postal Service and including a signature.
CIP	**Continuation-In-P**art - An application filed during the lifetime of an earlier Nonprovisional Application, repeating some substantial portion or all of the earlier Nonprovisional Application and adding matter not disclosed in the earlier Nonprovisional Application.
Claims	Define the invention and are what aspects are legally enforceable. The specification must conclude with a claim particularly pointing out and distinctly claiming the subject matter which the Applicant regards as his invention or discovery. The claim or claims must conform to the invention as set forth in the remainder of the specification and the terms and phrases used in the claims must find clear support or antecedent basis in the description so that the meaning of the terms in the claims may be ascertainable (clearly understood) by reference to the description.
Confirmation Number	A four-digit number that is assigned to each newly filed patent application. The confirmation number, in combination with the application number, is used to verify the accuracy of the application number placed on correspondence filed with the USPTO to avoid misidentification of an application due to a transposition error (misplaced

digits) in the application number. The USPTO recommends that Applicants include the application's confirmation number (in addition to the application number) on all correspondence submitted to the USPTO concerning the application.

Continuation Application

A second application for the same invention claimed in a prior Nonprovisional Application and filed before the first application becomes abandoned or patented.

Continuing Application

A Continuation, Divisional, or Continuation-In-Part patent application.

Customer Number

A number assigned by the USPTO that is used to simplify the submission of an address change, to appoint a Practitioner, or to designate the fee address for a patent. Customer numbers are primarily used by attorneys and law firms, and must be requested using the "Request for Customer Number" form (PTO/SB/125).

Dependent Claim

A claim that refers back to (depends on) and further limits a preceding dependent or independent claim. A dependent claim shall include every limitation of the claim from which it depends.

Deposit Account

An account that is established in the USPTO, upon payment of a fee for establishing such an account, for the convenience in paying any fees due, in ordering services offered by the USPTO, copies of records, etc.

Design Patent Application

An application for a patent to protect against the unauthorized use of new, original, and ornamental designs for articles of manufacture.

Design Patent

May be granted to anyone who invents a new, original, and ornamental design for an article of manufacture.

Disclaimer

A patentee, whether of the whole or any sectional interest therein, may, on payment of the fee required by law, make disclaimer (give up all or part of the owner's rights to enforce claims) of any complete claim, stating therein the extent of their interest in such patent. Such disclaimers are required to be in writing and recorded in the USPTO, and are considered as part of the original patent to the extent of the interest actually possessed by the disclaimant and by those claiming under him. Any patentee or Applicant may disclaim or dedicate to the public the entire term, or any terminal part of the term (from a certain point in time through the projected end of the entire term), of the patent granted or to be granted. There are two types of disclaimers: a statutory disclaimer and a terminal disclaimer.

Disclosure	In return for a patent, the inventor gives as consideration a complete revelation (describes it) or disclosure of the invention for which protection is sought.
Divisional Application	A later application for an independent or distinct invention disclosing and claiming (only a portion of and) only subject matter disclosed in the earlier or parent application.
Drawing	Patent drawings must show every feature of the invention as specified in the claims. Omission of drawings may cause an application to be considered incomplete but are only required if drawings are necessary for the understanding of the subject matter sought to be patented.
EBC	Electronic Business Center – includes links to Patents EBC. A web page containing hyperlinks to all online systems for conducting electronic commerce with the USPTO.
EFS	Electronic Filing System (for patent applications). Supports secure electronic filing of Patent application documents via the Internet.
ePAS	**E**lectronic **P**atent **A**ssignment System
EPO	**E**uropean **P**atent **O**ffice
Election of Species	Where restriction between species is appropriate, an election of species is needed. Species are referred as examples or figures in the specification.

Express Abandonment

A patent application may be expressly abandoned by filing a written declaration of abandonment identifying the application in the USPTO. Express abandonment becomes effective when an appropriate official of the USPTO takes action thereon. Express abandonment of the application may not be recognized by the USPTO before the date of issue or publication unless it is actually received by appropriate officials in time to act.

Priority Mail Express mailing label

Patent correspondence delivered to the USPTO via the "Priority Mail Express Post Office to Addressee" service of the USPS which is considered filed in the USPTO on the date of deposit with the USPS, shown by the "date-in" on the "Priority Mail Express" mailing label.

Fee

An amount of money charged for a particular service or product supplied by the USPTO.

Filing date

The date of receipt in the Office of an application which includes (1) a specification containing a description and, if the application is a Nonprovisional Application, at least one claim, and (2) any required drawings.

Final Office Action (rejection)

An Office Action on the second or any subsequent examination or consideration by an Examiner that is intended to close the prosecution of a Nonprovisional Application.

FOA

Final Rejection – see definition under **Final Office Action**

GAU

Group Art Unit - see definition under Group Art Unit.

Group Art Unit

May be abbreviated "AU", "GAU" or "Grp art Unit" on USPTO correspondence. A working unit responsible for a cluster of related patent art.

IAC

Inventors Assistance Center (formerly Patent Assistance Center) - 1-800-786-9199.

IDS

See **Information Disclosure Statement**

IFW	**I**mage **F**ile **W**rapper – an electronic version of a patent application, including image and/or text versions of the bibliographic information, all papers as filed, and all office actions and correspondence related to that application.
Independent Claim	A claim that does not refer back to or depend on another claim.
Information Disclosure Statement	A list of all patents, publications, U.S. applications, or other information submitted for consideration by the USPTO in a Nonprovisional Application to comply with Applicant's duty to submit to the USPTO information which is material to patentability of the invention claimed in the Nonprovisional Application. The IDS must include a list of all patents, publications, U.S. applications, or other information submitted for consideration by the USPTO. The USPTO provides forms for use in the submission of an IDS, the PTO/SB/08a and PTO/SB/08b.
Invention	Any art of process (way of doing or making things), machine, manufacture, design, or composition of matter, or any new and useful improvement thereof, or any variety of plant, which is or may be patentable under the patent laws of the United States.
Inventor	One who contributes to the conception of an invention. The patent law of the United States of America requires that the Applicant in a patent application must be the inventor.
IP	**I**ntellectual **P**roperty
Kind Codes	WIPO Standard ST. 16 codes include a letter, and in many cases a number, used to distinguish the kind of patent document (e.g., publication of an application for a utility patent publication, plant patent, or design patent) and the level of publication (e.g., first publication, second publication, or corrected publication).
Letters Patent	See under Patent

Maintenance Fees	Fees for maintaining in force a patent based on an application filed on or after December 12, 1980.
MPEP	Manual of Patent Examining Procedure
Multiple Dependent Claim	A dependent claim which further limits and refers back to the alternative to more than one preceding independent or dependent claim. Acceptable multiple dependent claims shall refer to preceding claims using the terms "or, any one of, one of, any f, either." A multiple dependent claim may not depend on another multiple dependent claim, either directly or indirectly.
NOA	**N**otice of **A**llowance
Non-Final Office Action	An Office Action made by the Examiner where the Applicant is entitled to reply and request reconsideration or further examination, with or without making an amendment.
Nonprovisional Patent Application	An application for patent that includes all patent applications (i.e., utility, design, plant, and reissue) except provisional applications. The Nonprovisional Application establishes the filing date and initiates the examination process. A Nonprovisional Application must include a specification, including a claim or claims; drawings, when necessary; an oath or declaration; and the prescribed filing fee.
Notice of Allowability	A notification to the patent Applicant that the application has been placed in condition for allowance.
Notice of Allowance and Fues Due	A notification to the Applicant that they are entitled to a patent under the law and requesting payment of a specified issue fee (and possibly a publication fee as well) within three (3) months (non-extendable) from the mailing date of the Notice of Allowance.
NPL	**N**on-**P**atent **L**iterature – documents and publications that are not patents or published patent applications but are cited as references for being relevant in a patent prosecution. For example, a magazine article or doctoral thesis relevant to a claimed invention might be

cited as non-patent literature. Typically, references cited in an application are grouped into; domestic patents and patent application publications; foreign patents; and non-patent literature.

OED — **O**ffice of **E**nrollment and **D**iscipline

OPLA — **O**ffice of **P**atent **L**egal **A**dministration

PA — **P**atent **A**gent

PAIR — **P**atent **A**pplication **I**nformation **R**etrieval. Provides secure access for customers who want to view current patent application status electronically via the Internet.

Paralegal — Patent Professional

Parent Application — The term "parent" is applied to an earlier application of the inventor disclosing a given invention.

Patent — A property right granted by the Government of the United States of America to an inventor "to exclude others from making, using, offering for sale, or selling the invention throughout the United States or importing the invention into the United States" for a limited time in exchange for public disclosure of the invention when the patent is granted.

Patent application — See under Application (patent)

Patent application publication — Pre-grant publication of patent application at eighteen (18) months from priority date.

Patent Infringement — Unauthorized making, using, offering to sell, selling or importing into the United States any patented invention.

Patent Number — Unique number assigned to a patent application when it issues as a patent.

Patent pending — A phrase that often appears on manufactured items. It means that someone has applied for a patent on an invention that is contained in the manufactured item. It serves as a warning that a paten may issue that would cover the item and that copiers should be careful because they might infringe if the patent issues. Once the patent issues, the patent owner will stop using the phrase "patent pending" and start using a phrase such as "covered by U.S. Patent Number XXXXXXX." Applying the patent pending phrase to an item when no patent application has been made can result in a fine.

Patentable	Suitable to be patented; entitled by law to be protected by the issuance of a patent.
PTAB	**P**atent **T**rial and **A**ppeal **B**oard.
PG Pub	Pre-Grant Publication of patent application at eighteen (18) months from priority date.
POA	**P**ower **of A**ttorney – formal assignment to another of the right to legally act on your behalf.
Practitioner	One who stands for or acts on behalf of another. A patent attorney or patent agent may represent the inventors named in a patent application.
Priority Claim	Claims under 35 USC 119(a)(e) and 35 USC 120 for the benefit of the filing date of earlier filed applications.
Provisional Patent Application	A Provisional Application for patent is a U.S. national application for patent filed in the USPTO under 35 USC 111(b). It allows filing without a formal patent claim, oath or declaration, or any information disclosure (prior art) statement. It provides the means to establish an early effective filing date in a Nonprovisional Application filed under 35 USC 111(a) and automatically becomes abandoned after one year. It also allows the term "Patent Pending" to be applied.
PTA	**P**atent **T**erm **A**djustment.
PTO	**P**atent and **T**rademark **O**ffice.

Publication Number	A number assigned to the publication of patent applications filed on or after November 29, 2000. It includes the year, followed by a seven digit number, followed by a kind code. Example 200011234567A1.
RCE	Request for Continued Examination. A request filed in an application in which prosecution is closed (e.g., the application is under final rejection or a notice of allowance) that is filed to reopen prosecution and continue examination of the application; requires the filing of a submission and payment of a fee.
Practitioner	Registered Patent Practitioner
Registration Number	A registered patent attorney/agent is assigned a registration number that must include on patent correspondence and forms when representing others before the USPTO; individual Applicants do not have a registration number and should leave this field blank on patent forms.
Restriction Requirement	If two or more independent and distinct inventions are claimed in a single application, the examiner may require the Applicant to elect (designate) a single invention to which the claims will be restricted (limited to). This requirement is known as a requirement for restriction (also known as a requirement for division).
Small Entity	For purposes of small entity determination – means an independent inventor, a small business concern, or a nonprofit organization eligible for reduced patent fees.
Specification	A written description of the invention and the manner and process of making and using the same.
Statutory Disclaimer	Under 35 USC 253 (paragraph 1) and 37 CFR 1.321(a), the owner (in part or in entirety) of a patent may relinquish all rights to a complete claim or claims of the owner's patent.
Substitute Specification	An application which is in essence a duplicate of a prior (earlier filed) application by the same Applicant abandoned before the filing of the

substitute (later filed) application; a substitute application does not obtain the benefit of the filing date of the parent application.

Surcharge Due

An additional fee that may be required due to late or insufficient payment of fees.

Technology Center

A unit of several Group Art Units in the mechanical, electrical, chemical, or design area, managed by one or more Group Directors.

Terminal Disclaimer

Also "TD"; a statement filed by an owner under 35 USC 253 (paragraph 2) and 37 CFR 1.321(b) or (c) to disclaim or dedicate to the public the entire term or any portion of the term of a patent or patent to be granted. A TD may be filed for the purpose of overcoming a judicially created double patenting rejection.

USPTO

United **S**tates **P**atent and **T**rademark **O**ffice, designation became effective April 3, 2000, a result of the American Inventors Protection Act of 1999.

USPS

United **S**tates **P**ostal **S**ervice

Utility Patent Application

Protect useful processes, machines, articles of manufacture, and compositions of matter.

Utility Patent

May be granted to anyone who invents or discovers any new, useful, and nonobvious process, machine, article of manufacture, or composition of matter, or any new and useful improvement thereof.

Window close

Time period after which a utility patent (that issues from an application filed on or after December 12, 1980) expires if a maintenance fee has not been paid. A petition must be filed along with the appropriate fees to reinstate an expired patent.

Window open

Time period when a maintenance fee can be paid with or without a surcharge.

Withdrawn Claim

A non-elected claim. "Withdrawn" is the status identifier that should be used for claims that were not elected (chosen by the Applicant to remain under consideration) in response to a restriction requirement.

Withdrawn Patent

An allowed application for patent in which the Applicant files correspondence to withdraw the patent from issue; thus preventing it from issuing on the patent issue date. The printed document is sometimes available on the day of publication, but is later retracted and will not be available in the patent database. No copy of the patent document will appear on the official USPTO website.

Index

● ● ●

(References are to chapter and chapter sections)

Made in the USA
Lexington, KY
10 June 2017